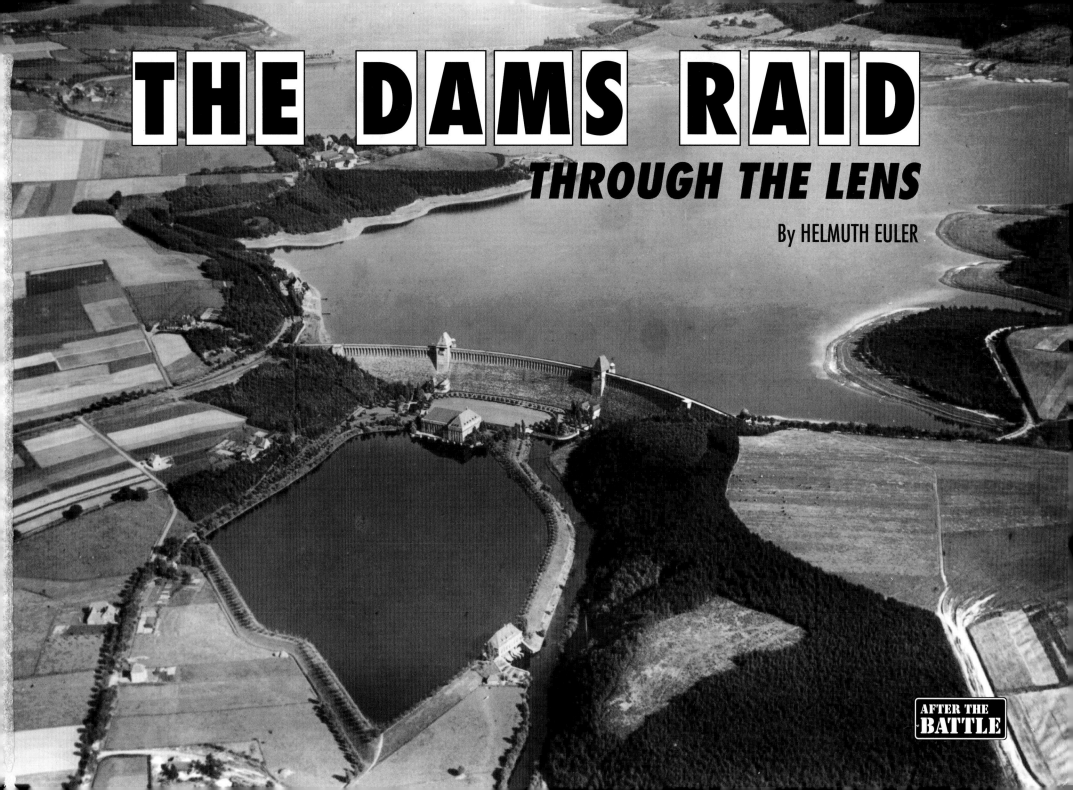

THE DAMS RAID
THROUGH THE LENS

By HELMUTH EULER

AFTER THE
BATTLE

Credits

ISBN: 1 870067 27 4
© Helmuth Euler/*After the Battle*, 2001
Translated by Michael Ockenden
Designed by Winston G. Ramsey, Editor-in-Chief *After the Battle*

PUBLISHERS
Battle of Britain International Limited, Church House, Church Street, London E15 3JA

PRINTERS
Printed in Great Britain by Heronsgate Ltd, Basildon, Essex.

PHOTOGRAPHS
All the photographs are from the author's archive, save for the following:
Australian War Memorial: *Page 224 left.*
Commonwealth War Graves Commission: *Page 92 top left.*
J. A. H van den Driesschen: *Page 216 both.*
Imperial War Museum: *Page 16 right, 17 right, 20 right, 21 left and centre, 23 top left, 24 top right and bottom, 26 left, 27 left, 30 top right, 31, 48 bottom right, 49, 86 right, 97, 111, 158, 159, 160 right, 161 bottom, 162, 163 both, 164 both, 165 both, 166, 167, 168, 208, 209 right, 220.*
Kardar Luftbild: *Page 53.*
University of Keele: *Page 106 left, 108 right.*
Heinz Leiwig: *Page 181 left.*
Lincolnshire Aviation Heritage Centre: *Page 226 bottom.*
Mike McCormac: *Page 51 bottom left and right, 52 top left and right.*
National Physical Laboratory: *Page 19 right.*
Public Record Office: *Page 40, 41.*
Royal Air Force Museum, Hendon: *Page 34 left.*
Royal Air Force, Scampton: *230, 231, 232, 233.*
Winfried von Rüden: *Page 213, 219 left.*
Ruhrverband Essen: *Page 5 right.*
Transport Road Research Laboratory: *Page 10 bottom.*
Ullstein Bilderdienst: *Page 222 top right.*
Wasser und Schiffahrtamt Hannoversch-Münden: *Page 76.*
Werkfoto Preussenelektra: *Page 7 bottom.*

MAPS
Landesvermessungsamt Nordrhein-Westfalen, Bonn.

ENDPAPERS
Front left: The vital Möhne dam, critical for the supply of water and hydro-electric power for the German war machine in the Ruhr, pictured after the attack on the night of May 16/17, 1943. The ruined building in the foreground was the home of Franz Müller which lay some 300 metres from the local inn at Günne run by Adolf Nölle. His story appears on page 120.

Front right: The flooded valley at Guntershausen, some 46 kilometres below the Eder — the second dam attacked that night. Although its importance to German industry was minimal — its main purpose being to regulate water levels — the prestige factor to the Royal Air Force in breaching two of Germany's biggest dams in a single stroke was immeasurable.

Rear left: Although an exact death toll has never been established, around 1,400 people were drowned in the tidal waves which bore down the Möhne and Eder valleys. This is the state funeral for the victims at Neheim (see page 126).

Rear right: Eight of the Lancasters failed to return. RAF casualties were 53 killed in action with three men taken prisoner. These are the graves of the crew of AJ-M in Rheinberg War Cemetery, north of Krefeld (see page 60).

FRONTISPIECE
The Möhne dam before the raid, courtesy of Foto-Dülberg/H. Windgassen, Soest.

REAR COVER
A rare sight — the Möhne dam in full flow with water cascading from the 105 overflow vents. (Photo by the author.)

Contents

Introduction

Operation 'Chastise' has become a legend in the annals of military history, possessing as it does the traditional military attributes of originality, surprise and heroism, coupled with a dramatic outcome. In Germany, the victims of the catastrophe have not been forgotten, and following the publication of my book *Als Deutschlands Dämme brachen* in 1975, many German eyewitnesses came forward with additional reports, photographs and film material about the night attacks against the Möhne and Eder dams. Also, with the passage of 50 years, previously-classified records have now been released and other hitherto unknown documents made public which were included in my second book *Wasserkrieg* published in 1992.

During the night of May 16/17, 1943, 19 Lancaster bombers of the RAF's newly-formed No. 617 Squadron launched a low-level attack against four dams in the Ruhr. Within an hour, the special 'bouncing' bombs had smashed two of the main targets, the massive dams in the Möhne and Eder valleys. The Sorpe was damaged but the Ennepe withstood the attack. Eight Lancasters did not return.

Yet though it had been based on a series of experiments whose results had been accurately predicted, the first air raid to have been conceived within the context of engineering technology proved a failure. Its target was the arsenal of the Third Reich but the anticipated strategic advantages for the Allies failed to materialise and production continued unhindered. Even at a time when Britain needed victories in the air — and the operation certainly bolstered British civilian morale — was it worth the cost in time and materials, coupled with the loss of eight bombers and the lives of 53 men?

How did the Royal Air Force manage to breach the Möhne and Eder dams, which together held back 336 million tonnes of water? From an examination of original documents it is clear that the Air Ministry had, in September 1937, already identified German dams and reservoirs as potential targets in any new war, and in October of the same year the Möhne and Sorpe were specifically named. With the outbreak of hostilities in September 1939, RAF Bomber Command concentrated on the notion that if the nerve centre of the German military economy could be paralysed, the war would be shortened considerably.

By the beginning of 1943 many of the RAF's proposals had been put forward, agreed and listed, but with this came the realisation that conventional techniques could not be used to destroy the dams. Tactics such as torpedoes, remote-controlled flying boats filled with explosives, the synchronised detonation of sea mines, or sabotage units dropped by parachute had all been considered for use against the Möhne dam. Initially, Barnes Wallis believed the dams could be brought down with a 10-ton earthquake bomb but in May 1943 such a device was impossible to deliver and drop accurately. Wallis was not the first to recognise the German dams as important targets, but he was the one who came up with the brilliant idea of using a bouncing bomb to unleash the waters pent up behind the Möhne and Eder dams.

Barnes Wallis tinkered with his bomb theories for three years in the face of resistance from aviation experts. When the decision was taken on February 26, 1943 to implement Operation 'Chastise', there were no detailed drawings of the special weapon. No. 617 Squadron, under Wing Commander Guy Gibson, had just seven weeks to practise low-level flying, and the first and only test with a live bomb was successfully carried out only three days before the attack.

The decision to give priority to 'Upkeep' (the dam-busting bomb) over 'Highball' (the anti-surface vessel bomb) was not taken at the Air Ministry in London but in Washington where RAF Chiefs-of-Staff were conferring with their American opposite numbers. The Air Ministry asked for a decision and on May 14 a message from the United States brought the news they had been hoping for — the attack was to go ahead. Two essential factors had to coincide: the required water levels behind the dams and a full moon. The latest possible date when 'Chastise' could successfully be carried out was May 26 for only then would these two criteria exist.

The Dams Raid was undoubtedly Bomber Command's most spectacular operation of the Second World War, and it has been described by the official British military historian as 'the most precise bombing attack ever delivered and a feat of arms which has never been excelled'.

The scale of the devastation unleashed by a single bomb — in this case 'Upkeep' — was not exceeded until the atomic bomb was dropped on Japan in 1945. During the course of Germany's longest night, over 200 square kilometres of land were flooded and some 1,400 people lost their lives — the highest number to date in an air raid.

This, then, is the story of that attack, graphically told 'through the lenses' of the photographers who recorded the scenes before, during and after the operation.

HELMUTH EULER, 2001

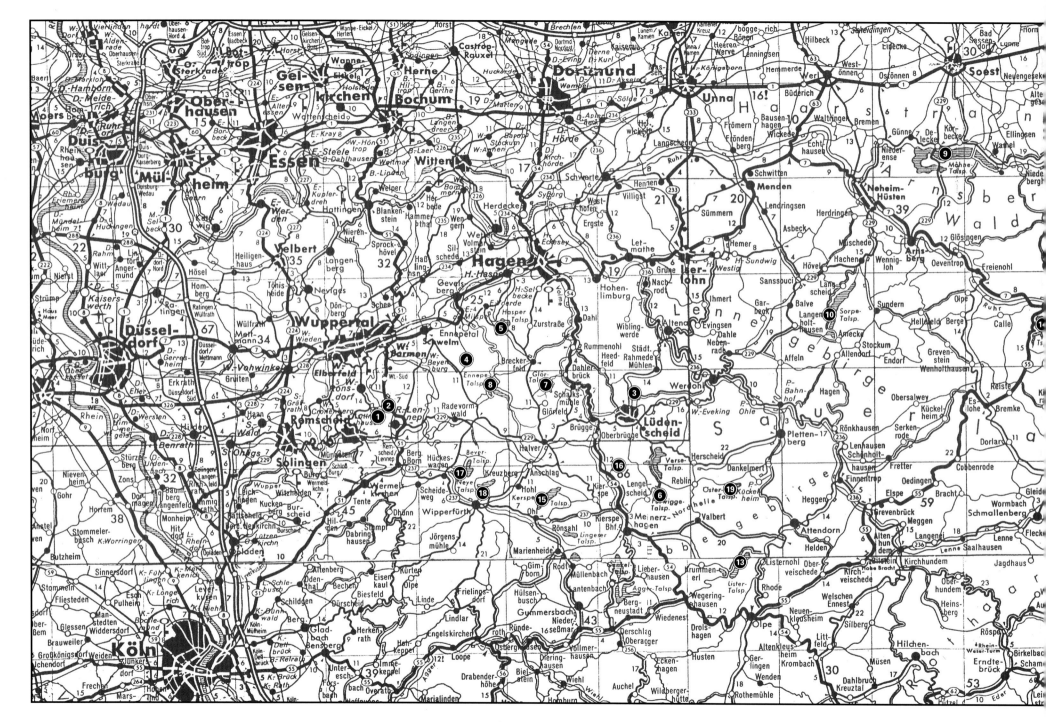

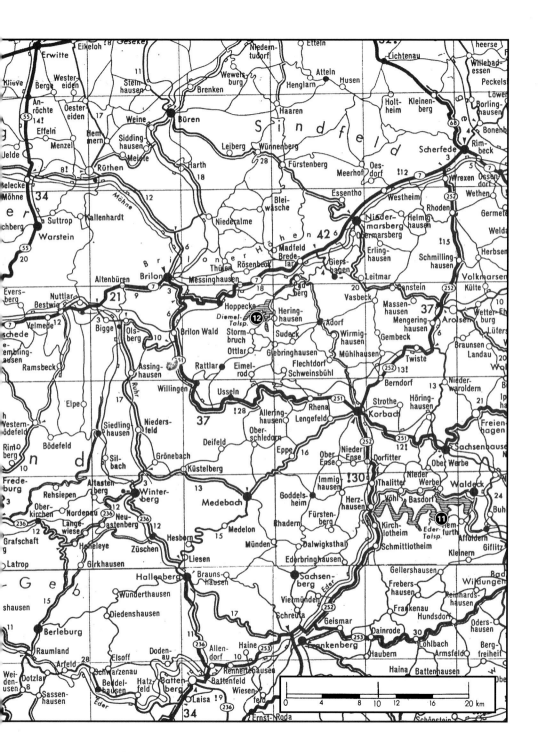

The Möhne, 120 kilometres east of Cologne, was the largest to be completed in the Ruhr.

Dam-building in the Ruhrgebiet

The construction of dams is one of the most important technical achievements of mankind. Engineers have always tried to store water in large quantities, be this to provide drinking water for towns, irrigation for fields during droughts, or the protection of inhabited areas from floods. However, the construction of artificial reservoirs is not an invention of the 19th and 20th centuries and important dams had already been built in ancient times. For thousands of years the building of dams has gone hand in hand with the development of cities, for settlements of any size have always required an adequate supply of water. Contemporary writers tell of 'Lake Moeris' situated in Fayum Oasis, 50 miles south of Cairo where, with the help of dams and canals, a masterpiece of civil engineering stored up the floodwaters of the Nile for use during dry periods; more than 1,800 years BC one of the most fertile provinces of ancient Egypt was created by means of a dam. However, the oldest existing dam is that at Sadd-el-Kafara built 2700-2600 BC in Wadi Garawi 20 miles south of Cairo. Built for protection against flood-water with a 40-foot-high wall, it was destroyed before completion due to an unexpected flood. The remnants can still be seen today.

In Germany, important dam-building works took place in the 16th and 17th centuries in the Harz region where water power was used for smelting and metal processing in the mining industry. Traditional metalworking was also an important economic factor in the Sauerland and Bergisches Land (the region of North Rhine-Westphalia between the Rhine, Sieg and Ruhr rivers) where, for hundreds of years, mills and forges had harnessed the water power of the many brooks and streams in the valleys. However, all this changed with the advent of modern industrialisation. Businesses expanded and the population grew rapidly, both being equally dependent on ever-increasing demand for water which could no longer be provided by traditional pumping stations.

The Ennepe, some 12 kilometres east of Wuppertal was built between 1902-04, this picture showing the 'heaven's ladder' method of construction. The dam wall was raised by 10 metres in 1912 which increased the capacity to 12.6 million cubic metres of water.

The industrial revolution led to new technical developments in the construction of reservoirs. This in turn prompted some cities to plan their own reservoirs for the storage of drinking water. The great pioneer of German dam building was Dr. Ing. Otto Intze, Professor at the University of Technology at Aachen. In 1891, and without building permission, the city of Remscheid, 30 kilometres east of Düsseldorf, completed Germany's first dam in the Eschbach valley [1] to provide a reservoir for drinking water. Professor Intze employed the latest civil engineering techniques when he drew up his plans for the dam wall and he kept the local government in Düsseldorf informed of the progress of the works. However, the authorities were reluctant to accept responsibility for the dam's ability to withstand the pressure of water and, as a result, building permission was withheld, yet the dam was completed and the authorities presented with a fait accompli.

Remscheid's success spurred on the neighbouring town of Lennep to build a dam of its own and Professor Intze and Albert Schmidt, a local chartered building engineer, paved the way for the project. The Panzertalsperre [2] had just been completed when building permission came through! It was not long before other reservoirs were constructed in the Bergisches Land — a region which can truly be considered as the birthplace of modern dam building — and soon a multiplicity of artificial lakes appeared around the River Wupper. However, the reputation of the Bergisches Land was soon to be challenged by the Sauerland.

The second half of the 19th century saw a sharp growth of industry and population in this region between the Rivers Emscher and Ruhr. Within a few decades, a predominantly agricultural area had been transformed into the 'Ruhrgebiet' which, with its coal and steel reserves, was to become the centre of heavy industry in Germany. In order to supply the rapidly expanding cities and their factories with sufficient water, the river that gave its name to the region was run dry. Pumping stations in the Ruhr valley sprouted like mushrooms. Scant consideration was paid to the problem created by over-extraction and

this sparked off a typhus epidemic in Gelsenkirchen in 1901 caused by poor water quality in the mains supply. The river was just able to meet the demands without help until the end of the 19th century although during some summers, when there was below-average rainfall, a catastrophic water shortage prevailed in the lower reaches of the Ruhr. It was only when the quantities extracted shot up within a few years from 90 million cubic metres (1893) to 135 million cubic metres (1897) and then to more than 500 million cubic metres, that the natural supply proved insufficient. The demands on the water reserves were so great they could no longer be guaranteed without recourse to large-scale engineering solutions in the form of dams. With the help of the cities of Altena and Gevelsberg, the first two dams in the drainage basin of the Ruhr, the Fuelbecke [3] and Heilenbecker [4], with a storage capacity of 7 million cubic metres and 4.5 million cubic metres respectively, were built in 1896 to supply local drinking water.

However, the thirst of the Ruhrgebiet seemed insatiable and on December 10, 1899 the Ruhrtalsperrenverein (Ruhr Valley Dams Association) was established with the stated aim 'to improve the water level of the River Ruhr in terms of quantity and composition by the furthering of dam building in the drainage basin of the river'. Generous subsidies were made available by the Association to support small dam-building co-operatives, and in 1904 dams in the valleys of the Hasper [5], Fürwigge [6], Glör [7] and Ennepe [8] were officially opened providing a combined volume of 16.1 million cubic metres. All four were built according to plans drawn up by Professor Intze.

The setting up of the Ruhr Valley Dams Association, involving the water extraction companies and those using the river to power machinery, was originally voluntary, but given a legal framework in 1913 with the passing of the Ruhr Valley Dams Legislation. This law made it possible to levy financial contributions from all those involved in the water industry. Because of the pressing need for more water, the Ruhr Valley Dams Association had already (in 1906) decided on a major project, the Möhne dam [9]. This, with its initial reservoir capacity of some 135 million cubic metres, far exceeded what had

The Sorpe was Germany's largest earthen dam. The concrete core — the backbone of the dam — is shown under construction. When completed in 1935 it reached a height of 69 metres.

hitherto been the conceived limits for such constructions in Europe. The dam wall of granite masonry blocks stretched across a 650-metre-wide bend in the valley and rose 37.3 metres above its floor. The foundations did not simply extend down to the bedrock but were excavated a further three metres in order to prevent any movement of the wall due to water pressure. The total height was therefore 40.3 metres to the crest with a width of 34.2 metres at the base, the thickness of the wall at its crown being 6.25 metres. Construction began in 1908 and was completed in 1912. (It was officially opened on July 12, 1913.)

Fifteen kilometres south-west from the Möhne dam stands the Sorpe dam [10] forming — when completed in 1935 — the second biggest reservoir in the Sauerland. In contrast to the Möhne, the Sorpe was constructed with an earth embankment comprising rubble and an inner concrete core. The dam came into service in 1935 and consists of 3.25 million cubic metres of rubble and 130,000 cubic metres of concrete. For many years the 69-metre-high Sorpe was Germany's highest earthen dam, surmounted by a crest 700 metres long and ten metres wide. With its capacity of 70 million cubic metres, the Sorpe dam forms a reservoir with sufficient resources to supplement the others in the drainage basin of the Ruhr during the so-called 'double dry years'. (The latter term describes the situation when the rainfall is below average for two consecutive years and when the other reservoirs are unable to meet the needs of the Ruhrgebiet.) It also has another special feature — a 'one-year plus reserve'. This means that its reservoir has a capacity greater than the annual average of waters entering from the drainage basin. As a result, water flowing into the Sorpe must be carefully husbanded as it takes a long time to be replenished. In the 1950s, the ingress of water was increased further by means of additional channels from neighbouring river valleys, yet the amount of electricity generated at the Möhne and Sorpe dams is insignificant in terms of other hydro-electric plants.

Some 70 kilometres south-east of the Möhne, lies the Eder dam [11]. This was built thanks to Prussian legislation passed in 1905, the content of which included a law relating to the planning and construction of the Mittelland Canal designed to link the River Elbe

By far the largest reservoir in Germany — the Eder — was built between 1908 and 1914.

Kaiser Wilhelm II inspects the construction work on the Eder dam in August 1912.

with the Rhine. The stated aim was 'to improve the rural economy, reduce flood damage and construct a network of inland waterways'. The western section of the canal as far as Hanover was completed first, and to ensure it had sufficient water, guaranteed quantities had to be drawn from the River Weser throughout the year, but without endangering navigation on that river. This required the building of dams in the area where waters fed the Weser. So came about the construction of the gigantic (at the time) Eder reservoir (1908-14) with a capacity of 202 million cubic metres and the Diemel dam [12] (1912-24) with a capacity of 20 million cubic metres.

The Eder dam, a slim construction with no clay apron at the front, is eight metres higher than the Möhne. Although the wall of the Eder is 200 metres shorter, it nevertheless holds back an additional 70 million cubic metres of water. Another reason for the creation of the 27-kilometre-long Eder reservoir was to provide protection against flooding, since the Eder had shown itself to be the most turbulent river in the Hessen region. Floods in 1840, 1881 and 1890 had caused great destruction, but in future the waters were to be captured within the Eder reservoir and stored for use during dry periods. The difference in water levels would also be exploited for the generation of electricity at power stations situated at the dam itself and also at the end of the stilling basin which serves as the lower basin for the Waldeck 1 power station.

Other dams serving the Ruhrgebiet are the Lister (1912) [13] of 22 million cubic metres; the Henne (1905) [14] with 11 million cubic metres; the Kerspe (1912) [15] comprising 15.5 million cubic metres; Jubach (1906) [16] of just over one million cubic metres; the Bever (1898 and 1939) [17] of 27 million cubic metres; the Neye (1909) [18] of 6 million cubic metres, and the Oester (1906) [19] of 3 million cubic metres. (By comparison, the pre-war US Boulder Dam, renamed Hoover Dam in 1947, completed in 1936 has a reservoir capacity of 38,547 million cubic metres. One of the largest dams existing today — the Kariba in Zimbabwe — holds 180 billion cubic metres of water — 1,400 times as large as the Möhne reservoir.)

Air Attacks on Reservoirs and Dams

As early as September 1937, the RAF had prepared detailed intelligence reports on the largest German dams. The preferred targets of the Air Staff were the armament factories of the Ruhr — the heart of the German defence industry — with the associated waterways of the River Weser and the Mittelland Canal along which war materials would be transported. If the dams could be destroyed, at a stroke the Ruhr would be drained of water and the hydro-electric power stations put out of action.

The following year, with the Second World War looming, the 18th meeting of the Bombing Committee was convened at the Air Ministry at Adastral House, Kingsway, on July 26, 1938, the topic under discussion being 'Air Attacks on Reservoirs and Dams'.

The prevailing view had always been that targets of this nature would be extremely difficult to attack from the air and that any such attacks would be uneconomical. For this reason the importance and far-reaching consequences of a successful strike on specific dams within the territory of potential enemies had thus far not been fully appreciated, and these targets did not figure in the current edition of the Manual of Air Tactics.

Air Vice-Marshal W. Sholto Douglas, the Assistant Chief of the Air Staff, chaired the meeting and opened the debate saying that recent investigations had indicated that certain reservoirs in Germany and Italy formed what might be termed an 'Achilles heel' in those countries in that their industrial power system was based on power derived almost entirely from these sources. He said that it was the object of the meeting 'to enquire into the extent to which effective air action against the dams of the reservoirs and similar targets would be possible'.

The information currently available was briefly summarised and circulated as Bombing Committee Paper No. 16. This described the types of construction and siting of the dams, notes on the potentialities of different weapons of attack, and also on the probability of hitting such targets by high-altitude bombing.

The minutes record that Squadron Leader C. G. Burge, representing the Air Targets Sub-Committee of Air Intelligence, reported that 'the amount of water consumed in the whole of Germany was only three times that of the Ruhr' and that 'the bulk of it was obtained from one large reservoir contained by a single-arch dam known as the Möhne dam'. He added: 'There were also four or five other reservoirs in Germany which fed the inland waterways. The destruction of these dams, he was informed, would leave the waterways high and dry and, as water transport figured very largely in the German transportation system, the extra traffic thrown on the roads and railways would very soon tend to cause chaotic conditions. The recent drought had caused several of these reservoirs to dry up, and the whole of two or three large stretches of waterways were inactive for three or four weeks, thus throwing a very heavy burden on the railways.'

Squadron Leader Burge mentioned that at a recent meeting of the Air Ministry Transportation Targets Committee, Mr Hawkins, an expert on dam construction, had strongly recommended an attack on the lower face as being the best method, the end in view being to fracture the structure, when it was considered that the pressure of the water would probably do the rest.

Dr R. Ferguson of the Research Department at Woolwich agreed that 'if a semi-armour-piercing bomb could be used to attack the target almost normal to its surface with sufficient striking velocity, that the bomb, when inside the target, would do immense damage'. He considered however, that some sort of specially-designed propelled bomb would be necessary in order to obtain the required velocity at low altitudes. He said that it was known that a 500lb semi-armour-piercing bomb, when propelled, had penetrated five feet into the concrete. The thickness of the dam at a depth of 40 feet was approximately 12 feet. If a bomb could be driven into the wall to a depth of five feet, the remaining seven feet should be severely damaged, and the damage thus obtained would be immeasurably greater than that caused by an ordinary bomb, fused for delayed-action, which detonated on the surface of the target.

Group Captain Norman Bottomley of Bomber Command enquired which would have the greater effect — a bomb of 1,000lbs detonated under water on the high water side, or a similar bomb a short distance on the low water side of the structure. Dr Ferguson

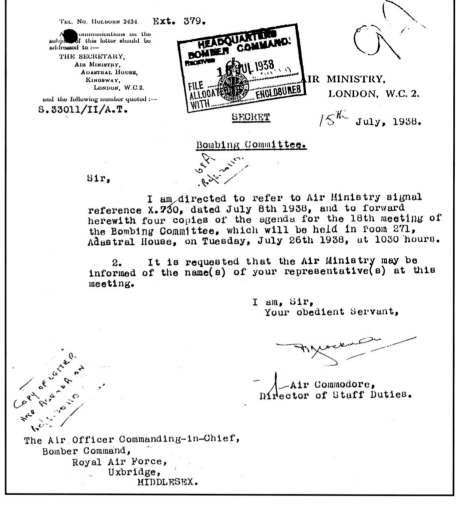

One might say that the operation to destroy the German dams in the Ruhr began on Tuesday, July 26, 1938 at a meeting chaired by Air Vice-Marshal W. Sholto Douglas, the Assistant Chief of the Air Staff. The Air Ministry was represented by Air Commodore R. P. Willcock, Group Captain A. Gray, Wing Commander H. V. Rowley, Wing Commander C. P. Brown, Wing Commander L. F. Pendred, Squadron Leader J. D. F. Bruce, Squadron Leader C. G. Burge and Mr R. Struthers and Mr E. M. Lake. Group Captain N. H. Bottomley, Group Captain J. F. Summers and Squadron Leader V. B. Bennett represented Bomber Command with Wing Commander G. H. Boyce present for Coastal Command. Group Captain R. B. G. Neville represented No. 25 (Arm) Group and Wing Commander W. R. Cox No. 1 Air Armament School. The Research Department at Woolwich was represented by Wing Commander F. R. Alford and Dr R. Ferguson, while Major R. Purves and Squadron Leader J. L. Wingate were present from the Royal Aircraft Establishment at Farnborough. The Admiralty representative was Lieutenant-Commander V. W. L. Proctor with Colonel I. Simpson for the War Office. The Air Ministry secretary was Flight Lieutenant F. G. Brockman.

Group Captain Bottomley enquired whether there were many dams in this country of the types which had been discussed, which an enemy could attack in the same way and, if so, were any defensive measures being taken? It was stated that there were several large reservoirs in Wales feeding Birmingham and Liverpool but no one at the meeting could voice an opinion as to what defensive measures were being contemplated.

At the end of the discussion the Committee were of opinion that the destruction of reservoir dams through the medium of attack from the air would, with certain qualifications, be a feasible operation. It was considered that low-level or low-dive attacks on these targets were the most likely to be successful, and were the most desirable from the operational point of view.

The committee concluded that 'the single-arch dam is the most likely type upon which attack will be required and the weapons recommended, on the basis of existing information (in order of priority), are: (a) a number of 18-inch torpedoes; (b) large general-purpose bombs; (c) 500lb general-purpose bombs; (d) 500lb anti-submarine bombs'.

The chances of success with options (c) and (d) were considered to be less favourable than with (a) and (b), but in the event of an emergency in the immediate future, it might be found that 500lb GP, and anti-submarine bombs were the only weapons available for immediate use.

Finally, the meeting reported that 'at the present time, it is considered that the attack should be directed primarily against the high water side of the dam. Attack against the lower side is considered less likely to be effective unless a bomb can be devised which will develop sufficient striking velocity to achieve the necessary amount of damage at low altitudes.'

Historic Kingsway, carved out of a slum area in London's West End at the end of the 19th century, where Adastral House, with the wireless masts on its roof, the new headquarters of the Royal Air Force, was opened at its southern end in 1919. Room 271 was the scene of the historic meeting in 1938 to examine the possibilities of destroying the German dams.

replied that a bomb fused with a short delay dropped on the high water side would be the most effective, but he pointed out that a bomb with a high charge-to-weight ratio would be necessary, and that it would have to fall very close to the wall. Wing Commander H. V. Rowley of the Air Ministry remarked that the only large bomb which was now available was the 2,000lb armour-piercing which had a very small charge-weight ratio and would therefore be practically useless for the purpose. As general-purpose bombs of 1,000 to 2,000lbs in weight would not be available for some time, and the largest bomb then available was only of 500lb, consequently he felt inclined to favour the torpedo as being the most suitable weapon for attack from the high water side.

Major R. Purves of the Royal Aircraft Establishment stated that the standard 18-inch torpedo had a range of 1,500 yards, and could be set to run between 5 and 45 feet below the water. The weight of the explosive in the warhead was just under 400lbs. If dropped 300 or 400 yards from the face of the dam it would reach the correct depth. It could be fitted with a net-cutter which was so efficient that ships had now abandoned the net system of protection.

Squadron Leader Burge then suggested that the element of uncertainty as to the outcome of the attack could be reduced by attacking on both sides of the dam, with bombs and/or torpedoes. This would give a double chance of success. In this connection Dr Ferguson said that the 500lb anti-submarine bomb already in service, which had a charge-weight ratio of 55 per cent and which could be carried in any bomber, would be better than a 500lb general-purpose bomb when dropped on the high water side. It would, however, break up in the event of a direct hit on the wall.

It was ironic that almost exactly six years later — on Friday, June 30, 1944 — the Germans came to within an ace of achieving retribution with a direct hit on the building. In the third worst V1 incident to befall London, a flying bomb struck the road just 40 yards in front of Adastral House, completely demolishing the ten-foot-high blast wall in front of the entrance and killing 48, the majority of the 200 casualties being passers-by.

Dr Barnes Wallis — the inventor of the bouncing bombs — photographed after the war in his office at Burhill, Walton-on-Thames, where his theory about the bombs took shape. A large photograph of the Möhne dam hangs on the wall (see page 169). Sir Barnes Wallis died on October 30, 1979 at the age of 92 having been knighted for his war services in 1968.

Barnes Wallis Goes to War

When war broke out Barnes Wallis was assistant chief designer of Vickers-Armstrong's Aviation Section at Weybridge. Here, quite independently of the Air Ministry, he concerned himself with how the energy sources of the Axis powers, Germany and Italy, might be eliminated. Specialist publications provided him with the necessary background information on the German dams, and he was firmly of the opinion that knocking out the water reserves of the Ruhr would severely curtail steel production for the German armament industry as the production of each tonne of steel required 100 tonnes of water. Articles in publications such as *Zeitschrift für Bauwesen* (Journal for Building Construction), *Zeitschrift für die gesamte Wasserwirtschaft*, (Journal for the National Hydro Economy) *Zeitschrift für Bauwesen* in the *Schweitzerische Wasserwiftschaft* (Building Construction in the Swiss Hydro Economy) and *Das Gas- und Wasserfach* (Gas and Water Industry) showed Wallis the technical minutiae of the German reservoirs.

By the end of 1940 Wallis believed that a heavy bomb dropped from 40,000 feet and weighing 10 tons would penetrate deep into the soil around the dams and that shock waves to the foundations would bring about the collapse of the whole structure. (Wallis was able to realise this idea in 1945 when his 10-ton 'Grand Slam' bombs were employed to destroy U-Boat bunkers and railway viaducts.) However, back in 1940, there was neither the 'earthquake bomb' nor an aircraft large enough to deliver and drop it accurately. Consequently, the Air Ministry did not attach a great deal of importance to the theory of the big bomb, believing that technical considerations made the proposal impossible to carry out. Nevertheless, from August 1940, Wallis managed to test streamlined model bombs in a wind tunnel at Teddington.

At the same time, a series of experiments to determine the amount of explosive necessary to destroy a dam began in October 1940 at the Road Research Laboratory at Harmondsworth, which was directed by Dr William Glanville. The RRL had been heavily involved with military matters since the outbreak of the war and had considerable experience in building models for predicting explosions and their effect. Dr Glanville discussed these problems in detail with Wallis and agreed — it would appear completely off the record — to initiate a series of tests on various model dams. He put together a team under Dr A. R. Collins and gave the responsibility for measuring the effects on the models to one of his scientific advisors, Mr D. G. Charlesworth.

The basis of these experiments was very simple. The scaled-down models were constructed of a similar material to those in Germany (and one in Sardinia) and these were subjected to relatively smaller amounts of explosive so that they would behave in the same way as the originals. Dr Collins explains how they went about it.

'Sir Reginald Strading, Chief Scientific Adviser to the Ministry of Home Security, who had a connection with Wallis through Professor A. J. S. Pippard, discovered that there was a small, unused concrete gravity dam in the Elan Valley water supply system of the City of Birmingham which was available for tests with explosives and he wrote to the corporation accepting responsibility on behalf of the Ministry for any costs that might be incurred.

'It had also been established that a model would reproduce accurately the effects of an explosion on a structure if the same materials were used and all the linear dimensions, including those of the explosive, were reduced by the same ratio. This rule, however, applied only to the effects caused directly by the explosion and a model would not necessarily represent the final effects on the structure as a whole because these would depend also on the type of structure, the site and the extent of the direct damage and the existing static loads including those due to gravity.

A wartime aerial view of the Road Research Laboratory at Harmondsworth. It was here that test explosions were carried out on scale models of the Möhne dam and of the Nant-y-Gro dam at Rhayader in Wales which had been secured for large-scale tests once the experiments on the models had been conducted. The area used for the testing can be seen top right.

Left: **The Director of the Road Research Laboratory was Dr W. H. Glanville.** Right: **Dr A. R. Collins oversaw the tests for Barnes Wallis and discovered by chance that a relatively small explosive charge, if placed in direct contact with the wall, would cause it to collapse.**

'In many instances the final results could be deduced easily but, in the case of a gravity dam which depended on its own weight for stability, the reliability of a model test was uncertain because gravity could not be scaled. It was, nevertheless, hoped that some means of circumventing this problem might be found and, in the first week of October 1940, Wallis visited the RRL and discussed plans for the research with Dr Glanville, Dr A. H. Davis (Assistant Director at the Laboratory) and myself. Without indicating how the choice had been made, Wallis suggested that the three main targets should be the Möhne and Eder masonry gravity dams in Germany and the Santa Chiara di Ula multiple-arch dam on the Tirso River in Sardinia. Of these dams Tirso was much the most vulnerable and, as it was not attacked, it can be dealt with very briefly, though the experimental work occupied several months. The maximum thickness of the reinforced concrete arches was only about five feet and preliminary tests on sections of concrete pipe indicated that a charge of about 3000lb of explosive would be likely to breach at least one of the arches if it were detonated in the water up to about 50ft away. This was confirmed by tests on an accurate 1:25 scale model built at the Building Research Station which showed also that a contact charge of about only a few hundred pounds might well be effective and that an attack with anti-submarine bombs or torpedoes would be possible.

'The problems posed by the Möhne and Eder dams were much more formidable. Both dams were massive structures built of cyclopean masonry and inherently stable even when cracked. The apparent impossibility of making allowance for the effects of gravity in a test on a model also added a major uncertainty. Of the two dams, Eder was the higher, but Möhne was the more conservatively designed and had a clay bank reaching almost to mid-height on the water face. It was therefore decided to use Möhne as the prototype for both dams, to confine the model to the centre section between two

Two models (above) **of the Nant-y-Gro dam were built to the scale of 1:10 for experiments before two tests were carried out on the actual dam in Wales to prove the theory in practice.**

Above: **To try to replicate the construction of the Möhne as near as possible, millions of tiny blocks were used to build the first test model at the Building Research Station at Garston near Watford.** *Below:* **For later models (in 1:50 scale), this time-consuming process was abandoned in favour of using mortar spread in layers.**

towers which were at approximately the third points of both dams, and to make it on a linear scale of 1:50. In view of the absence of previous experience and the uncertainty about the effects of gravity, it was also decided to make the model as accurately as possible by using a scaled-down form of masonry composed of mortar blocks 0.4 × 0.3 × 0.2 inches in size, and to lay them in the curved courses used in the prototype. This proved to be a tedious task requiring the production and laying by hand of some five million blocks which Dr Norman Davey and his colleague at the Building Research Station, Mr A. J. Newman, offered to undertake. The model was built on a small stream in the grounds of the Station.

'Wallis had estimated that his proposed ten-ton bomb would contain about seven tons of explosive and, on a scale of 1:50, this was represented by two ounces. He also suggested that, in a high-altitude attack by a squadron of aircraft, it could be expected that one bomb would fall in the reservoir within about 150ft of the dam. These parameters were, therefore, adopted as convenient starting points in the tests and preliminary experiments, using short lengths of concrete with a cross-section similar to that of the model, indicated that the effect would be significant but not so great as to prevent further tests.

'The true-to-scale model was fitted with a simple gauge to measure the horizontal deflection at mid-height at the centre, and the first charge of 2oz of gelignite was fired in the reservoir 3ft from the dam. The result was a short horizontal crack just below the crest and a vertical crack through the whole cross-section at the centre. The test was witnessed by several members of the Committee and it was agreed that the damage, if reproduced on the full scale, would require immediate repairs and perhaps a reduction in water level, but it could not be regarded as being enough to warrant an attack. The test was, therefore, repeated but this caused little more damage. Three more tests were made at the same distance of three feet, three at a distance of two feet, and, finally, two were made at a distance of one foot. Each of these caused a little more damage and the final effect was quite substantial. It was considered that, on the full scale, the same damage would require the

A deflective gauge was installed to record vibrations of the wall caused by underwater explosions at varying distances.

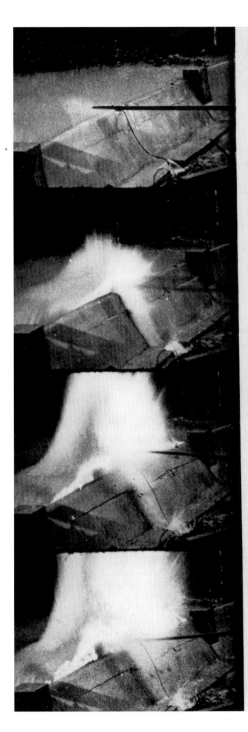
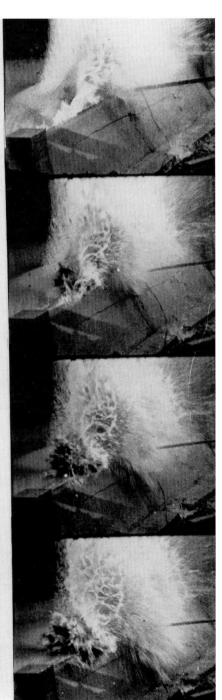

Left: **Slow motion cine footage shows the effects of two different experimental explosions on the model of the Möhne. The aim of the research was to establish the relationship between weight of explosive and the distance from the wall at which blasts became effective, depending on the varying water level in the reservoirs.** *Above and below:* **Author Helmuth Euler found the old model — which cost the princely sum of £34 13s to build — still standing at Garston.**

Following the model testing, in May 1942 the Nant-y-Gro dam at Rhayader was prepared for large-scale experiments.

reservoir to be drained and closer examination showed that the damage was more extensive than it appeared to be on the surface. The tests, however, represented a very heavy and extremely accurate attack that was very unlikely to be achieved in practice and it was therefore decided to continue with the investigation.

'It was, however, impracticable to construct more models by the time-consuming process used in making the first and the research team therefore devised a simpler method of representing the masonry construction by layers of mortar formed by a sliding template which allowed a model to be made in two weeks instead of the three months required by the original process. A test made to compare the two processes showed that while there were some differences in the behaviour of the models they were not important in comparison with other uncertainties.

'The BRS model had, however, been built on clay soil while the Möhne and Eder dams were founded on rock. The next test was therefore made to examine this factor with a new model built on an existing massive block of concrete. The results were, however, little different and it seemed at this time that there was only a remote possibility that a large gravity dam could be breached by the method proposed by Wallis. The Air Ministry, therefore, suggested that an attack might be made using a number of bombs or mines fitted with pressure-activated fuses which could be detonated by the shock wave from a normal bomb dropped further away from the dam so that the individual shock waves would amalgamate. Charlesworth investigated this proposal but found that the pressure-activated fuses would have to operate within one millisecond and this was regarded as being impracticable at the time.

'There was, however, a more promising development towards the end of 1941 when new and more powerful explosives were produced and one of these, plastic explosive (PE), was made available to the laboratory. After preliminary experiments, tests were made on some new models of Möhne and it was found that a one-ounce charge of PE at a distance of one foot caused significantly more damage than that achieved in the earlier tests with gelignite. Although the damage was still insufficient to warrant an attack with bombs dropped in the reservoir, the Committee felt that little further progress could be made without some information on the effects of scale and that the risks in making a test on the Elan Valley dam had to be accepted.

'The dam had been built at the turn of the century on a small stream, called the Nant-y-Gro on the bank of the Caban Coch Reservoir, to provide water for the construction of the main dam. It was made of mass concrete and was 30ft high at the centre, 180ft long, straight in plan and with a height/thickness ratio of 1.5 to 1.0. The reservoir was only 250ft long and any water released as a result of the test would flow safely into the main reservoir. A survey was made of the construction joints and cracks in the dam and the contours of the bed of the reservoir. Two models of the dam and reservoir complete with cracks and joints were then made at the laboratory and tested with one-ounce charges of PE at distances ranging from 6 inches to 24 inches and at depths of 18 inches and 24 inches.

'The results showed that the straight dam behaved in a way that was rather different from that seen in the Möhne models. There was no rebound effect resulting in forward movement, but there was evidence of a form of vertical 'bending' in which the blocks between the construction joints tilted away from the explosion and then fell back into place.

'Of this series of tests, that in which the charge was 9 inches from the dam and 18 inches deep produced enough damage to allow a comparison to be made, but not so much as to prevent another test on the Nant-y-Gro dam if required. The test was therefore repeated on the Nant-y-Gro dam with the ten-times equivalents of 62.5lb of TNT fired 7.5ft from the dam at a depth of 15 feet. The damage in both structures consisted mostly of cracking along the construction joints but some parts of the spillway walls were detached as a result of the reflected tensile stress forecast by Wallis but, as none of the effects would have been affected by gravity, they gave no indication of any way in which an allowance could be made for this factor.

'A solution to the problem was, however, found almost by chance shortly afterwards. Although Wallis had suggested to Tizard a direct hit on the water face of the dam, during the early stages of the investigation, he had rejected it in his paper to the Air Ministry and apparently agreed with the Committee that the idea was impracticable. Soon after the first test on the Nant-y-Gro dam, however the research team had to demolish a damaged model and decided to do this with a contact charge. The effect was unexpectedly severe and some parts of the model were projected more than 20ft downstream. When Glanville saw this result he reacted with a proposal for a means of allowing for the effect of gravity. He argued that as both the mass of the dam and the energy of the explosive varied with the cube of the scale, the distance travelled by any fragment of the structure would be the same irrespective of the scale. He therefore suggested that if the distance travelled by every fragment were reduced in proportion to the scale ratio, the model would then represent what would occur on the full scale. The model was, therefore, reconstructed in this way and the result was a realistic breach.

'Further tests on new models were then made with one-ounce contact charges at depths of 9 and 12 inches and with 4 and 8oz charges at a depth of 12 inches. After reconstruction of the models the results showed that a 4oz charge at a depth of 12 inches produced an adequate breach, and the Committee decided to reproduce this test on the Nant-y-Gro dam with the ten-times equivalent weight of explosive of 280lbs, provided by a 500lb anti-submarine bomb, at a depth of 10ft. The result was a breach 60ft wide and 24ft deep which was rather less wide and deeper than that forecast from the model, but was regarded as being more realistic and more reliable than the result with the tenth-scale model. It was, of course, not possible to reconstruct the Nant-y-Gro dam to represent the result at larger scales, but from the positions of the fragments it was deduced that an increase in scale of up to about five times would have little effect on the relative dimensions of the breach.'

While these tests were taking place, Wallis was preparing a long paper entitled *A Note on the Method of Attacking the Axis Powers*, the product of a year-long intensive period of thought, research and experimentation. It was finalised in March 1941 and some 100 copies were circulated in military and political circles, the outcome being the formation of a committee — the Aerial Attack on Dams Committee — to progress the matter further.

In general, the tests on the models had been disappointing and the first explosion on the real Nant-y-Gro dam shown here failed to breach the wall. Dr Collins thereby concluded that it would take in excess of 13 tons of explosive to be effective against the Möhne and of course no such bomb, or aircraft to carry it, then existed. However, this discouraging result was overturned when Collins set out to see what the charge would do if set off in contact with the face of the model dam at Harmondsworth. When he tested his theory, he was astonished to see how easily the model wall was breached by just 2oz of explosive with mortar flying 20 feet away. So a second test was ordered in Wales using a 500lb naval mine containing a scaled-up charge of 280lbs of explosive. This was suspended at the mid-point of the dam below the surface of the water and detonated on July 24. The result astounded those watching, indicating that 7,500lbs of explosive, if set off in contact with the Möhne dam wall, would breach it.

In preparing this report on the economic and moral consequences of the destruction of the German dams, the Ministry of Economic Warfare set out the pros and cons of each of the main targets. They also put forward the Lister, Ennepe and Henne as other possibilities and mentioned that there were another seven smaller dams within the Ruhr catchment area although the Möhne and Sorpe between them held 75 per cent of the total reservoir capacity. The Eder was the odd man out, seen here in profile via the model which was built in 1:40 scale in about 1910. Helmuth Euler discovered that it still stands off the northern shoreline near the Nieder-Werbe—Waldeck road (see map page 72). Normally submerged, the model was photographed one autumn when the water level had fallen sufficiently to expose it.

The Targets

On March 28, 1943, the RAF's Air Staff once again considered the targets in Germany and clarified the economic effect and the effect on morale of destroying the Möhne dam. At the same time they considered the increased impact if the Sorpe and Eder were to be simultaneously destroyed. This is their report drawn up on April 2, 1943.

ECONOMIC AND MORAL CONSEQUENCES OF THE DESTRUCTION OF GERMAN DAMS

Introduction

1. This memorandum assesses the probable economic and moral consequences of the destruction of the Möhne dam and the added effects which could be expected from the destruction of the Sorpe and Eder dams.

2. It has been prepared in consultation with the Scientific Advisers to the Minister of Production and with reference to the statements attributed to them in the introduction to the Combined Operations dossier on the Möhne dam. The latter document, on certain points of detail, over-states the expectations of the Scientific Advisers as to the probable economic effects and the following conclusions should be taken as representing their actual views.

3. Möhne Dam

(a) Although the precise nature of the catastrophe which would overtake the Ruhr valley as the result of the release of the greater part of the contents of this dam in the space of a few hours cannot be estimated in advance, it is agreed that there is every prospect that both the physical and the moral effects of the flood which would be produced are likely to be sufficiently great to justify this operation in themselves, even if there were no other significant effects.

(b) The destruction of this dam would not necessarily have any large or immediate effect on the supply of industrial and household water in the Ruhr area. This immediate source of the greater part of the Ruhr water supply is the underground water-bearing strata, supplemented by colliery water, water pumped back from the Rhine and water drawn from the Emscher river and canal systems. The purpose of the system of storage dams of which the Möhne dam is largest, is the conservation of rainfall, by means of which the level of the underground water can be maintained and protected from permanent depletion. In an emergency, a large and possibly adequate volume of water supplies might be obtainable for some months by drawing heavily on these underground supplies and depleting their level. Whether or not such depletion would proceed at a rate or reach the stage where economies in water consumption would have to be introduced would depend upon the amount of rainfall, the speed of repairs to damaged conservation works and the efficacy of emergency measures to obtain additional water (e.g. from the Rhine). If these factors were all unfavourable, a difficult situation might well develop by the end of the summer, but it is not possible to state that a critical shortage of water supplies in the Ruhr would be a certain and inevitable result of the destruction of the Möhne dam.

The model-making section at RAF Medmenham — the complex in Oxfordshire which housed the RAF's photo-reconnaissance interpretation unit — constructed models of the Möhne *(above)*, Eder and Sorpe reservoirs to the scale of 1:6000. On the morning of the raid three large boxes were unsealed at RAF Scampton and the targets revealed to the assembled aircrews. The models have been held by the Imperial War Museum in London since 1946.

The Sorpe model with the dam at its north-eastern end.

4. Sorpe Dam

The Sorpe dam is essentially complementary to the Möhne dam and its simultaneous or subsequent destruction would in general reinforce the effects of the destruction of the Möhne dam. In particular, its destruction would very greatly enhance the prospects of the development of a water supply shortage by the process described under section 3(b). For this reason the destruction of both dams would be worth much more than twice the destruction of one and it is most strongly urged, if the operational possibilities hold out any reasonable prospect of success, that an attack on the Möhne dam be accompanied, or followed as soon as possible, by an attack on the Sorpe dam.

5. Eder Dam

(a) The functions of the Eder dam are not related to those of the Möhne dam and Sorpe dam and its destruction would not therefore in any way supplement or reinforce the effects of the destruction of the Ruhr dams.

(b) The primary purpose of the Eder dam is flood prevention. The release of its waters would without doubt result in the inundation of large tracts of land in the Eder, Fulda and Weser valleys but the areas affected are likely to consist for the most part of agricultural land. It is unlikely that any densely populated industrial areas would be affected, apart from the possible inundation of the low-lying districts of the city of Kassel.

(c) Although the Eder dam plays some part in the conservation of water for maintaining the navigability of the lower reaches of the Weser and for supplying water to the Mittelland canal, it is unlikely that its destruction would lead to a critical situation in either case.

(d) The force of the flood released by breaching the dam would very probably result in the destruction of the four power stations situated below it. While not of major economic importance, this would constitute a useful measure of interference with the operations of the Preussenelektra electricity supply system.

MORAL EFFECTS

6. (a) The effects of the destruction of the Möhne and Sorpe dams would be witnessed by many thousands of persons who, whatever the true facts, would undoubtedly in view of the traditionally precarious nature of the Ruhr's water supplies become prey to every variety of alarmist rumour regarding the possibility of a shortage of drinking water, the risk of disease, and the inability of the fire services to deal with incendiary attacks. Exceptional opportunities would be presented for successful measures of political warfare.

(b) The destruction of the Eder dam would not be likely to affect directly any large centres of population (with the possible exception of the city of Kassel) and its effects would be experienced by many fewer people than in the case of the Ruhr dams. Since its functions are also less intimately connected with the daily life of large populated areas, the total moral effect, though by no means negligible, would inevitably be much smaller than in the case of the Ruhr dams.

A section of the Eder model. All were constructed by Medmenham using aerial photographs.

A Brilliant Idea

Ricocheting cannon balls have been known since the 16th century and aiming low was a technique used by naval gunners in the 17th and early 18th centuries to extend the range of their guns. In 1903, the German physicist Carl Wilhelm Ramsauer investigated the behaviour of high-velocity bodies striking water by firing brass balls with a diameter of 11mm and muzzle velocity of 610 metres per second onto the surface. These experiments demonstrated that when the angle of incidence is greater than seven degrees the ball enters the water but, when the angle is less, it skips over the surface. The mathematicians Cranz and Becker interpreted these results mathematically. Carl Julius Cranz is the father of modern ballistics and his pupil, Karl Becker, wrote important papers on the subject. However, the experiments carried out by naval gunners and Ramsauer did not involve the application of spin to the projectiles. Although rapid spin is an essential element for achieving certain effects in many ball games (tennis for example), the potential effect of spin on the flight of a ricocheting spherical projectile was not known until the subject was first studied by Barnes Wallis. He was the first to demonstrate that the range of ricocheting projectiles could be extended when backspin was added, which also gave greater power on impact. Called the 'Magnus Effect', it acts like aerodynamic lift and thereby increases the number of bounces.

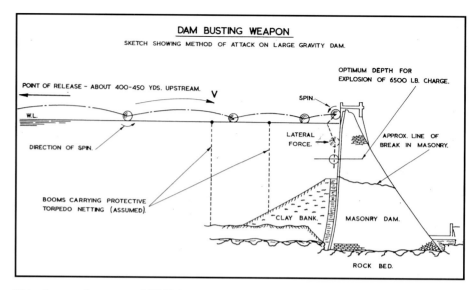

DAM BUSTING WEAPON
SKETCH SHOWING METHOD OF ATTACK ON LARGE GRAVITY DAM.

This diagram from one of Wallis's contemporary files demonstrates his theory of how a dam wall could be destroyed with a single bomb. Just 400 metres from the target, the cylindrical bomb, or rather mine, revolving with backspin, was to be released at a height of 60 feet. The initial bounces of 200 feet then gradually became shorter as the mine skipped over the torpedo nets and was driven against the dam wall. After rebounding from the freeboard of the dam, the mine spun under inertia back into contact with the wall and then crawled down until the hydrostatic fuse triggered the explosion at a depth of 30 feet four seconds later. The ensuing shock waves acted like an earthquake to bring down the dam.
Below: The catapult used by Wallis in later experiments is now on display at the Royal Air Force Museum at Hendon.

The story of the bouncing bomb started out on the terrace of Barnes Wallis's home, White Hill House, Effingham, Surrey (pictured in 1973). Barnes Wallis began firing marbles at a rainwater tub filled with water and got his children to measure the distance of the bounce when the marble hit a wooden board. His original idea came from the children's game of skipping a flat pebble across the surface of the sea.

The early crude experiments on his terrace using marbles were soon superceded by using specially-prepared spheres, approximately two inches in diameter, made of various substances and firing them down the length of the tank at the National Physical Laboratory at Teddington, Middlesex. *Above:* Looking rather like large golf balls, a number of the projectiles have survived to be displayed in the Barnes Wallis corner at Hendon. *Right:* The 670-foot-long No. 2 Towing Tank, used to carry out the experiments, has since been demolished to make way for a car park!

By the time Barnes Wallis arrived at the Road Research Laboratory the plan to attack the dams using conventional bombs seemed already dead. Yet he refused to be discouraged and remained convinced that success could be achieved if an explosive charge could be detonated against the dam wall. Consequently, in parallel with the experiments on model dams, he used the ship-testing facilities at the National Physical Laboratory at Teddington to check out his theories based upon the children's game in which pebbles are bounced off the surface of a pond. He had already carried out experiments in his own back garden using his daughter's marbles; now he carried his testing further with spherical projectiles made of wood, aluminium, steel and lead. These were catapulted along the tank so as to skip across the water before striking a simulated dam wall at the other end. In this way he hoped to establish the optimum weight, size, design, speed and bounce distance of the balls on the surface and thus determine the optimum skip technique.

And so the idea of the bouncing bomb was born: now all that was needed was some fine tuning to enable it to deliver a relatively small explosive charge accurately on the target. Extensive experiments proved that the number of bounces — and therefore also the range — of a spherical bomb is increased if it is dropped at low altitude at high speed with a rapid backspin. This would also enable the projectile to skip over torpedo nets or tear them easily. Then, after the bomb has hit the dam, the backspin would cause it to stay in close contact with the wall and crawl down its face to the critical depth where the explosion would bring about earthquake-like tremors in the wall. Wallis also had these experiments filmed at normal and high speed with cameras above and below the surface.

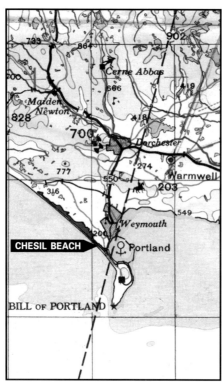

On December 4, 1942, Captain Mutt Summers *(left)*, Wallis's test pilot at Vickers-Armstrong, took off from the company's airfield at Weybridge in Wellington BJ895 en route for Chesil Beach near Portland. However the inert sphere broke up on hitting the sea.

A second attempt took place five days later followed by more flights in December, Wallis each time modifying and strengthening the 'bombs' to try to prevent them breaking up on impact. The 'bouncing' bomb theory was first proved possible on Saturday, January 23, 1943.

It was not until August 25, 1942, during a meeting at Vickers House in London, that Barnes Wallis finally convinced the representatives of the Ministry of Aircraft Production and Vickers-Armstrong of his ideas and, as a result, they decided to conduct tests using a spherical bomb. On December 4 a Wellington bomber took off from Weybridge with Captain Mutt Summers, a test pilot from Vickers, at the controls and Wallis in the bomb-aimer's position. For this first trial, a section of sea off Chesil Beach in Dorset had been chosen and a camera set up on the ground to film the results. Because the modified Wellington with its projecting bomb was not recognised, anti-aircraft defences opened fire but fortunately the aircraft was not hit. However, when the bomb struck the water, it promptly disintegrated.

The casing having been reinforced, the next flight took place on December 9. A flash from the cockpit of the Wellington signalled to the observers and the RAF cameraman that the bomb had been released. A white stripe had been painted on it to make it possible for the rotation to be seen. Further test drops from between 45 and 220 feet followed on December 15 at a speed of 230-255 mph with a bomb rotation speed of between 250 and 750 rpm. Wallis later rowed out in a boat to inspect the casings, finally locating one which was still intact but badly damaged.

A third trial took place on January 9, 1943 and a fourth on the 23rd of the month resulting in a 'skip' of 13 times and one the following day of a spectacular 20 times! On each occasion, different modifications were carried out to the casings until a further test on February 5 achieved a range of over 1,300 yards.

By the end of 1942 Wallis had completed a follow-up report entitled *Air Attack on Dams* and submitted it to a number of senior military and political figures. On January 28 he showed the films of the Chesil Beach tests to a gathering of high-ranking staff from the Air Ministry, Admiralty and Ministry of Aircraft Production. The Admiralty pressed for initial priority to be given to the further development of the bomb, which was required urgently for use against surface vessels, particularly the battleship *Tirpitz*, and at the end of January an order for 250 such weapons was placed on behalf of the Royal Navy.

However, Wallis wanted first to use his brainchild against the German dams which he regarded as being more important than German warships. He also felt that premature use of the new weapon could give away the secret of the bouncing bombs to the Germans, who would then turn their dams into impregnable fortresses. Wallis therefore proposed that both weapons — the anti-ship bomb code-named 'Highball' and the larger 'Upkeep' for attacking the dams — should be developed simultaneously. Wallis also intended to develop another version under the code-name of 'Baseball' which was to be fired at warships from motor torpedo boats. All the various types of bouncing bomb came under the combined code-name of 'Golf Mine'.

However, as early as February 10, Wallis received his first set-back when Air Vice-Marshal F. J. Linnell, Head of Research and Development at the Ministry of Aircraft Production, told him that all work on the project was to be halted immediately. The only consolation was that the 'Highball' programme could continue, especially with regard to its use by Mosquitos which were to carry two small bouncing bombs. On February 13 the head of

At first, Air Chief Marshal Sir Arthur Harris *(left)*, C-in-C of Bomber Command, was implacably opposed to the very concept of the new weapon when he was told about it by his Senior Air Staff Officer, Air Vice-Marshal Robert Saundby *(right)*.

RAF Bomber Command HQ was located at High Wycombe, Buckinghamshire. This is the Air Staff Block with Harris's office at the left-hand end. From there it was just a short walk from the end door towards the camera position to reach the underground Operations Block.

Bomber Command, Air Chief Marshal Sir Arthur Harris, was fully briefed on the dams proposal by Group Captain S. C. Elsworthy, the same day that members of the Aerial Attack on Dams Committee were entertaining doubts as to whether the new bombs could be operationally available by April.

On February 14 the Senior Air Staff Officer at Bomber Command HQ at High Wycombe, Air Vice-Marshal Robert Saundby, summarised the operation against the dams to Sir Arthur, attaching a copy of Wallis's paper *Air Attacks on Dams* saying that a final decision needed to be made by February 15. He explained that an uprated bomb of 10,000lbs containing a 6,500lb explosive charge would need to be carried in a specially-modified Lancaster for the attack on the Möhne dam. He also stated that the squadron concerned would have to be relieved of its duties for two to three weeks beforehand to carry out training. Saundby ended by saying that the operation would not be difficult as it would be carried out at night by the light of a full moon using the new radio altimeters.

Sir Arthur returned the report the same day with a curt hand-written note:

'This is tripe of the wildest description. There are so many ifs & ands that there is not the smallest chance of it working. To begin with the bomb would have to be perfectly balanced round its axis, otherwise vibration at 500 rpm would wreck the aircraft or tear the bomb loose. I don't believe a word of its supposed ballistics on the surface. It would be much easier to design a "scow" bomb to run on the surface, bust its nose in on contact, sink & explode. This bomb would of course be heavier than water & exactly fit existing bomb bays. At all costs stop them putting aside Lancs & reducing our bombing effort on this wild goose chase. Let them prove the practicalities of the weapon first.'

In spite of this depressing reply, which ended with Harris's prediction that 'the war will be over before it works — & it never will', a meeting was held the following day at the Air Ministry attended by Wallis and his pilot Captain Summers at which it was decided to go ahead with the construction of one of the larger dam-busting bombs and to have one Lancaster modified with cradles to test it. This decision was minuted to Sir Arthur on February 18. Harris replied immediately to Air Chief Marshal Sir Charles Portal, the Chief of Air Staff, the tone of his response repeating his earlier misgivings.

'. . . all sorts of enthusiasts and panacea mongers now careering round MAP [the Ministry of Aircraft Production] suggesting the taking of about 30 Lancasters off the line to rig them up for this weapon, when the weapon itself exists so far only within the imagination of those who conceived it . . . that some entirely new weapon, totally untried, is going to be a success. . . . I am now prepared to bet that the Highball is just about the maddest proposition as a weapon that we have yet come across — and that is saying something. . . . I am prepared to bet my shirt (a) that the weapon itself cannot be passed as a prototype for trial inside six months; (b) that its ballistics will in no way resemble those claimed for it; (c) that it will be impossible to keep such a weapon in adequate balance either when rotating it prior to release or at all in storage; and (d) that it will not work when we have got it. Finally we have made attempt after attempt to pull successful low attacks with heavy bombers. They have been, almost without exception, costly failures. . . . I hope you will do your utmost to keep these mistaken enthusiasts within the bounds of reason and certainly to prevent them setting aside any number of our precious Lancasters for immediate modification.'

One can picture the scene in Harris's office when Barnes Wallis entered with his test pilot. The Bomber Command chief is reported to have greeted them frostily: 'What the hell do you damned inventors want?'

The following day, February 19, Portal had the opportunity to see for himself the results of the Chesil Beach tests when Wallis arranged a screening at Vickers House. Also in attendance was the First Sea Lord, Admiral Sir Dudley Pound. On the strength of the film, the latter declared Highball to be 'the most promising secret weapon yet produced by any belligerent'. Portal, already convinced, decided that he would make three valuable Lancaster bombers available for test purposes until such time as the bouncing bombs were ready for production. He informed Sir Arthur of his decision later the same day, declaring: 'If you want to win the war bust the dams'.

On February 21 Wallis took the bull by the horns and went with Matt Summers to Harris's headquarters at High Wycombe. The interview had been set up by Air Vice-Marshal Sir Ralph Cochrane commanding No. 5 Group, the man who would have the responsibility of organising the attack if it went ahead. He had persuaded his chief that he must give the matter further consideration. Sir Arthur had acquiesced but he was in an abrasive mood and shouted at Wallis as soon as he came through the door: 'What the hell do you damned inventors want? My boys' lives are too precious to be thrown away by you!'

After he had calmed down and his staff had been dismissed, Sir Arthur agreed to watch the film that Wallis had brought with him, Air Vice-Marshal Saundby acting as projectionist. Despite the unpleasant atmosphere, Wallis explained the various types of bomb and also the targets. Underwater shots of the Teddington tests aroused Harris's curiosity but he remained sceptical. However he let slip that the Chief of the Air Staff had already agreed the conversion of three Lancasters so Wallis finally realised that he was getting somewhere.

The following day the encouraging news that the Ministry of Aircraft Production had authorised the modification of two Mosquito fighter-bombers for Highball tests, was quickly negated when Wallis was summoned to London to see the chairman of Vickers-Armstrong, Sir Charles Craven. He told Wallis in no uncertain terms that he was making a thorough nuisance of himself at the Air Ministry and, by involving Vickers-Armstrong directly or indirectly, he was damaging the firm's interests. Sir Charles then ordered Wallis to stop all work on the large bomb forthwith. In the circumstances, Wallis's reaction was understandable — he offered to resign.

Nevertheless Wallis continued working and two days later he was invited to attend a conference at the Ministry of Aircraft Production to be chaired by Air Vice-Marshal Linnell. In the presence of representatives from the Air Ministry and Vickers-Armstrong (including Sir Charles), Linnell explained that the Chief of the Air Staff now wanted every effort to be made on the development of the aircraft and bombs, and that the project to breach the dams would now have priority so that the operation could be carried out by May 26, the latest optimum date before the water level would fall too low.

While Wallis was highly delighted at the unexpected turn of events, nevertheless there were now just three months left for the manufacture of the Upkeeps; to design and perfect the mechanism for supporting and rotating them aboard the aircraft; to modify the Lancasters and, more important than anything, to train the crews to drop the new bombs accurately. He shared his thoughts at the time when he wrote on February 27 that 'it appears that we are to go ahead at full speed, and my only fear now is that this important decision may have been arrived at too late'.

The project was given top priority at both the Vickers-Armstrong and Avro factories. In addition to the three Lancaster bombers that were already being modified, a further 20 were now to receive the same treatment. Avro were given the job of modifying the bomb bays of the Lancasters and strengthening the fuselage at this point. Furthermore, they were to construct the release mechanism and install the motor for rotating the bomb. Meanwhile, Vickers-Armstrong were to deal with the attachment arms to carry the bomb

As we now know, Harris was proved wrong and Wallis right — the new bomb did work — and very successfully. Here, 30 years later, Sir Barnes shows his wife a sectionalised Upkeep on display at the RAF Museum at Hendon.

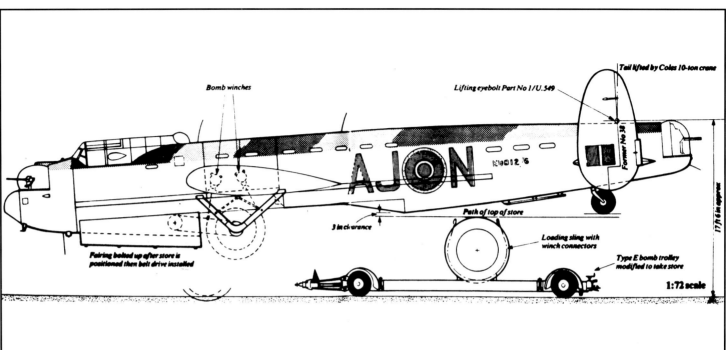

Bomb winches

Lifting eyebolt Part No 1/U.549

Tail lifted by Coles 10-ton crane

Former No 34

Path of top of store

3 in clearance

Loading sling with winch connectors

Fairing bolted up after store is positioned then belt drive installed

Type E bomb trolley modified to take store

1:72 scale

After seeing film of the Chesil Beach tests, the Chief of the Air Staff, Air Chief Marshal Sir Charles Portal *(above)*, **took it on himself to order modifications to be made to three Lancasters to drop the bomb. However, Wallis's idea of having a spherical bomb had to be abandoned because of a shortage of the necessary quality steel so a cylindrical design, which could be constructed from sheet metal, was substituted.** *Right:* **Ironically, this drawing is reproduced from a German bomb-disposal manual — as we shall see they captured one of the weapons intact after the raid.**

and the manufacture of the bomb itself. An order was placed for 120 Upkeeps: 60 inert bombs for practice and 60 filled with the powerful explosive RDX, it being estimated that the mere filling of the bombs would take over three weeks.

By February 28 Wallis had completed a set of plans for the Upkeep. Initially he had wanted a bomb of 7ft 6in in diameter but the high-grade steel necessary to fabricate a spherical bomb was in very short supply so he had to settle for a cylindrical shape which could be rolled from sheet steel and welded together. The necessary diameter would then be achieved by over-packing with wood cladding held on by steel bands. Three naval-type hydrostatic pistols were to be used to ensure that the device would detonate at a precise depth, and a self-destruct charge was incorporated to prevent an intact weapon falling into enemy hands. The test bombs, painted grey, were filled with concrete while the live Upkeeps were dark green.

A testing range had been earmarked at a secluded stretch of the north Kent coast at Reculver close to the airfield at Manston. Cameras were set up on the shore to record both the lateral skip of the bombs and any horizontal deviation. The first modified Lancaster was ready on April 8 and it was flown to Manston two days later by Captain Summers with Barnes Wallis aboard. Ground testing of the spinning mechanism followed to check the balance of each bomb which could be fine-tuned by the addition of steel plates at either end and by Tuesday morning, April 13, all was ready.

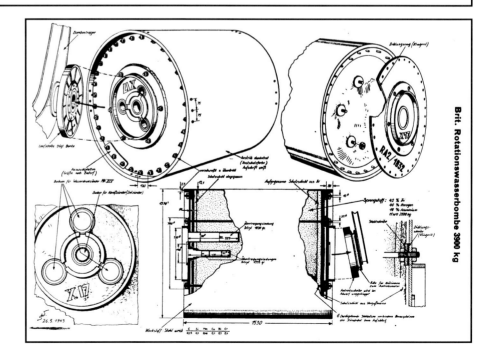

Brit. Rotationswasserbombe 3900 kg

23

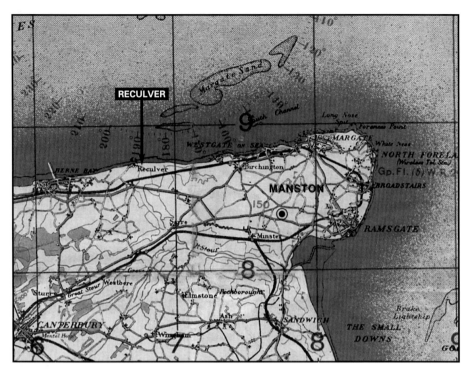

Testing with the modified Lancasters and the full-size Upkeep was switched to the north Kent coast at Reculver, which was both isolated from prying eyes and conveniently situated not far from the aerodrome at Manston.

For the first drop, another Vickers test pilot, Captain R. C. Handasyde took off carrying a scaled-down inert Upkeep in the Wellington which had been used in the Chesil Beach testing. Dropped from an altitude of 80ft, the wooden packing disintegrated when the bomb hit the water although the cylinder itself remained intact. The woodwork on two more bombs tested that day by a Lancaster piloted by Squadron Leader M. V. 'Shorty' Longbottom also broke up. Over the next few days, the bracing bands were strengthened but when the same thing happened at the next test held on Sunday, April 18, Wallis decided to dispense entirely with the wooden casing. The first bare cylinder was dropped three days later but it, too, shattered on impact. Though Wallis was not present, he soon determined that the reason was that the pilot had released the bomb too high at 185ft. Wallis emphasised that the bombs must be dropped from exactly 60ft, at a ground speed of 232mph, to induce the desired skip effect and on April 28 the first really successful drop resulted in the bomb bouncing six times over 670 yards. Further test drops over the next three days, and on through the first week of May, confirmed the height and speed criteria.

On May 13 a live Upkeep was dropped for the first time by Squadron Leader Longbottom five miles off the North Foreland coast at Broadstairs. Released from 75ft with a backspin of 500 rpm, it cleared a distance of 800 yards in seven huge skips before sinking and exploding four seconds later. The detonation created a plume of water over 750 feet high some 200 to 300 yards wide.

Since the go-ahead had been given on February 26, less than three months had passed — an almost unbelievable time in the development of an entirely new weapon from conception to operational use. Now there were just three days left.

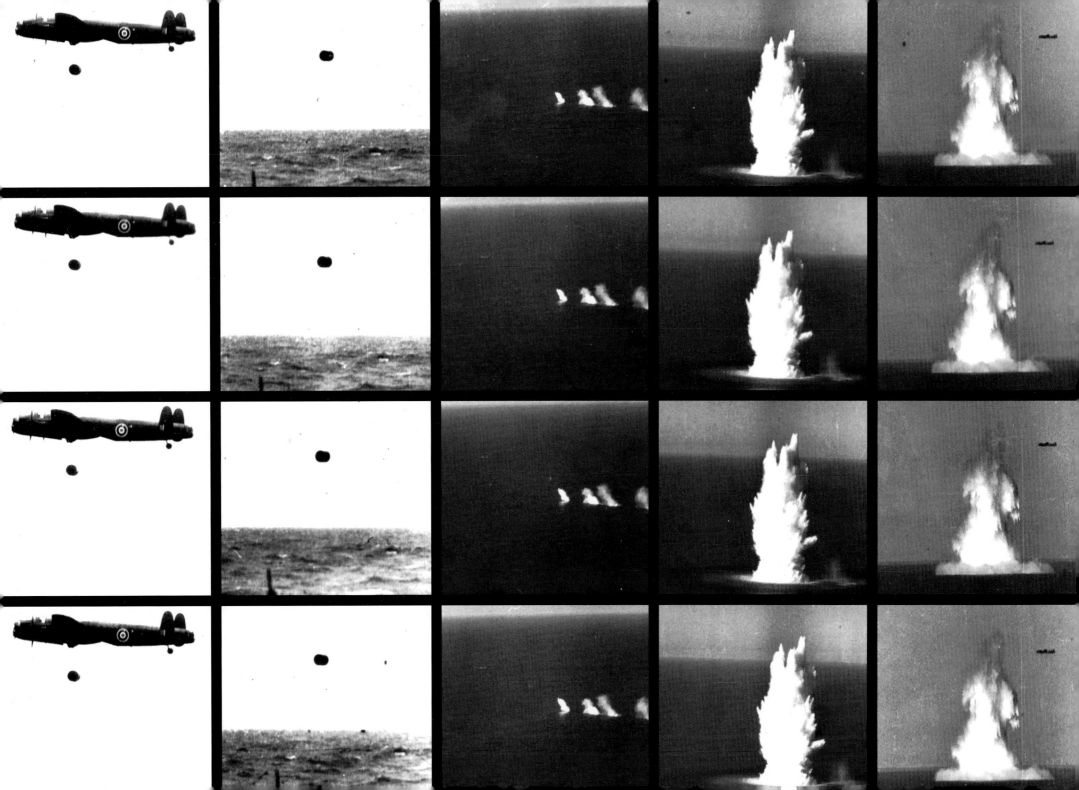

Left: **Air Vice-Marshal Sir Ralph Cochrane, the Air Officer Commanding No. 5 Group, had his headquarters at St Vincents, a country mansion at Grantham built circa 1867.** *Above:* **This picture dates from 1979 when it was purchased by South Kesteven District Council for office accommodation by which time the wartime Operations Block in the grounds had been demolished. Today it is a private residence.**

Squadron X

On March 15, 1943, Sir Arthur Harris ordered Air Vice-Marshal Cochrane, the AOC of No. 5 Group, to organise the operation against the dams. Harris specified that an entirely new squadron must be formed for the job and that it was to be led by Wing Commander Guy Gibson, currently the CO of No. 106 Squadron based at Syerston, Nottinghamshire. Initally, Gibson was posted to No. 5 Group headquarters at Grantham, Lincolnshire, ostensibly with the task of writing a book to describe the work of aircrews in

Wing Commander Guy Gibson, 24 years old. On March 25, 1943, on the completion of his third operational tour at which time he had logged a total of 642 hours on 170 sorties, he was awarded a bar to his DSO. Gibson had been a keen Scout and used to wear a leather strap on his left wrist, with the Boy Scout fleur-de-lis — unfortunately not visible in this picture. He is wearing a German Mae West, reputedly taken from a Heinkel 111 that he had shot down when he was on night fighter ops.

bomber and fighter squadrons. However two days later was he was summoned to see the AOC and asked if he would be willing to lead a very important operation. With the prospect of being relieved of his present laborious task, Gibson agreed although he went back to the book-writing project the following year. Published after Gibson's death, *Enemy Coast Ahead* describes the follow-up meeting held with the AOC on March 18:

'In his office was another man, one of the youngest base commanders in the Group, Air Commodore [sic] Charles Whitworth. The Air Vice-Marshal was very amiable. He told me to sit down, offered me a Chesterfield and began to talk.

'"I asked you the other day if you would care to do another raid. You said you would, but I have to warn you that this is no ordinary sortie. In fact it can't be done for at least two months." (I thought, hell, it's the *Tirpitz*. What on earth did I say "Yes" for?)

'"Moreover", he went on, "the training for the raid is of such importance that the Commander-in-Chief has decided that a special squadron is to be formed for the job. I want you to form that squadron. As you know, I believe in efficiency, so I want you to do it well. I think you had better use Whitworth's main base at Scampton. As far as aircrews are concerned, I want the best — you choose them. W/C Smith, the SOA will help you pick ground crews. Each squadron will be forced to cough up men to build your unit up to strength. Now there's a lot of urgency in this, because you haven't got long to train. Training will be the important thing, so get going right away. Remember you are working to a strict timetable, and I want to see your aircraft flying in four days' time. Now up you go upstairs to hand in the names of your crews to Cartwright; he will give you all the help you want."

'"But what sort of training, sir? And the target? I can't do a thing—"

'"I am afraid I can't tell you any more just for the moment. All you have to do is pick your crews, get them ready to fly, then I will come and see you and tell you more."'

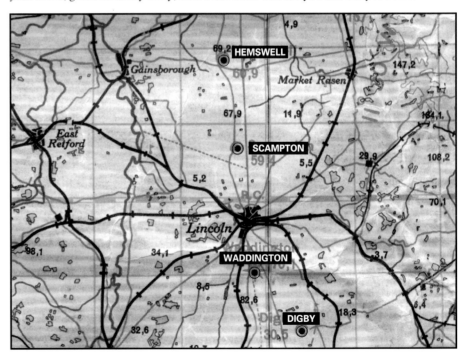

Scampton, the base selected for Gibson's new squadron, lay four miles north of Lincoln and was partly located on an old First World War landing ground which had ceased to exist by the early 1920s.

Left: RAF Scampton, base of No. 617 Squadron. Eleven years after the raid, the scenes are recreated on the same hallowed ground in Lincolnshire for the film *The Dam Busters* released in 1955. On the right, the Sergeants' Mess where the final briefing with the model dams took place. With the expansion of the RAF to meet developments in Germany during the 1930s, the Air Ministry turned first to abandoned First World War landing grounds when looking to build the required new airfields. The Scampton aerodrome site proved suitable although a larger acreage was required taking in farmland to the south in the parish of Scampton, a village to the west of the B1398, which was compulsory purchased in 1935. Work took the best part of two years and the RAF appeared before completion. The camp area was placed in the south-east corner and accessed from the A15 which formed the eastern border of the station. Substantial flat-roofed, brick buildings predominated and four Type C hangars were erected. The weapons' stores were further north on the eastern side of the airfield. With the outbreak of war, the most frequent operational commitment of the Hampdens of Nos. 49 and 83 Squadrons then resident was minelaying approaches to the enemy's ports. The first two Bomber Command VCs went to men from the Scampton squadrons. On August 12, 1940, Flight Lieutenant Roderick Learoyd's No. 49 Squadron Hampden was badly damaged by ground fire when he pressed home a low-level attack on the Dortmund-Ems canal. The award was made for his conduct in this action and bringing back the badly mauled bomber safely to base. Sergeant John Hannah, a wireless operator/gunner in a No. 83 Squadron Hampden gained his award for successfully fighting a fire in the rear of the crew compartment which resulted from a direct flak hit in the bomb-bay. In December 1941, No. 83 Squadron began to receive Avro Manchesters with No. 49 using the type the following April. This troublesome aircraft had limited operational use before it was gradually phased out in favour of the Lancaster. No sooner had No. 83 converted to the Lancaster than it was selected as one of the squadrons for the new Pathfinder Force and departed to Wyton. Its replacement was No. 57 Squadron from Feltwell. In fact, this former No. 3 Group Wellington squadron was re-built with Lancaster crews and aircraft, becoming operational in October when the photo *(right)* was taken. Six days before No. 617 was formed at the airfield, a bomb accidentally released from a No. 57 Squadron Lancaster detonated and destroyed four visiting aircraft from No. 50 Squadron parked nearby. (Construction of concrete runways began only in August 1943.)

The new unit came into being on March 17 simply as X Squadron, the Air Ministry not getting round to allocating it a number for another few days. Officially, No. 617 Squadron was created at Scampton, Lincolnshire, on March 21; unique in the history of the RAF as it was the only squadron formed with the specific purpose of carrying out a particular operation. That same day, Gibson's hand-picked crews began assembling at their new base. They came from several Commonwealth countries: Great Britain, Australia, New Zealand, Canada and also the USA, and by the 27th some 700 personnel, including ground staff, had arrived at Scampton.

Gibson had already been down to meet Barnes Wallis and view the test films before he received his 'most secret' orders on the 27th. Although no specific targets were listed, they stated that the attacks would involve 'low-level navigation over enemy territory in moonlight with a final approach to the target at 100 feet at a precise speed'.

Speculation and rumours were rife amongst the crews as to the targets yet Gibson was unable to be frank. In his welcoming address he told them that 'you're here to do a special job . . . which, I am told, will have startling results. Some say it may even cut short the duration of the war. What the target is I can't tell you. Nor can I tell you where it is. . . . I needn't tell you that we are going to be talked about. It is very unusual to have such a crack crowd of boys in one squadron. There are going to be a lot of rumours — I have heard a few already. We've got to stop these rumours. We've got to say nothing . . . because security is the greatest factor.'

(In fact, security remained a factor long after the war and Gibson could not reveal Barnes Wallis's identity in his book and the shape of the bomb could only be guessed at when the film *The Dam Busters* was made in 1954-55. This must have made the film's technical adviser smile for he was none other than the former station commander at Scampton, Group Captain Charles Whitworth! Details of the Upkeeps were not released until 1963.)

Virtually no photography exists, either of the training flights, or of the actual operation against the dams but in May 1977, on the 34th anniversary of the raid, the RAF staged a recreation at Derwent Reservoir — Target 'C' to the crews in 1943. *Above:* **Squadron Leader Kenneth Jackson flew the RAF's last airworthy Lancaster (PA474) from Scampton to make six low passes over the dam west of Sheffield where the twin towers were used to simulate those on the German dams.** *Right:* **This rather blurred shot was taken on or before May 16, 1943 by Flying Officer Bellamy — unfortunately the aircraft code is not discernable.**

Training started at once, Gibson undertaking one of the first flights to the Derwent Reservoir west of Sheffield to see how difficult it would be to keep to Wallis's specified height of 150 feet. Although Gibson's log-book fails to record this particular flight on March 28, he nearly flew into the water when attempting a circuit at dusk. The following day the true nature of the squadron's mission was revealed to him when he was shown the target models at No. 5 Group HQ.

Intensive training followed, initially using Lancasters borrowed from other squadrons, flying along prepared routes to three locations: Target 'A', Eyebrook Reservoir at Uppingham in Leicestershire; Target 'B', Abberton Reservoir south-west of Colchester in Essex; and Target 'C', the Derwent Reservoir.

The specially-modified Lancasters began arriving at Scampton on April 8 and on the 11th the first of two aircraft was equipped with special simulated night-flying equipment. This consisted of fitting blue celluloid over the perspex in the cockpit and gunners' positions and the crew wearing amber-tinted goggles which would give the impression of flying at night.

By the end of April the crews had logged upwards of 1,000 hours and Gibson could report that all his pilots were proficient at low-level night flying. The difficulty of map-reading near the ground using sheet maps had been solved by making up strip maps on rollers of the particular route to be followed. Other aids had also been developed to help the crews.

YEAR 1943.		AIRCRAFT		PILOT, OR 1ST PILOT	2ND PILOT, PUPIL OR PASSENGER	DUTY (INCLUDING RESULTS AND REMARKS)
MONTH	DATE	Type	No.			
—	—	—	—			— TOTALS BROUGHT FORWARD
APRIL	1	LANCASTER	3	SELF	CREW	LOCAL.
						CREW. P/O TREVOR.
						P/O SPAFFORD
						F/LT TREVOR. ROPER
						F/LT HUTCHISON.
						P/O DEERING
						STT PULFORD.
"	4	"	B	"	"	To Lake Nr Sheffield.
"	5	"	D	"	"	SCOTTISH X COUNTRY. LAKES.
"	9	"	D	"	"	BASE - DERWENT RESERVOIR
"	11	MAGPIE	—	"	"	- UPPINGHAM RES. - BASE.
				SELF	F/LT MAY.	LOCAL MANSTON.
						CRASHED IN FIELD. OK.

Gibson first flew over the same reservoir on March 28 although his log-book records his maiden flight with No. 617 as having taken place on April 1. He gives his first sortie to Derwent on April 4 but undoubtedly he was hard-pressed to keep his paperwork up to date.

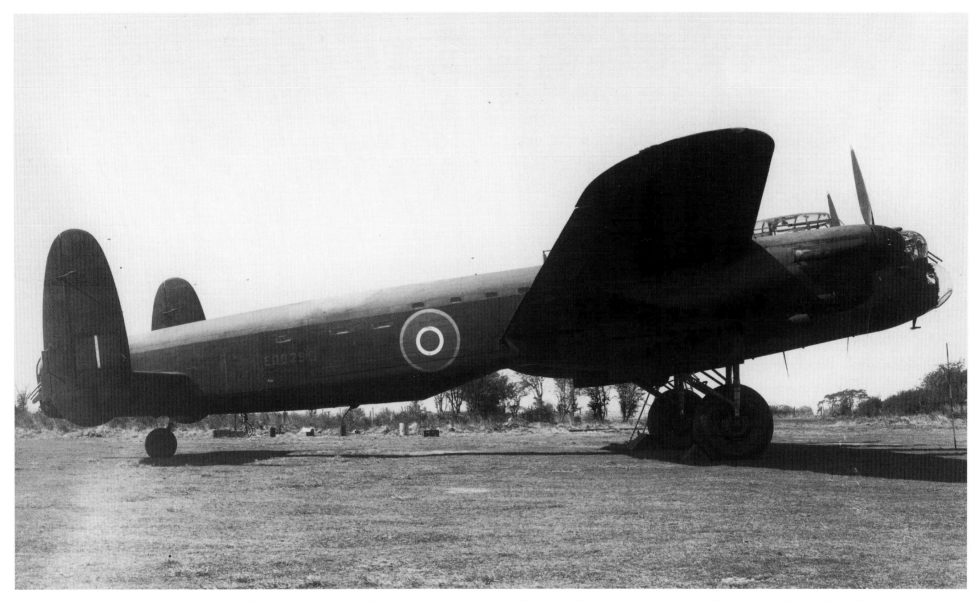

On May 13, Lancaster ED933/G, piloted by Squadron Leader Henry Maudslay, was damaged when the huge column of water from the impact of a full-size Upkeep striking the sea off Reculver hit the tailplane. Although the crew were switched to another aircraft (ED937/G), the accident reduced the number of serviceable machines on the strength of the squadron to 18. Fortunately there was a spare (ED825/G illustrated *above*) at Boscombe Down and an urgent call went out for it to be brought up to Scampton. However, it had not been fitted with the spotlights which were to serve as an altimeter on the final run-in nor the VHF radios which had been specially provided for air-to-air communication during the attack.

Also one of its engines was suspect. Nevertheless, the American pilot on the squadron, Flight Lieutenant Joe McCarthy, had no hesitation in claiming the aircraft when his own Lancaster AJ-Q (ED923/G) became unserviceable at the last minute due to a coolant leak. Yet this switch of aircraft does not appear to have filtered through to the Squadron Operations Record Book which still lists McCarthy's aircraft (with a handwritten alteration to the '3') as ED923G. This has led to much confusion over the years as to which aircraft he took to Germany. On the raid, ED825/G carried the sqadron code AJ-T. (The 'G' suffix indicated that the aircraft was fitted with secret equipment that needed to be 'Guarded'.)

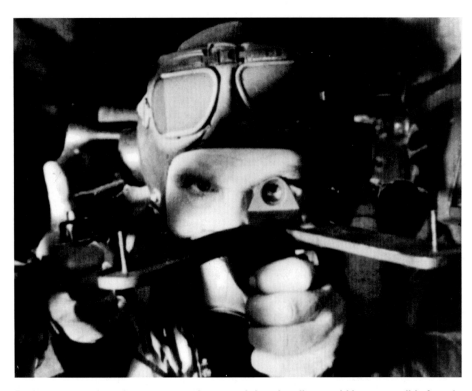

During the actual run-in, crews were instructed that the pilot would be responsible for taking the correct line to the target and the navigator for the aircraft's height. Range from the target was down to the bomb-aimer while the flight engineer would take care of the ground speed. The wireless operator would look after the rotation rate of the mine. Gibson's original orders given to him on March 27 stated that the mine was to be released visually at an estimated range to be judged either by a landmark on a nearby shore or by timing so many seconds after passing an easily identified location. In the event this was nowhere near accurate enough so a method had to be developed to ensure the weapon would be dropped plus or minus 40 yards either side of the correct release point. The improvised 'bomb-sight' which was introduced was recreated *(above)* in the feature film *The Dam Busters* and was not dissimilar to the actual thing.

To help maintain level flight close to the ground, the Royal Aircraft Establishment perfected the positioning of two spotlights — one in the bomb bay and the other in the front camera slot beside the bomb-aimer — set to converge at the right height just in front of the starboard wing where the navigator could see them and direct the pilot down to the point where they joined to make a figure of eight. (The height was reduced from 150 feet to 60 feet on May 5 to prevent the bomb from breaking up on hitting the water.)

Then, a simple way had to be found to guide the bomb-aimer in releasing the mine at the correct distance in front of the dam wall. Although a Y-shaped gadget was made up with a peep-hole and two nails which would marry up with the towers on the dams at the correct distance, some crews experimented with tape markers stuck on the perspex. Two white cricket sight-screens were set up 700 feet apart at the Wainfleet bombing range on the Wash to simulate the twin towers on the dams and, although the crews were still left in ignorance as to the real target, most believed that it would either be U-Boat pens or the *Tirpitz*.

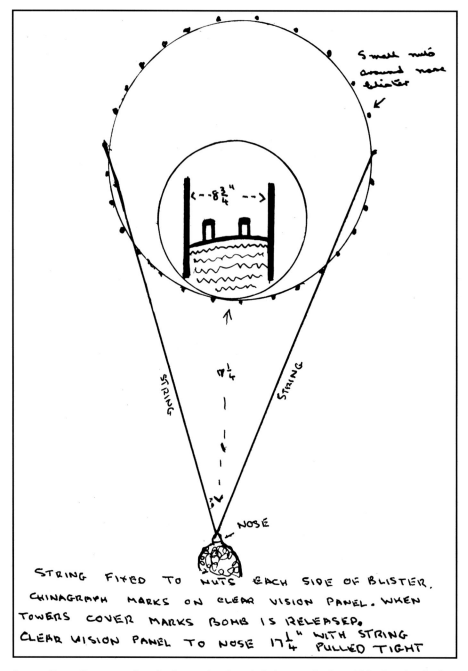

As an alternative, some bomb-aimers developed their own devices. This drawing by Len Sumpter shows a string bomb-sight.

Gibson's aircraft (ED932/G), coded AJ-G, pictured with its Upkeep showing the driving gear. Pressing the bomb release caused the V-shaped attachment arms to open and free the weapon. Some ten minutes before release, the mine had to be set in rotation, anti-clockwise, at 500 rpm having been carefully balanced on the ground to avoid vibrations.

View of 'G' George looking rearwards with the squadron's hangar (No. 2) faintly visible in the background. Gibson's office was located above the crew rooms overlooking the tarmac. (This historic aircraft was scrapped in 1947.)

Good air-to-air communications were essential but interference when using the normal TR 1196 R/T sets fitted to the Lancasters broadcasting on 5005 kc/s was very bad, particularly at night. Various tests were carried out but by the end of April the problem had still not been solved. The Royal Aircraft Establishment was consulted and suggested the best solution would be to fit VHF TR 1143 sets as used in fighter aircraft which operated in the 100-124 mc/s band. On May 6 the decision was taken to fit VHF R/T in all the aircraft and, following a superhuman effort, this task was completed within three days. On May 9 tests were carried out between two Lancasters and good voice reception was achieved up to a range of over 50 miles although when the aircraft descended to 200 feet the range was reduced. Nevertheless, Gibson was now satisfied for the success of the whole operation depended very much on communication between the attacking aircraft. Contact with control at Group HQ back in Grantham would be by Morse on 3680 kc/s using the following code-words:

PRANGER	Attack Target X [the Möhne]
NIGGER	Target X breached divert to Target Y [the Eder]
DINGHY	Target Y breached divert to Target Z [Sorpe]
DANGER	Attack Target D [Lister]
EDWARD	Attack Target E [Ennepe]
FRASER	Attack Target F [Henne, later changed to Diemel]
MASON	All aircraft return to Base
APPLE	First Wave listen out on Button 'A' [one of the VHF channels]
CODFISH	Jamming on Button 'A' change to Button 'C'
MERMAID	Jamming on all R/T, control by W/T
TULIP	No. 2 take over control at Target X
CRACKING	No. 4 take over control at Target Y
GILBERT	Attack last resort targets as detailed

Thirty years later, Gibson's cap lies on his desk, his office preserved as a shrine to his memory. On the extended apron the Vulcans of No. 617, the squadron having been reformed at Scampton in May 1958 as part of Britain's V-bomber force. They were joined in 1973 by No. 27 Squadron and two years later by a third Vulcan squadron, No. 35. In between the office and the tarmac . . . the grave of Nigger.

A final dress-rehearsal was carried out on the evening of Friday, May 14, Gibson recording that they carried out 'attacks' on Uppingham and Colchester lakes. There was little flying on Saturday as ground crews laboured to fit the Upkeeps and carry out last-minute checks. That evening, Gibson gave an informal briefing to his deputy flight commanders and his chief bomb-aimer but, as the meeting finished, Group Captain Whitworth personally broke the news that Nigger had been run over outside the main gate earlier that evening. *Above:* Richard Todd, who portrayed Guy Gibson in *The Dam Busters*, is told (incorrectly by his batman) that Nigger has been killed.

On May 7 all leave was cancelled and four days later training flights began for real using inert Upkeeps filled with concrete launched against targets set up on the beach at Reculver. Although Vickers-Armstrongs were still testing the bomb there, the squadron carried out its first sortie to the bombing range on the north Kent coast on May 11. Guy Gibson noted in his log-book for his three-hour flight that day: 'Low level Upkeep dropped at 60ft. Good run of 600 yards'.

As each Upkeep arrived at Scampton it had to be balanced, much like the wheels of a motor car, so that it would spin smoothly and, by May 13, 56 live mines had been delivered. There were a further two at Manston. The following day, 19 serviceable Lancasters (one had been damaged when the column of water from the initial impact of the Upkeep with the sea hit the tailplane) took off at 21.50 hours on what was to be their final full-squadron exercise. They were in the air for over three hours as they mounted mock attacks on the British reservoirs which were standing in for the German dams.

On the evening of May 15, Gibson took his key personnel aside for an informal briefing with Barnes Wallis in the privacy of Group Captain Whitworth's house. There, his deputy, Flight Lieutenant John Hopgood; Flight Lieutenant Robert Hay, the squadron's chief bomb-aimer, and his two flight commanders, Squadron Leaders Henry Maudslay and Henry Young, were let into the secret but the remainder of the crews would have to wait until the morrow before being told.

With all now ready, the day ended on a depressing note when Gibson's black labrador, Nigger, was run over outside the main gate. It was an ill omen for the coming operation for the code-word 'Nigger' had been chosen to be the signal that the Möhne had been successfully breached.

Nigger.

The grave of a Black Labrador Dog. Mascot of 617 Squadron owned by Wing Commander Guy Gibson, V.C., D.S.O., D.F.C

Nigger was killed by a car on the 16th May 1943. Buried at midnight as his owner was leading his Squadron on the attack against the Mohne and Eder Dams.

Gibson: 'And so I went back to my room on the eve of this adventure with my dog gone — the squadron mascot . . . Then I was alone in my room looking at the scratchmarks on the door Nigger used to make when he wanted to go out, and feeling very depressed.'

Aerial Reconnaissance

Meanwhile, the targets in Germany were being kept under close surveillance, both to monitor the level of the water in the reservoirs and to check on any new defence installations. The water level was important because experiments had shown that the explosive effect from the mine decreased sharply with reduced water pressure, the ideal level being around five feet below the top for the Möhne dam. Yet at the same time the water level should not be at its maximum as at least three feet of exposed wall was required to stop the mine on its final bounce. On February 19, air reconnaissance photos indicated that the water level was six feet below the top of the Möhne but by the beginning of April it had increased to within two feet of the top.

The optimum point for the actual detonation was at a depth of 30 feet and with the mine in contact with the wall. The chance of achieving a breach would be considerably reduced if an explosion occurred at a greater depth because of the increased thickness of the wall towards its base but the hydrostatic fuzes were claimed to be accurate to within one or two feet. Tests on models established that just one contact detonation should bring about a collapse.

All this and more was discussed in detail at a meeting chaired by the Assistant Chief of the Air Staff, Air Vice-Marshal Bottomley, on May 5 to try to determine the best time to mount the operation. Other factors in the equation were the need for the raid to be scheduled during the period of a full moon to aid navigation, the next phase occurring between May 14 and May 26. Wallis explained that it would be necessary to carry out one further photo-reconnaissance sortie to check on the water level but Bottomley was very concerned about more over-flying lest the targets be compromised.

After discussing all the various aspects, it was decided that an attack in May was preferable because the risk of failure increased considerably from June onwards due to a drop in water level amounting to around ten feet per month. Orders were therefore issued for a further reconnaissance to be carried out forthwith and that the pilot was to be instructed that in case of an emergency he was to bale out rather than try to force-land so that the film would be destroyed in the crash.

Opposite: **German gunners with their 2cm FlaK on the platform on top of one of the towers at the Möhne. There was a third gun on the roadway at the northern end.** *Above left:* **The dam was protected by a double line of torpedo netting but what had mystified the air photo interpreters in Britain were the peculiar tall objects along the roadway which had not shown up on the February 19 sortie** *(above).* **Three more light AA guns are positioned in a field to the north-west of the dam near the village of Günne (top left). The shores of the lake around the peninsula with the Haus Delecke restaurant (above the compass rose) appear light in colour indicating that the reservoir has not yet filled up to the level required for the attack.**

The aerial pictures which had been taken on April 4 and 5 had also given rise to some anxious speculation about the defences. Photographic interpreters described objects which had shown up on the roadway crossing the Möhne dam as looking like posts but, from their shadows, they appeared much wider at the bottom than the top. It was not possible to establish the exact size of these upright objects but some were grouped by the dam parapet and others in front of the parapet by the wall. Various explanations were put forward: that essential repairs were being carried out . . . the wall of the dam was being raised to increase water capacity . . . or, more serious, they were defensive measures, possibly some form of anti-aircraft rocket, in response to rumours of an impending air strike. In fact, they were artificial Christmas trees which the Luftwaffe was using to try to camouflage the dam so as to make it look like a spit of land extending from the Arnsberg Forest!

What was ominous were platforms about 20 by 15 feet which had appeared on top of the towers and light flak guns were believed positioned on each. Three more sandbagged gun emplacements were pinpointed in a field below the dam to the north-west. However, the interpreters felt that the tightening of the torpedo nets in front of the wall of the dam since the previous pictures were taken on February 19 did not in itself indicate a security leak as a check on the earlier prints showed that the boom was then somewhat neglected. As the water level rose during the winter months, some of the spacers between the chains would inevitably need replacing and it was obviously now time to adjust the boom.

Yet what did give cause for concern was the realisation that a Most Secret paper written in 1942 detailing the test explosions at the Road Research Laboratory and at the Nant-y-Gro dam, had fallen into civilian hands in the United States. Seventy sets of this illustrated document, in which the Möhne dam was specifically named, had been circulated and four copies had been sent to the USA to stimulate interest in heavy bombs and aircraft carriers. In September that year, one had been passed to Dr von Karman at the California Institute of Technology as he was also working on the theory of big bombs so it could be assumed that its contents might well have been circulated unwittingly to third parties. The fear now was that the precautions which appeared to have been put in place to protect the dam might be as a result of the contents of the report having reached Germany.

In fact the objects were dummy conifers — actually a framework draped with camouflage netting to make them look like trees — which had been added beside the roadway in an attempt at camouflage. This is the view from the southernmost tower of the Möhne.

On May 14 the dams were photographed one final time to check the water level and to look for any further defensive measures. The Möhne pictures still showed a dark straight line along the parapet and, although the interpreters could not determine exactly what it was, they speculated that it could be either a drainage channel or a belt of wire. The boom holding the torpedo net was still floating between 100 to 300 feet from the dam but otherwise there appeared to be no further changes.

Print from the April 5 sortie by No. 541 Squadron showing the clumps of artificial trees along the edge of the roadway although not identified as such at the time.

The Eder through the lens on May 9 with the two hydro-electric power stations operated by the Preussische Elektrizitäts AG arrowed.

```
R.A.F. Form 683.                    SECRET.          (L) 10346.  Wt. 3086-1335.  120M.  8/42.  T.S. 700

                                   CYPHER MESSAGE.                       1 A.

To—                                              Date      15.5.43.
        HQ Bomber Command                                Receipt      Despatch
                                                 Time of    1130
From—   Air Ministry Whitehall AX457 15th May    System

        MOST SECRET                              Serial No.  Y3976

        Operation CHASTISE immediate attack of targets X Y Z
        approved.   Execute at first suitable opportunity.

                                       T.O.O.  150900Z
   MOST  IMMEDIATE                     T.O.R.  151125B
```

Countdown

On May 5, the Prime Minister boarded the *Queen Mary* en route for the United States and the forthcoming 'Trident' conference in Washington. The agenda was to resolve the differences between the two countries as to the future of Anglo-American operations and a series of meetings were scheduled with the President and the Combined Chiefs-of-Staff. And it was in Washington, during the conference, that the ultimate decision was made to go ahead with the attack on the German dams.

The Air Ministry in London had already apprised the RAF delegation in Washington as to the invention of the new weapon in a Most Secret telegram on April 12:

'We have been developing a spherical bomb which will be dropped from low-flying aircraft and act in the nature of a surface torpedo. The bomb is suspended in the bomb-bay and given a backward spin of about 500 revs. per minute before dropping. This initial spin lengthens initial flight before impact on water, increases the angle of incidence of ricochet and serves to counter the action of the water drag and the tendency of the sphere to roll under water. Investigations so far show that the spherical bomb will not be checked by booms carrying protective torpedo netting.

'The following are brief details of spherical bombs at present being developed:

Weapon A.
Weight 960lbs. Charge weight 600lbs; Diameter 35in. Bomb sinks between 10 to 20 feet per second and is exploded at pre-set depth by hydrostatic fuze. Range of weapon depends on speed and height of drop but at about 100 feet and at 300 mph range would be about 1,250 yards, weapon striking target with probable velocity of 150 mph. Two of these bombs can be carried in Mosquito.

Weapon B.
Weight 11,000lbs; charge weight 7,000lbs; diameter 84in. Characteristics similar to those of Weapon A. One can be carried in Lancaster.

'Primary purpose of Weapon A is the attack of capital ships in harbour protected by booms and other ships either in harbour or at sea. Primary purpose of Weapon B is to destroy important enemy dams, intention being to use it in moonlight conditions.

'Thirty Mosquitos are being modified for Weapon A and twenty Lancasters for Weapon B. Initial trials are being held this week and will be attended by representatives of General Andrews and Admiral Stark who alone have been informed.

'Experiments up-to-date indicate that the weapons are technically feasible but we cannot guarantee success until we have seen results of the trials. The potentialities, however, are so great that we have taken a gamble and pressed on with development of the weapon as quickly as possible.

'In view of the fact that the enemy may be able to take effective counter-measures against the weapons, particularly in their use against capital ships in harbour and important dams, it is most important that the highest possible degree of secrecy should be observed in discussing the weapons. Intended to launch major initial operations simultaneously so as to exploit surprise and avoid possible counter-measures. Danger of enemy coming to know of weapon is an argument for initial use at early date. Particulars of code-names and covering plan will be sent to you in subsequent signal. Date of initiation of these operations not yet decided but you will be kept informed on results of all preliminary trials.

'Please inform personally Generals Marshall and Arnold and Admiral King and impress on them at the same time the absolute need for secrecy.'

A supplementary signal advised that Weapon A was code-named 'Highball' and Weapon B 'Upkeep', and that operations using Weapon A would be called 'Servant' and those using Weapon B 'Chastise'. In recommending that the Upkeep operation be authorised with effect from the following day, as it was no longer felt that its prior use would prejudice Highball, the following reasons were given:

'Development trials of Upkeep showed spherical form to be unsuitable and simple cylinder now employed. In this form shape and fittings give no indication of method of discharge or surface running principle.

'Very short running ranges now being employed. Range will be 450 yards including air path. Method of attack might well engender belief that special form of depth charge had been dropped between boom and dam. This would be confirmed by attack on Target "Z" in which aircraft will fly close and parallel to dam face. Bounces at this short range closely resemble normal skip effect when a bomb is dropped short.

'In view of above, highly improbable enemy would associate Upkeep with principle of spherical weapon suitable for employment against ships where long range would be essential.'

Churchill was still in the United States when the necessity of making a decision over mounting Operation 'Chastise' became urgent, and on May 13 the Air Ministry sent a signal to Washington for the Combined Chiefs-of-Staff:

'Reasons demanding immediate employment of Upkeep are as follows:

'(i)   Subject to final confirmation by reconnaissance flown today, water levels believed now satisfactory for attack this moon period. Chances of success will be seriously reduced by even slight falls below optimum level of 5 feet below spill. Heavy withdrawals possible in coming weeks and postponement to June would gravely prejudice success.

'(ii)   23 operational Lancasters "frozen" for this special operation which will include the three objectives "X", "Y" and "Z". Further operations of this character considered impracticble in view of enemy counter-measures. Postponement till June means loss of normal bombing effort from these aircraft for further month.

'(iii) Subject to one further test today, weapon now satisfactory and crews have reached peak of training and are keyed up for this very hazardous operation. Delay undesirable on these accounts.'

The following day, the Chief of the Air Staff, Sir Charles Portal, gave the green light for Operation 'Chastise' to go ahead.

R.A.F. Form 683.

SECRET.

(L) 10346. Wt. 23086-1335. 120M. 8/42. T.S. **700**

6/7

CYPHER MESSAGE.

To—	Officer Commanding Scampton (R) Bomber Command.	Date	16.5.43.	
			Receipt	Despatch
		Time of	1610	1645
From—	5 Group A 7 16th May.	System		

Serial No. Y3990.

Executive operation Chastise 16/5/43 zero hours

22/48B.

T.O.O.161510B
T.O.R.1607/16

G/C OPS (ww)

1 6 MAY 1943

The signal to Washington requesting the go ahead was despatched at 6.55 p.m. on Thursday, May 13. Early Friday morning, Air Chief Marshal Sir Douglas Evill, the Vice-Chief of the Air Staff who was standing in while Portal was in Washington, followed this with a personal cypher for his chief reporting that the live test drop of Upkeep (see pages 24-25) had proved entirely satisfactory and requesting that the separate operation (i.e. excluding Highball) be approved for immediate action. Washington responded at 2.40 p.m.: 'For reasons stated by you, Chiefs-of-Staff agree to immediate use of Upkeep without waiting for Highball'. (Although it has been claimed that Winston Churchill personally authorised the operation, there is no documentary evidence to back this up; neither does Churchill mention it in his autobiographical account of the Second World War.) The decision was relayed to Sir Arthur Harris's HQ at High Wycombe at 9 a.m. on Saturday, May 15, ordering the attack to take

place at the 'first suitable opportunity' (see telegram *opposite*). The time of receipt of the message was confirmed at 11.25 a.m. Once No. 5 Group was informed, the draft operational order (No. B976) was finalised with the operation to take place 'on the first suitable date after 15th May'. Three 'last resort' targets were added to the plan: Target 'D' — the Lister Dam; 'E' — the Ennepe; with the Diemel having replaced the Henne as Target 'F'. Twelve numbered copies of the order were produced (No. 7 being reproduced in facsimile on the following pages), copies Nos. 1 and 2 being sent to Scampton for the attention of Group Captain Whitworth. Not produced here are Appendix 'A' covering routes and timings; Appendix 'B' signals procedure and target diversions, and Appendix 'C' which gave night and moon tables. *Above:* The final signal on Sunday afternoon from No. 5 Group to Whitworth (Officer Commanding Scampton) authorising the raid to be carried out that night.

NO. 5 GROUP OPERATION ORDER NO. B.976

APPENDIX 'A' - ROUTES AND TIMINGS.

APPENDIX 'B' - SIGNALS PROCEDURE FOR
TARGET DIVERSIONS, ETC.

APPENDIX 'C' - LIGHT AND MOON TABLES.

INFORMATION.

General.

1.   The inhabitants and industry of the Ruhr rely to a very large extent on the enormously costly water barrage dams in the Ruhr District.   Destruction of TARGET X alone would bring about a serious shortage of water for drinking purposes and industrial supplies.   This shortage might not be immediately apparent but would certainly take effect in the course of a few months.   The additional destruction of one or more of the five major dams in the Ruhr Area would greatly increase the effect and hasten the resulting shortage.   TARGET Z is next in importance.

2.   A substantial amount of damage would be done, and considerable local flooding would be caused immediately consequent on the breach of TARGET X.   In fact it might well cause havoc in the Ruhr valley.   There would be a large loss of electrical capacity in the Ruhr partly caused by destruction of hydro-electric plants, but also due to loss of cooling water for the large thermal plants.

3.   In the Weser District the destruction of the TARGET Y would seriously hamper transport in the Mittelland Canal and in the Weser, and would probably lead to an almost complete cessation of the great volume of traffic now using these waterways.

4.   The reservoirs usually reach their maximum capacity in May or June, after which the level slowly falls.

Enemy Defences.

5. (a) TARGET X.

There are three objects on the crest of this dam which may each be a light A.A. gun.   A light 3-gun A.A. position is situated below and to the N. of the dam with a possible searchlight position nearby.   A double line boom with timber spreaders is floating on the main reservoir at 100 to 300 feet from the dam.   No other A.A. position or defence installation is known.

(b) TARGETS Y and Z.

Information about the defences of these two dams will be given when P.R.U. sorties have covered these areas.   (Information has now been issued).

(c) The last resort targets are unlikely to be defended.

INTENTION.

6.   To breach the following dams in order of priority as listed:-

(a) TARGET 'X' (GO 939)
(b) TARGET 'Y' (GO 934)
(c) TARGET 'Z' (GO 960)
(d) Last Resort Targets:-
        (i)   TARGET 'D' (GO 938)
        (ii) TARGET 'E' (GO 935)
        (iii) TARGET 'F' (GO 933)

/EXECUTION ....

EXECUTION.

Code Name.

7.   This operation will be known by a code name which will be issued separately.

Date of Attack.

8.   The operation is to take place on the first suitable date after 15th May, 1943.

Effort.

9.   Twenty Special Lancasters from 617 Squadron.

Outline Plan.

10.   The twenty special Lancasters of 617 Squadron are to fly from base to target area and return in moonlight at low level by the routes given in APPENDIX 'A'.   The Squadron is to be divided into three main waves, viz:-

(a) 1st Wave. Is to consist of three sections, spaced at ten minute intervals, each section consisting of three aircraft.   They are to take the Southern route to the target area and attack Target X.   The attack is to be continued until the Dam has been clearly breached.   It is estimated that this might require three effective attacks.   When this has been achieved the leader is to divert the remainder of this wave to Target Y, where similar tactics are to be followed.   Should both X and Y be breached any remaining aircraft of this wave are to attack Z.

(b) 2nd Wave. Is to consist of five aircraft manned by the specially trained crews who are to take the Northern route to the target, but are to cross the enemy coast at the same time as the leading section of the 1st wave.   This 2nd wave are to attack Target Z.

(c) 3rd Wave. Is to consist of the remaining aircraft and is to form an airborne reserve under the control of Group H.Q.   They are to take the Southern route to the target but their time of take-off is to be such that they may be recalled before crossing the enemy coast if the 1st and 2nd waves have breached all the targets.

Recall will probably not be possible unless the first section of the 1st Wave is at POSITION 51°51' N., 03°00'E. by Civil Twilight (EVENING) + 30 minutes and the 3rd Wave must be at this position 2 hours 30 minutes later.   Orders will be passed to aircraft on the Special Group frequency if possible before they reach the enemy coast instructing them which target they are to attack.   Failing receipt of this message aircraft are to proceed to X, Y and finally last resort targets in that order, attacking any which are not breached.   Officer Commanding, R.A.F. Station, Scampton, is to arrange for individual aircraft to be detailed to specific last resort targets.

Detailed Plan.

11.   The 1st Wave is to take off in three sections each of three aircraft and fly to the target at low level by the route given in Appendix 'A'.   Sections are to be spaced at intervals of ten minutes and are to fly in open formation.   Height is not to exceed 1,500 feet over England.   On leaving the English Coast aircraft are to descend to low level and set their altimeters to 60 feet using the Spotlight Altimeters for calibration.   The QFF at various stages of the route is to be carefully noted.   Aircraft are to remain at low level for the flight to the target and on the return journey at least until crossing a point 03°00'E.

12.   An accurate landfall on the enemy coast is important but on no account should aircraft turn back if their landfall is not quite accurate.   The routes selected should be free of all major opposition from flak but good map reading and crew co-operation is essential to keep aircraft on track.   The enemy coast is to be crossed

/as low as possible ....

as low as possible both going in and coming out even if it is necessary to climb a little later for map reading.

13.   On arriving at a point 10 miles from the target the leader of each section is to climb to about 1,000 feet. On seeing this all other aircraft are to listen out on V.H.F. Each aircraft is to call the leader of the Wave on V.H.F. on arriving at the target. Spinning of the special store is to be started ten minutes before each aircraft attacks. The leader is to attack first and is then to control the attacks on TARGETS X and Y by all the other aircraft of the 1st Wave using the Signals procedure given in APPENDIX 'B'.

14.   Number 2 of the leading section of the 1st Wave is to act as deputy leader for the whole of the attack on the 1st Wave during the attack on TARGET X. Should the leader fall out No. 2 of the leading section is to take over leadership, and No. 3 deputy leader-ship, for the attack of TARGET X. For the attack of TARGET Y Number 4 is to take over deputy leadership, or if No. 1 is absent he is to take over leadership, in which event No. 7 is to be the deputy leader. All other aircraft are to return to base after completing their attack. The first three aircraft are to return by Route 1, the second three by Route 2 and the last three aircraft of this wave by Route 3.

15.   The direction of attack of TARGET X is to be at right angles to the length of the target. The general direction of attack is, therefore, to be S.E. to N.W. Aircraft are not to be diverted to TARGET Y until TARGET X has been breached. If TARGET X is breached, up to two additional aircraft may be used, at the discretion of the leader, to widen the breach in TARGET X providing at least three aircraft are diverted to attack TARGET Y.

16.   Destruction of the Dam may take some time to become apparent and careful reconnaissance may be necessary to distinguish between breaching of the dam and the spilling over the top, which will follow each explosion.

17.   When TARGET X is seen to be breached beyond all possible doubt the leader is to divert the remainder of the first Wave to TARGET Y by W/T and V.H.F. where similar tactics are to be used for the attack of this target. The general direction of attack of TARGET Y is to be from N.W. to S.E. If target Y is seen to be breached beyond all possible doubt all remaining aircraft of the 1st Wave are to be diverted by the leader to attack Target Z independantly using the same tactics as the 2nd wave.

18.   For the attacks of both Targets X and Y the special range finder is to be used, the height of attack is to be 60 feet and the ground speed 220 m.p.h.

19.   The 2nd Wave is to take off and fly to Target Z at low level by the Northern Route given in Appendix 'A'. Aircraft are to cross the enemy coast in close concen-tration, but not in formation, at the same time, although at a different point, as the leading section of the 1st Wave. Aircraft of this Wave will be controlled on the alternative V.H.F. channel. The special stores are not to be spun for the attack of Target Z. Aircraft are to attack this target from N.W. to S.E. parallel to the length of the dam and are to aim to hit the water just short of the centre point of the dam about 15 to 20 feet out from the edge of the water. Attacks are to be made from the lowest practicable height at a speed of 180 m.p.H. I.A.S. Aircraft are to return to base independently. First two aircraft by Route 1; second two aircraft by Route 2 and the last by Route 3.

20.   The 3rd Wave is to consist of the remaining aircraft and is to form an airborne reserve under the control of Group Headquarters. They are to fly to Target X in close concentration, but not in formation, at low level by the Southern route given in Appendix 'A'. These aircraft are to be at Position 51°52'N., 03°00'E. 2 hours 30 minutes after the leading section of the 1st Wave have crossed this point on their outward route to the target. Orders for the 3rd Wave will be passed to all aircraft on the special Group frequency, if possible before they reach the enemy coast, instructing them which target to attack. Failing receipt of this message aircraft are to proceed to X, Y and, finally, last resort targets in that order attacking any which are not breached. The 3rd Wave are to use tactics of attack

/similar to those ...

similar to those used by the 1st Wave when attacking Targets X and Y except that attacks on last resort targets are to be made independantly. After attacking, aircraft are to return to base independantly at low level by any of thre three return routes given in Appendix 'A'. Aircraft attacking early should take Route 1; the next aircraft Route 2 and the last Route 3.

Method of Attack.

21.   Aircraft are to use the method of attack already practised. The pilot being responsible for line, the Navigator for height, the Air Bomber for range and the Flight Engineer for speed.

22.   The interval between attacking aircraft is to be not less than three minutes on all targets.

23.   On all targets except Target Z each aircraft is to fire a red verey cartridge immediately over the dam during the attack. Aircraft attacking Target Z are each to fire a red verey cartridge as they release their special store.

24.   All aircraft are to fly left hand circuits in each target area keeping as low as possible when waiting their turn to attack.

Time of Attack.

25.   The time of attack of each target by each wave is not important to within a few minutes. The time of crossing the enemy coast is, however, all important. ZERO HOUR, which will be given in the executive order, is, therefore, to be the time at which the first section of the 1st wave are to be at POSITION 51°52'N., 03°00'E. on the outward route to the target. This time will probably be Civil Twilight (EVENING) ± 30 minutes. At this time aircraft of the 2nd Wave should be about Position 53°19'N., 04°00'E.

Routes.

26.   As in Appendix 'A'.

Diversions.

27.   The whole essence of this operation is surprise, and to avoid bringing enemy defences to an unnecessary degree of alertness, diversionary attacks must be carefully timed. H.Q.B.C. will be asked to arrange the maximum possible diversionary attacks so that the first enemy R.D.F. or other warning of the diversionary attacks occurs 20 minutes after the leading section of the 1st wave crosses the enemy coast. No diversionary attacks should be despatched which would cross the enemy coast for a period of one hour preceding the 3rd Wave. 15 minutes after the 3rd Wave cross the enemy coast further diversionary attacks should be made at maximum strength and should continue, if possible until the 3rd wave are clear of enemy territory on the return journey. Diversionary attacks below 2,000 ft. should not be made in the area bounded by the points (51° 00'N., 03°20'E), (51°20'N., 06°30'E)., (51°00'N., 10°00'E)., (52°00'N., 09°00'E.). (53°20'N., 06°00'E.). H.Q.B.C. will also be asked to arrange suitable weather reconnaissance to report in particular on the visibility in the target area at least in sufficient time to recall the Lancasters before they cross the enemy coast if the weather is unsuitable.

Armament.

28. (a) **Bomb Load.** - Each Lancaster is to carry one special modified store (UPKEEP)

(b) **Ammunition.**- All guns to be loaded with 100% night tracer (G VI).

Fuel.

29.   The Lancasters may take off at a maximum all up weight of 63,000 lbs. at +14 boost. As the modified store now weighs about 9,000 lbs. 1750 gallons of petrol can be carried.

/Navigation ...

5

Navigation.

30. H.Q.B.C. are requested to arrange for the Eastern Chain, Stud 5 to be switched on at Z - 20 minutes and to remain on for the whole of the operation. This should assist in making an accurate landfall on the enemy coast at the correct time.

31. The route is to be carefully studied before flight and the oustanding features, obstructions and pinpoints noted, particularly water pinpoints. E.T.A.'s at each are to be carefully calculated and if any pinpoint is not found on E.T.A. a search is to be made before proceeding to the next pinpoint. Aircraft may climb to 500 feet shortly before reaching each pinpoint if necessary to help map reading.

32. The maximum use is to be made of the Air Position Indicators.

Synchronisation of watches.

33. All watches are to be synchronised with B.B.C. time before take off on the day of the operation.

Secrecy.

34. Secrecy is VITAL. Knowledge of this operation is to be confined to the Station Commander, O.C. 617 Squadron and his two Flight Commanders until receipt of the EXECUTIVE signal. After crews are briefed they are to be impressed with the need for the utmost secrecy because of the possibility that the operation may be postponed should weather reconnaissance prove the weather to be unsuitable.

Reports.

35. Each aircraft as soon as possible after it has attacked is to report by W/T on the normal Group operational frequency in accordance with APPENDIX 'B'.

Special Devices.

36. MANDREL and TINSEL are not fitted.

37. IFF is NOT to be used on the outward journey but normal procedure is to be followed on the homeward flight. Any aircraft returning early is NOT to use IFF except after Z + 30 minutes for the 1st and 2nd Waves and after Z + 3 hours for the 3rd Wave.

Nickels.

38. Nickels are not to be dropped.

INTERCOMMUNICATION.

Wireless Silence.

39. Strict W/T and R/T silence is to be maintained until after Z + 30 minutes for the 1st and 2nd Waves and after Z + 3 hours for the 3rd Wave. Any aircraft returning early is NOT to break W/T or R/T silence and is NOT to identify on MF/DF except after Z + 30 minutes for the 1st and 2nd Waves and after Z + 3 hours for the 3rd Wave. Aircraft returning before that time are to cross the English Coast at 1,500 feet at the point of exit and proceed direct to base or the nearest suitable airfield. Otherwise normal operational signals procedure is to be used except as modified by Appendix 'B'.

MF/DF Section.

40. Section D is to be used if required in accordance with Paragraph 39.

Executive Order.

41. The executive order for the operation will be given by EXECUTIVE followed

/by the code word ...

by the code word allotted, the date on which the operation is to take place and the time of Zero Hour in British Double Summer Time.

42. ACKNOWLEDGE BY TELEPRINTER.

H. Satterly G/C.

Senior Air Staff Officer,
No. 5 Group,
Royal Air Force.

Ref:- 5G/101/54/Air.
Date:- 16th May, 1943.

DISTRIBUTION.

External.	Copy No.
Group Captain J. N. H. Whitworth, DSO., DFC.	1 and 2.
Headquarters, Bomber Command. (Deputy C.-in-C, personally, or in his absence, Group Captain N, W. D. Marwood-Elton, D.F.C.).	3, 4 and 5.

Internal.		
Action Copy (Ops, II),	6	Not to be issued until after despatch of Executive Signal.
C.S.O.	7	
File,	8	
Spares,	9, 10, 11, and 12.	

Opposite: **Aircraft on the Möhne reservoir. D-833 was a Junkers T13 seaplane based on the reservoir at Delecke giving pleasure flights in the halcyon days before the war. In the background the spur of land over which the Lancasters would begin their run-in. Ferdinand Nölle was a special constable from Günne: 'In 1936, just two days after Hitler had marched into the Rhineland, we were patrolling the Möhne dam in our civilian clothes. We did our training at evening classes. An Oberleutnant recommended that we should be in uniform and so we put on our firemen's uniforms. The duty room was in the power station in front of the dam. After the war began, for some time before the raid, people in Neheim [the nearest town downstream] started phoning in to complain. They said we should let some of the water out so as to reduce the danger if there was a raid. But nothing happened. One day they set up a barrier and put the dam off limits for all civilian traffic. Shortly after this, a commission came over from Luftgaukommando Wehrkreis [Air Defence District] VI at Münster with General der Artillerie August Schmidt to inspect the dam. These gentlemen were standing between the two towers and pointing over at the Heve basin. I went up closer to them and heard the General say: "That's where it (the torpedo?) will be dropped". A civilian who was with him said it would be 700-800 metres away and added that it wouldn't come out of the Heve basin. If it did that it would hit the Möhne-Strasse and not the dam. The General didn't say exactly what it was that would be dropped. I made a report about this conversation, and it all got entered into the log-book as well.'**

OPERATION 'CHASTISE', MAY 16/17, 1943

No. 617 SQUADRON PERSONNEL

The awards are those given specifically for the raid. The † indicates killed on Operation 'Chastise'; * prisoners of war.

Aircraft	Pilot	Flight Engineer	Navigator	Wireless operator	Bomb-aimer	Front gunner	Rear gunner
			FIRST WAVE				
AJ-G ED932/G	W/Cdr G. P. Gibson (VC)	Sgt J. Pulford (DFM)	P/O T. H. Taerum (DFC)	Flt Lt R. E. G. Hutchison (Bar DFC)	P/O F. M. Spafford (DFC)	F/Sgt G. A. Deering (DFC)	Flt Lt R. A. D. Trevor-Roper (DFC)
AJ-M ED925/G	Flt Lt J. V. Hopgood†	Sgt C. Brennan†	F/O K. Earnshaw†	Sgt J. W. Minchin†	P/O J. W. Fraser*	F/O G. H. F. G. Gregory†	P/O A. F. Burcher*
AJ-P ED909/G	Flt Lt H. B. M. Martin (DSO)	P/O I. Whittaker	Flt Lt J. F. Leggo (Bar DFC)	F/O L. Chambers (DFC)	Flt Lt R. C. Hay (Bar DFC)	P/O B. T. Foxlee	F/Sgt T. D. Simpson (DFM)
AJ-A ED877/G	Sqn Ldr H. M. Young†	Sgt D. T. Horsfall†	F/Sgt C. W. Roberts†	Sgt L. W. Nichols†	F/O V. S. MacCausland†	Sgt G. A. Yeo†	Sgt W. Ibbotson†
AJ-J ED906/G	Flt Lt D. J. Maltby (DSO)	Sgt W. Hatton	Sgt V. Nicholson (DFM)	Sgt A. J. B. Stone	P/O J. Fort (DFC)	Sgt V. Hill	Sgt H. T. Simmonds
AJ-L ED929/G	Flt Lt D. J. Shannon (DSO)	Sgt R. J. Henderson	F/O D. R. Walker (Bar DFC)	F/O B. Goodale	F/Sgt L. J. Sumpter (DFM)	Sgt B. Jagger	P/O J. Buckley (DFC)
AJ-Z ED937/G	Sqn Ldr H. E. Maudslay†	Sgt J. Marriott†	F/O R. A. Urquhart†	WO2 A. P. Cottam†	P/O M. J. D. Fuller†	F/O W. J. Tytherleigh†	Sgt N. R. Burrows†
AJ-B ED864/G	Flt Lt W. Astell†	Sgt J. Kinnear†	P/O F. A. Wile†	WO2 A. Garshowitz†	F/O D. Hopkinson†	F/Sgt F. A. Garbas†	Sgt R. Bolitho†
AJ-N ED912/G	P/O L. G. Knight (DSO)	Sgt R. E. Grayston	F/O H. S. Hobday (DFC)	F/Sgt R. G. T. Kellow	F/O E. C. Johnson (DFC)	Sgt F.E. Sutherland	Sgt. H. E. O'Brien
			SECOND WAVE				
AJ-E ED927/G	Flt Lt R. N. G. Barlow†	P/O S. L. Whillis†	F/O P. S. Burgess†	F/O C. R. Williams†	P/O A. Gillespie†	F/O H. S. Glinz†	Sgt J. R. G. Liddell†
AJ-W ED921/G	Flt Lt J. L. Munro	Sgt F. E. Appleby	F/O F. G. Rumbles	Sgt P. E. Pigeon	Sgt J. H. Clay	Sgt W. Howarth	F/Sgt H. A. Weeks
AJ-K ED934/G	P/O V. W. Byers†	Sgt A. J. Taylor†	F/O J. H. Warner†	Sgt J. Wilkinson†	P/O A. N. Whitaker†	Sgt C. McA. Jarvie†	F/Sgt J. McDowell†
AJ-H ED936/G	P/O G. Rice	Sgt E. C. Smith	F/O R. MacFarlane	Sgt C. B. Gowrie	F/Sgt J. W. Thrasher	Sgt T. W. Maynard	Sgt S. Burns
AJ-T ED825/G	Flt Lt J. C. McCarthy (DSO)	Sgt W. Radcliffe	F/Sgt D. A. McLean (DFM)	Sgt L Eaton	Sgt G. L. Johnson (DFM)	Sgt R. Batson	F/O D. Rodger
			THIRD WAVE				
AJ-C ED910/G	P/O W. Ottley†	Sgt R. Marsden†	F/O J. K. Barrett†	Sgt J Guterman†	F/Sgt T. B. Johnston†	Sgt F. Tees*	Sgt H. J. Strange†
AJ-S ED865/G	P/O L. J. Burpee†	Sgt G. Pegler†	Sgt T. Jaye†	P/O L. G. Weller†	WO2 J. L. Arthur†	Sgt W. C. A. Long†	WO2 J. G. Brady†
AJ-F ED918/G	F/Sgt K. W. Brown (CGM)	Sgt H. B. Feneron	Sgt D. P. Heal (DFM)	Sgt H. J. Hewstone	Sgt S. Oancia (DFM)	Sgt D. Allatson	F/Sgt G. S. MacDonald
AJ-O ED886/G	P/O W. C. Townsend (CGM)	Sgt D. J. D. Powell	P/O C. L. Howard (DFC)	F/Sgt G. A. Chalmers (DFM)	Sgt C. E. Franklin (Bar DFM)	Sgt D. E. Webb (DFM)	Sgt R. Wilkinson (DFM)
AJ-Y ED924/G	F/Sgt C. T. Anderson	Sgt R. C. Patterson	Sgt J. P. Nugent	Sgt W. D. Bickle	Sgt G. J. Green	Sgt E. Ewan	Sgt A.W. Buck

Ranks held during wartime are confusing. The normal 'Substantive' peacetime rank was complicated by a wartime structure which made provision for 'War Substantive', 'Temporary' and 'Acting' ranks. Basically, the full Substantive rank only applied to officers holding regular commissions; War Substantive was awarded to officers receiving time promotions and also to officers holding Temporary or Acting rank for certain periods; and Temporary rank was given for promotions by the Air Ministry to fulfil vacancies in the war establishment. Acting rank was bestowed by Commands and Groups to officers performing, temporarily, duties of certain higher ranks. Officers could hold Acting ranks of two or, exceptionally, three grades higher than their Substantive rank for a considerable period before promulgation to a War Substantive rank. For example, Guy Gibson had held the Acting rank of Wing Commander since April 13, 1942 but his Substantive rank was Squadron Leader. (It is the policy of the Commonwealth War Graves Commission to ignore the word 'Acting'.) Although all the ranks have been checked with those given in the squadron

Operations Record Book, there are a number of discrepancies, particularly where the individual was killed on the raid. We have confirmed that the ranks for the dead inscribed by the Commission on their headstones are correct although they do not correspond with squadron records in every case. On the 617 ops list, Charles Roberts (AJ-A) given as a Sergeant, should be a Flight Sergeant, likewise Allan Cottam (AJ-Z) was a Warrant Officer Class 2. On AJ-B, Abram Garshowitz was also a Warrant Officer Class 2 and Francis Garbas a Flight Sergeant. On AJ-E, both Samuel Whillis and Alan Gillespie were Pilot Officers. On AJ-K, Vernon Byers was a Pilot Officer, James Warner a Flying Officer, Arthur Whitaker a Pilot Officer and James McDowell a Flight Sergeant. On AJ-S, both James Arthur and Joseph Brady were Warrant Officers Class 2. The correct rank of Bill Townsend, the pilot on AJ-O, was Pilot Officer, not Flight Sergeant, as he was promoted on March 16, 1943. Likewise Flight Sergeant Fraser in AJ-M had been commissioned on March 14, 1943 so should also be accorded the rank of Pilot Officer.

Three minor dams were added to the target list in case the Möhne, Eder or Sorpe were, for any reason, unable to be attacked. The Diemel (20 million cubic metres of water, [12] on the map on pages 4-5), mid-way between the Möhne and Eder, was designated Target F.

The other two lay within the clutch of dams in the Ruhrgebiet. *Above:* Target E ([8] on the map) was the small Ennepe retaining 12 million cubic metres while Target D *(below)* was the Lister [13], the southernmost dam, the reservoir holding 22 million cubic metres of water.

First Wave against the Möhne and Eder dams

Sunday morning saw a hive of activity at Scampton as the heavy Upkeeps were hoisted into the bomb bays and belts of tracer rounds were loaded for the .303 Brownings. As the massive steel casing of the mines affected the magnetic field, the compasses on each Lancaster had to be swung both with and without the Upkeep on board. Then came the briefing for pilots and navigators in the large first-floor room of the Officers' Mess (see page 28) where the models of the dams were unveiled and charts, sectional maps and aerial photographs were also displayed, analysed and evaluated.

The Möhne dam, Target X, with the reference number GO 939, lay seven miles to the south of Soest and 26 miles east of Dortmund. The Sorpe dam — Target Z (GO 960) — was six miles south-west of the Möhne as the crow flies, and it was hoped that a ridge surmounted by the church tower at Langscheid would not directly impede a parallel approach to the dam. Target D (GO 938) was the Lister where the attack was to go in over the village of Eichen. The Ennepe — Target E (GO 935) — lay some 19 miles to the south of Dortmund where, even at high water level, a small island protruded from the reservoir about 300 yards in front of the dam. The Henne — Target F (GO 936) — was the fourth target within the catchment area of the River Ruhr, and lay near Meschede but, due to the possibility of heavy flak near the town, the dam was deleted from the final target list.

The two other dams lay within the catchment area of the River Weser. The Eder — Target Y (GO 934) — lay 50 miles to the south-east of the Möhne and, although this was undefended, the hilly terrain would make a low-level night attack extremely difficult. The sixth target, replacing the Henne as Target F, was the Diemel dam (GO 933), situated 20 miles north of the Eder, and this, like the Lister and the Ennepe dams, was assigned to the list of 'last resort targets'.

Left: **A post-war shot of the old Sergeants' Mess — latterly the Airmen's Mess. The main briefing was held in the large room on the first floor** *(right)* **but other offices were also used.**

A final briefing for all the 132 men due to fly with him that night began at 6 p.m. when Wing Commander Guy Gibson introduced Barnes Wallis, who described the bomb and presented sectional diagrams of the dams and the arguments for their destruction. Standing before a huge map of Western Europe, with red strips showing the flight paths to the targets, Air Vice-Marshal Cochrane then took the floor and prophesised that the forthcoming operation would go down in history and be a devastating blow to the German war machine.

Gibson reminded his audience of the take-off arrangements. The first wave of nine aircraft destined for the Möhne, Sorpe and Eder dams would leave the ground in three groups of three at ten-minute intervals. The second wave, comprising five Lancasters, would fly straight to the Sorpe while the third wave of five aircraft would take off 2½ hours later to serve as back-up. He told the crews that if they had to abort for whatever reason, the Upkeeps were to be jettisoned and on no account brought back because of the danger of landing with such a heavy weapon still on board.

Gibson: 'At exactly the right time Hutch [seen in the picture *(right)* helping Gibson with his parachute harness] fired a red Very light and all the aircraft started up. There was to be RT silence until we crossed the enemy coast. The AOC walked into my ship and wished me the best of luck, and I replied with a sickly grin. An RAF photographer came running up and asked to take a picture — these men certainly choose the queerest times. Then we ambled out onto the runway in our formation and stood there waiting to take off.' *Opposite:* **This is the photo taken by Flying Officer Bellamy of the crew about to enter AJ-G. Gibson is reported to have called to the photographer as an afterthought: 'Make sure you send a copy to my wife!' Neither he nor his crew survived the war. L-R: The rear gunner, Flight Lieutenant Dick Trevor-Roper; the flight engineer, Sergeant John Pulford; the front gunner, Flight Sergeant George Deering; the bomb-aimer, Pilot Officer Fred Spafford; wireless operator, Flight Lieutenant Bob Hutchison; Gibson; and Pilot Officer Torger Taerum, the navigator. (As the official photographer at Scampton, Bellamy took a total of nine shots — see page 210. Only four were passed for publication of which these are two.)**

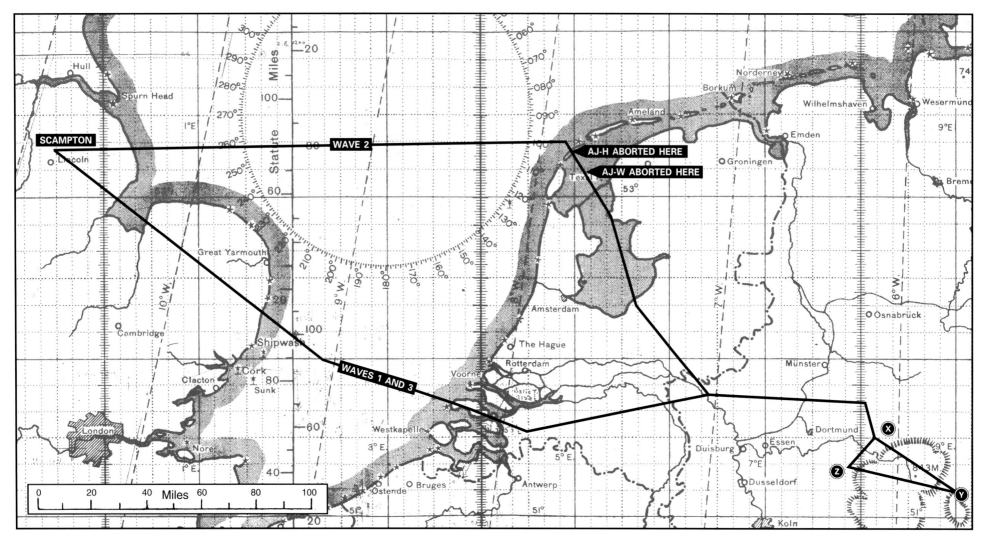

The planned routes to the targets. The Lancasters in the second wave, flying the longer northern leg, took off first at one-minute intervals: AJ-E at 21.28, AJ-W 21.29, AJ-K 21.30, AJ-H 21.31, with McCarthy's AJ-T delayed until 22.01. Gibson in AJ-G then led the first wave, taking off line abreast with AJ-M and AJ-P at 21.39; AJ-A, AJ-J and AJ-L took off all together at 21.47; and AJ-Z, AJ-B and AJ-N at 21.59. The back-up wave followed, taking off singly: AJ-C at 00.09, AJ-S at 00.11, AJ-F at 00.12, AJ-O at 00.14 and AJ-Y last at 00.15.

At 21.10, Flight Lieutenant Bob Hutchison, the wireless operator on board Gibson's Lancaster, fired a red Very light from the cockpit of AJ-G as the signal for the first and second waves to start their engines and taxi around the perimeter track. At 21.28, with Flight Lieutenant Bob Barlow at the controls, the first aircraft of the second wave (AJ-E) rolled across RAF Scampton's grass for its take-off. Taking the northerly route, the aircraft in this second wave had a longer flight path than those in the first wave and therefore were first to leave the ground. Operation 'Chastise' was finally underway. After a long run due to the heavy load, the five Lancasters of the second wave roared off one after the other, turning to the east in the direction of Sutton-on-

Sea on the North Sea coast. However, because of an aborted start due to a coolant leak in the No. 4 engine of AJ-Q, Flight Lieutenant Joe McCarthy had to hurriedly switch his crew to the reserve aircraft AJ-T (see page 31). Consequently, he had to try to make up a 20-minute delay.

At 21.39, a green from an Aldis lamp signalled that Gibson's Lancaster was clear for take-off. With Flight Lieutenant John Hopgood on his right in AJ-M and Flight Lieutenant Harold Martin to his left in AJ-P, the three Lancasters roared across the grass in formation and within 20 minutes the whole of the first wave was airborne. Forty minutes later they were coasting out over Southwold towards Holland.

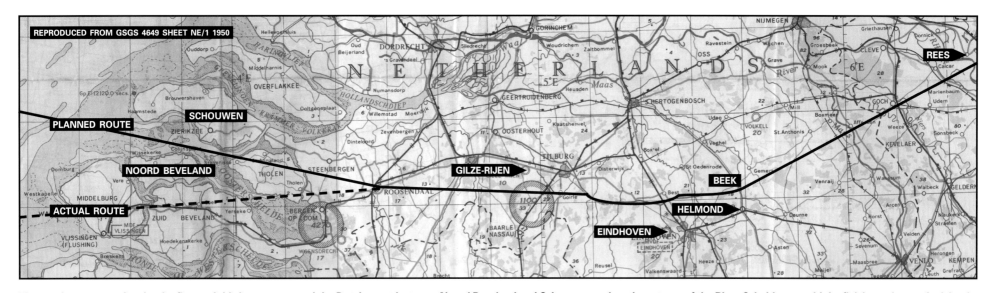

PLANNED ROUTE

ACTUAL ROUTE

SCHOUWEN

NOORD BEVELAND

GILZE-RIJEN

BEEK

HELMOND

EINDHOVEN

REES

The southern route taken by the first and third waves crossed the Dutch coast between Noord Beveland and Schouwen and up the estuary of the River Schelde to avoid the flak batteries on the islands.

The North Sea lay calm beneath them and from time to time, Aldis lamps flashed messages in Morse from aircraft to aircraft. Gibson mistakenly crossed the coast over the heavily defended island of Walcheren before correcting his course towards Roosendaal. Using one of the special roller maps in the bomb-aimer's position, Pilot Officer Fred Spafford kept constant check on their track which took them along the Wilhelmina Canal and between the German night fighter bases at Gilze-Rijen and Eindhoven. Close to the town of Helmond, the canal intersects the Zuid Willemsvaart (South Willems Canal) at right angles and from here the flight took them to a bend in the Rhine at Rees, then east towards Ahsen, past the small lakes near Dülmen. In the Borken area there was heavy flak and intense searchlight activity which briefly caught all three aircraft of the first flight. Gibson broke radio silence to issue a flak warning which Group HQ re-broadcast to all aircraft shortly afterwards, together with a position report. There was also heavy flak to the north of Hamm on the approach to Europe's largest marshalling yards.

After the war the two islands were linked together by the Oosterscheldedam.

The next landmark was Roosendaal, recognisable by the railway junction north of the town.

Carefully navigating between the two German night fighter bases of Gilze-Rijen and Eindhoven, east of Tilburg they picked up the Wilhelmina Canal which acted as a signpost for the next stage of the flight.

This took them to Beek, easily identifiable because of the T-junction where the Wilhelmina Canal (on the left) joins the Zuid Willemsvaart. (This is a modern picture, the fourth curving arm on the right being a post-war addition.)

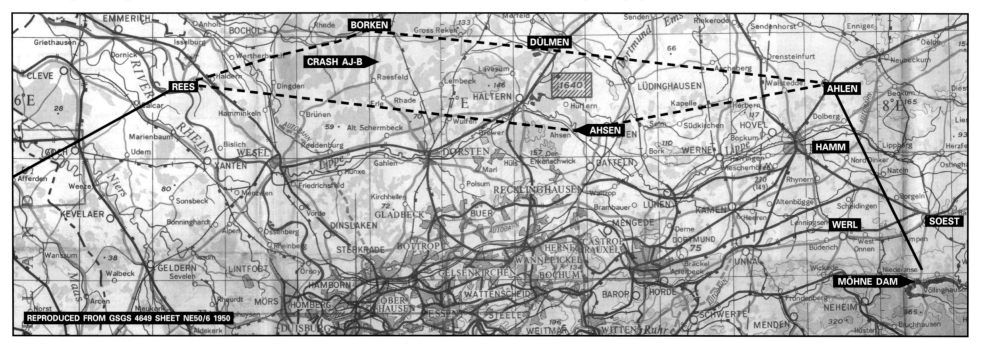

REPRODUCED FROM GSGS 4649 SHEET NE50/6 1950

Reaching the Rhine at Rees *(above)*, in the operational order the next turning point was to be at Ahsen where the course shifted a little to the north to Ahlen from where the route lay south-east between Soest and Werl (our author's home town) to reach the Möhne dam. However the leading machine ran into heavy anti-aircraft fire past Rees so the course was adjusted a little to the south. However, it appears that the aircraft must have reverted northwards, near to the planned track but it was a fatal decision for one of the machines. (The bridge in the photo was built after the war, the only method of crossing the river in 1943 being by ferry. In March 1945, this was also the location for the 21st Army Group's assault across the Rhine by the British Second Army, Rees being very badly damaged in the process.)

The searchlight position in front of what was then the Fasselt-Welchering farm near Raesfeld, just a mile or so south-west of Marbeck where AJ-B came down. It was not until the aircraft had roared past at tree-top height that this searchlight came into action and began sweeping the sky for the attackers. In the background can be seen the extension of the same high-tension power line which was the Lancaster's undoing.

Flight Lieutenant Astell clipped the top of one of the pylons at the farming hamlet of Marbeck. A note written by the local policeman listed the names of only three of the crew and gave a meagre list of personal possessions recovered: emergency rations . . . money . . . a ring . . . a cigarette case . . . a watch . . . a bunch of keys . . . a Canadian lighter . . . and an engraved wristwatch. In front of a shattered wing lies the body of one of the crew.

Eight minutes behind Gibson, the second flight of three aircraft led by Squadron Leader Henry Young (AJ-A), with Flight Lieutenant Dave Maltby to his right (AJ-J), and Flight Lieutenant Dave Shannon (AJ-L) to his left, followed in their wake. They also encountered flak near Dülmen and arrived over the Möhne dam at 00.20.

The final flight of three aircraft in the first wave, led by Squadron Leader Henry Maudslay (AJ-Z), with Flight Lieutenant Bill Astell (AJ-B) on his right and Pilot Officer Les Knight (AJ-N) on his left, had taken off at 21.59, their flight over the North Sea taking somewhat longer due to headwinds. As they crossed the Dutch frontier into Germany Astell was following close behind Maudslay and Knight when, near Marbeck, while flying at the prescribed low level but without having been picked out by searchlights or engaged by flak, AJ-B hit an electricity pylon. Sister Roswitha Reiming witnessed the crash.

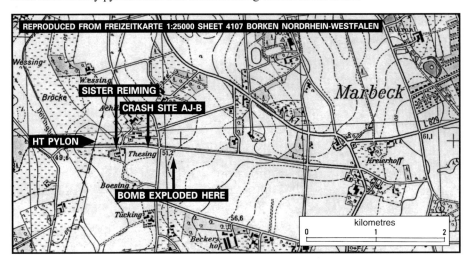

Flight Lieutenant Astell hit a pylon near the farmhouse of the Thesing family. His Upkeep detached from the aircraft and exploded 150 yards away.

'During the war I was working as a maid for the Thesing family whose farm was situated in the countryside near Marbeck. On many a night, fires made the sky glow red over the Ruhr as the bombs rained down. Getting on towards midnight on May 16, I was standing outside with old Herr Thesing watching low-flying aircraft, which we took to be German. First of all a four-engined aircraft came from the side over the neighbours' houses. One or two minutes later a second aircraft came past from the same westerly direction but nearer to us. This was followed two minutes later by a third. This one flew into the top of an electricity pylon 150 to 200 metres from the Thesings' farmhouse; it was not on fire at the time. Suddenly the aircraft was engulfed in flames. It rose a little, flew over our house and crashed 200 metres away in a field. About two minutes after this, a bomb exploded and left a crater so big you could have put a house into it. Seven men were killed in the crash. The blast blew out all the windows in the house; all the doors and the roof were badly damaged, too. There was an air raid warning on at the time but the flak batteries defending Marl didn't start firing until the bomber had already crashed. The searchlights at Marbeck also shone straight up into the sky after this. The enemy aircraft were flying so low that the searchlights couldn't have lit them up anyway. We were all quite sure they were our own aircraft and were just about to call the others from the cellar when the crash happened. It lit up our house as it burned. One thing struck me: at the roadside just 50 metres from the bomb crater, there was a statue of St Josef with the baby Jesus in his arms. This wasn't touched at all. It didn't even lose a finger. Not like all the damage to the buildings further away.'

William Astell *(left)* **and his crew are now buried in Reichswald Forest War Cemetery in Germany (five kilometres south-west of Kleve). All the graves lie in Plot 21 with six of the crew side by side in Row D: Astell Grave 13; Sergeant John Kinnear Grave 14; Pilot Officer Floyd Wile Grave 15; with Flight Sergeant Francis Garbas, Flying Officer Donald Hopkinson and Warrant Officer Abram Garshowitz collectively (because their remains could not be individually identified) in Graves 16-18. Sergeant Richard Bolitho alone lies behind in Grave 1 of Row E.**

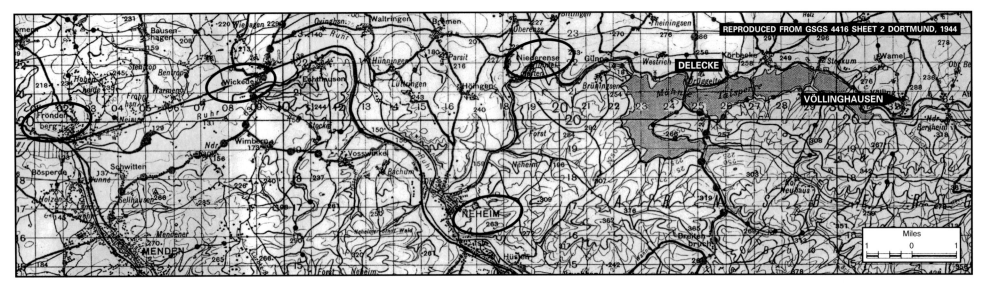

REPRODUCED FROM GSGS 4416 SHEET 2 DORTMUND, 1944

Primary Target X: The Möhne dam

Wing Commander Guy Gibson arrived over the Möhne reservoir at 00.15 leading the aircraft of the first wave. One by one, the Lancasters assembled in an anti-clockwise holding pattern ten kilometres south of Völlinghausen over the Arnsberg forest. Gibson called up AJ-B but in vain for the Lancaster was already a burning wreck on the ground near Marbeck. Gibson assessed the situation and sized up the flak. Everything seemed to be just as forecast at the briefing with three batteries on the dam wall and three more in the valley. Now in position, Gibson confirmed that the attack would go in from above the forester's house, Grüne Hoffnung, across the centre of the Heve promontory — the wooded, flat spit of land between the Heve basin and the Delecke bridge — and then for a mile over the water in a straight line to the centre of the dam wall. Over the VHF radio, Gibson assigned five of the remaining eight Lancasters to the attack, with Hopgood as his second in command in the event that anything should happen to him.

Target X viewed before the war from the south-west with the main power station between the dam and the equalising basin.

Seen from just a little north of east, the subsidiary power plant can be seen on the far side of the basin.

A table of numeric codes had been drawn up to simplify the notification of success or otherwise back to Group Headquarters using the prefix 'Goner'. As we have seen, each target had been assigned a code-letter — Möhne X, Eder Y, Sorpe Z, (confusingly changed to A, B and C in the signals order) Lister D, Ennepe E and Diemel F — and this letter was to be added after the following number code: 'Goner 1' special weapon released, failed to explode; 'Goner 2' special weapon released, overshot dam; 'Goner 3' special weapon released, exploded more than 100 yards from dam; 'Goner 4' special weapon released, exploded 100 yards from dam; 'Goner 5' special weapon released, exploded 50 yards from dam; 'Goner 6' special weapon released, exploded 5 yards from dam; 'Goner 7' special weapon released, exploded in contact with dam; 'Goner 8' no apparent breach; 'Goner 9' small breach in dam; 'Goner 10' large breach in dam. Therefore 'Goner 78C' would signify that the Upkeep had been released at the Sorpe and it had exploded in contact with the dam but with no apparent effect.

In the face of the heaviest opposing fire imaginable, Gibson proposed to go in first. He descended to the prescribed height and held his speed with the bomb rotating at 500 rpm. As Pilot Officer Fred Spafford, the bomb-aimer, saw the towers on the target coincide with the markings on his sight he released the weapon and the bomb exploded at 00.28. From his grandstand seat the rear gunner, Flight Lieutenant Dick Trevor-Roper, saw the bomb bounce three times before a great plume of water rose up. For a moment they thought the wall had been breached but the bomb had struck some 150 feet to the south of the centre of the dam. Gibson's wireless operator, Flight Lieutenant Bob Hutchison, signalled 'Goner 68A' back to base informing them of a miss.

Left: **The only photograph taken during the raid. Fourteen-year-old Heinz Vogt in Günne earned his place in the history books when he took this shot with his 6x9cm Agfa box camera using a five-minute exposure which recorded the tracer from the flak guns.**

With the lack of photography of the actual attack, no excuses then for including at this point in the story an enlargement from the only live Upkeep test (see page 25) to set the scene.

The remains of AJ-M, piloted by Flight Lieutenant John Hopgood *(inset)* **and hit by flak over the Möhne, scattered across a meadow ironically called Himmelpforten — Gateway to Heaven.**

Waiting for the waves to subside, five minutes later Flight Lieutenant Hopgood attacked in AJ-M. As the Lancaster approached the target, the other crews saw flak set an engine and wing ablaze. Then the Upkeep was released but too late and it bounced over the dam and exploded on the power station. With orange flames trailing behind it, Hopgood's Lancaster pulled away to crash near Ostönnen. Hopgood had tried unsuccessfully to gain height and three of the crew managed to bale out at almost tree-top height. Pilot Officers Tony Burcher and Jim Fraser landed safely but Sergeant John Minchin, already badly wounded by flak, was killed on impact when his parachute failed to fully deploy.

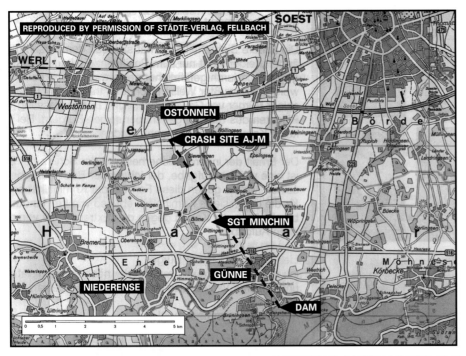

Pilot Officers Tony Burcher and Jim Fraser managed to bale out at low level and were taken prisoner, but the parachute of the third man to escape, Sergeant John Minchin, did not fully open and his body was found in a field on the Haarhöhe. With the exception of its tail section, the Lancaster disintegrated upon impact.

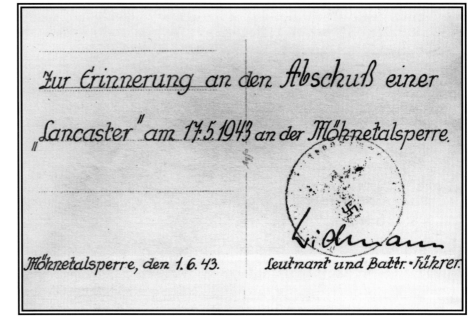

Above left and right: **Postcard sent by flak battery commander Leutnant Jörg Widmann on June 1, 1943 'in memory of the shooting down of a Lancaster on May 17, 1943 at the Möhne reservoir'.**

A member of the Möhne flak battery with a trophy of their victory recovered for their hutments situated near the Haus Delecke restaurant . . .

This inscription near the door was believed to have been written by WO2 Garshowitz — the wireless operator on Astell's AJ-B — as he had a reputation for being a practical joker. He even chalked one of the Upkeeps: 'Never has so much been expected of so few'!

. . . but the only relic from AJ-M which appears to have survived today is this engine plate taken at the time by a souvenir hunter.

The funeral of the five dead airmen took place with full military honours at 11.30 a.m. on the morning of May 20 at the Ostenfriedhof in Soest. Their remains were buried in three graves (numbered 8486, 8487 and 8488) and there they lay until their exhumation on August 14, 1947 for reburial in the large British War Cemetery at Rheinberg (24 kilometres north of Krefeld) which now contains over 3,000 dead. Helmuth Euler pictured their collective grave in Row E of Plot 17.

In August 1991, at the instigation of former Captain Paul Snook (right) of Major and Mrs Holt's Battlefield Tours, a small memorial plaque was erected close to the crash site near Ostönnen which was dedicated by Pastor Martin Gocht (centre). On the left, the former burgomeister of Ostönnen, Walter Rocholl. The crash site is not that easy to find but when coming from Niederense towards Ostönnen, just before the post-war autobahn, a farm track leads some 500 metres to the crash site which lies in a small valley. (See map page 60.)

Luftwaffenbefehlshaber Mitte   Den 19. Juni 1943.
Führungsabteilung

Az.: 8 c Nr. 11700/43 (Ia op 3 (LS) 3)

Betr.: Gefangenenaussage.

An den
Reichsminister der Luftfahrt u.
Oberbefehlshaber der Luftwaffe
-L. In. 13-

= = = = = = = = = = = = = = = = =

24. JUNI 1943

Nachstehend wird die Nachvernehmung des F/Sgt. F r a s e r (Bombenschütze), abgeschossen am 17.5.1943 bei Ostönnen b. Soest i. W., mit einer "Lancaster" der 617.Bo.Sqd., Scampton, abschriftlich bekanntgegeben:

F/Sgt. Fraser machte nach eingehender Befragung noch die folgenden Angaben:
Zum genauen Abwurf der bekannten Grosswasserbombe war die langgeschulte Zusammenarbeit von 4 Besatzungsmitgliedern erforderlich;

	der Pilot	hatte auf Höhe und Horizontalflug zu achten;
	der Bordmechaniker	hatte durch Bedienung von Gashebel usw. die vorgesehene Fluggeschwindigkeit einzuhalten;
	der Funker	war mit Bedienung des Ölmotors zwecks Rotationsantrieb der Grosswasserbombe betraut und hatte auf vorgeschriebene Umdrehungszahl derselben zu achten;
	der Bombenschütze	war für genauen Abwurf verantwortlich,
und	der Orter	bediente MG's in Bugkanzel.

F. gab als Flugzeuggeschwindigkeit 420 km/Std. (260 m/h) an; die Abwurfhöhe nannte er mit 18.25 m (60) Fuss). Der Ölmotor zum Rotationsantrieb der Grosswasserbombe musste 5-6 Minuten vor dem Ziel durch Zufluss aus Druckölleitung langsam angelassen werden. F. konnte angeblich nicht sagen, aus welcher Druckölleitung. Die zu erreichende Umdrehungszahl der Grosswasserbombe schrieb F. schliesslich mit 380 pro Min., die durch Tachometer kontrolliert wurde, nachdem er vorher von 400 bis 500 Umdrehungen pro Minute gesprochen hatte.

F. will sich als Bombenschütze nach vielen diesbezüglichen Übungsflügen eine eigene einfache Vorrichtung zur Anvisierung der Sperrmauer aus Sperrholz hergestellt haben. Er skizzierte diese Visiervorrichtung in Form eines gleichschenkeligen Dreiecks mit Basis von 6 Zoll und Höhe von 9 Zoll und erklärte dazu, dass er dieselbe dicht am Auge hielt und beim Anflug nur zu warten brauchte, bis sich der Abstand zwischen den Türmen der Sperrmauer bei vorgesehener Abwurfentfernung mit der Basis seines Visierdreiecks deckte. - Er nannte als ihm bekannten Abstand zwischen den Türmen auf der Sperrmauer der Möhnetalsperre 620 Fuss (etwa 195 m) und bezeich-
- 2 -

Although captured aircrews were obliged only to give their name, rank and number, Pilot Officer Jim Fraser spilt the beans when questioned at the Luftwaffe Transit and Interrogation Camp, popularly known as 'Dulag Luft', at Oberursel, just north of Frankfurt-am-Main. This is a translation of the German document dated June 19, 1943.

Luftwaffenbefehlshaber Mitte, Führungsabteilung. Statement from prisoner.
To Reich Air Minister and Commander-in-Chief of Luftwaffe.

'Herewith a copy of the interrogation report from F/Sgt *(sic)* Fraser (bomb-aimer), shot down on May 17, 1943 at Ostönnen near Soest i. W. in a Lancaster of 617 Bomber Squadron based at Scampton. After close questioning, F/Sgt Fraser provided the following information:

'To ensure the accurate delivery of what we know to be the large depth-charge, the co-operation (achieved after lengthy training) of four crew members was required. The responsibilities of the crew members were as follows:

The pilot:	**maintain height and ensure that the aircraft flew straight and level**
The flight engineer:	**adjust the throttles, etc, to maintain the required airspeed**
The wireless operator:	**operate the motor that rotated the large depth-charge, and maintain the required rotation speed**
The bomb-aimer:	**ensure the accurate release**
The navigator:	**man the machine guns in the forward turret**

'F gave the airspeed as 420 kph (260 mph); the height of release was given as 18.25m (60 feet). The motor that rotated the large depth-charge had to be started up *slowly* by opening a pressurised oil lead 5-6 minutes before the target. F claimed he could not say which pressurised oil lead. The required rotation speed was monitored by a tachometer. F finally *wrote* this as 380 per minute after he had previously given it *verbally* as 400 - 500 revolutions per minute.

'F claims that after many training flights for the mission he had, as bomb-aimer, made up his own simple device from plywood for aiming at the dam. He sketched this aiming device as an isosceles triangle with a base of *6 inches* and a height of *9 inches.* He explained that he held this up to his eye. On the bombing run, he had only to wait until the gap between the towers of the dam was covered by the base of the aiming triangle to know he was at the planned release distance. He gave the distance between the towers of the Möhne dam as 620 feet (about 195m) and the release point as *(as an example, he said)* 900 feet (about 275m). F jokingly wrote each of these figures twice. However, he crossed out the figure 900 just once when he was supposed to give a straight answer to the question concerning the distance of the release point from the dam. He at once hastily confirmed that he had only given this figure as an example. (Interrogation Officer's note: as the dimensions of F's home-made aiming device were *6in x 9in* it can reasonably be assumed that, with the distance between the towers known by him to be *620 feet,* the release point was *900 feet* in front of the dam wall.)

'When F was told that the recovered bomb weighed 3900kg (8599lbs), he said that he knew it to be 11000lbs (about 5000kg). However, he subsequently thought this latter figure could refer to the total weight of the special additional load.

'As far as the many training flights are concerned, F stated that the final exercise was carried out with a *cement bomb* of the same weight as the one used on the mission. However, he would not give any information as to the location of the place where the practice drop was carried out. The rotation of the cement practice bomb set up severe vibrations in the aircraft but there were hardly any vibrations before the release of the bomb on the target.
F confirmed the perceived view that the Lancasters engaged in the raid against the dams had been specially prepared and mentioned in passing that the preparations had taken about a year.

'F is very proud of his involvement in the raid on the dams; he also said that during the raid on Stuttgart on November 23, 1942 he dropped a 4000lb bomb on the main railway station and scored a hit.

'They were well informed by reconnaissance photographs as to the dams' weak defences and the location of anti-aircraft guns. In addition to accurate maps, models were also used to develop tactics for the raid. The bomb-aimer in Sqd Ldr Maudslay's crew was named by F as Fg Off Tytherleigh'.
(See note page 46 concerning Fraser's rank. He was subsequently sent to Stalag Luft 3 at Sagan. He returned to Canada after the war but has since died.)

This contemporary artist's impression of the attack by Montague Black appeared in Hutchinson's *Pictorial History of the War*. Although the illustration gives a good impression of the moment the dam collapsed, artistic licence has added a second non-existant dam in the right-hand corner. Also there are far too many flak guns and searchlights.

The third attack was launched by Flight Lieutenant Martin in AJ-P with Gibson flying alongside so as to confuse the German gunners. A great plume of water rose 150 feet in front of the northern side of the dam but Martin had to signal 'Goner 58A' indicating another miss. (When they had landed back at Scampton, it was revealed that the flak had hit an empty fuel tank.)

Then it was Squadron Leader Young's turn with AJ-A and he went in for the fourth bombing run. This time Martin flew parallel with him engaging the ground defences while at the same time Gibson flew over the dam from the south with all his lights on. Once again a plume of water shot up high over the dam and another miss was signalled as 'Goner 78A'.

64

Record of W/T Messages.

Time	From	Message
00.11	G	Flak warning at 51.48 N. 07.12 E.
00.12	Group	(As above – retransmitted on full power by Group H.Q.).
00.37	G	GONER68A
00.50	A	GONER78A
00.53	P	GONER58A
00.55	J	GONER78A
00.56	G	NIGGER
00.57	Group	NIGGER – retransmitted on full power by Group H.Q. Aircraft replied "Correct".

Note that Martin's signal (AJ-P, the third aircraft to go in) arrives *after* that of Young in AJ-A — the fourth Lancaster to attack.

Now Gibson ordered Flight Lieutenant Maltby in Lancaster AJ-J to go in for the fifth release while he and Martin flew alongside to engage the flak and a third Lancaster fired at the batteries on the dam from a point over Haarstrang. Maltby was spot on course and the bomb hit the dam in exactly the right place. Once again a plume of water shot 1,000 feet into the air, collapsing slowly in the moonlight, the shock waves in the water being clearly visible. Maltby's wireless operator had just sent another disappointing signal back to base — one more miss and Gibson had already ordered Shannon to carry out the sixth attack — when suddenly he saw the dam give way. Immediately all the flak stopped firing with the exception of one gun and at 00.56 Flight Lieutenant Hutchison transmitted the code-word 'Nigger' thus informing No. 5 Group that the Möhne dam had been breached. HQ repeated the message and requested confirmation so as to make quite sure there had been no misunderstanding. (The seismological station in Göttingen 130 kilometres away recorded the actual time as 00.49.)

The crews of the seven aircraft looked down at their handiwork with amazement; the sight of water shooting through the breach in the dam wall was indescribable — probably something that would never be experienced again from the air by human eyes.

As planned, Maltby and Martin then set course for home while the three aircraft still with Upkeeps on board — AJ-L (Flight Lieutenant Shannon), AJ-Z (Squadron Leader Maudslay) and AJ-N (Pilot Officer Knight) — now flew off to the south-east with Gibson and his second in command, now Squadron Leader Young, to the Eder reservoir, which was some 10-12 minutes flying time away.

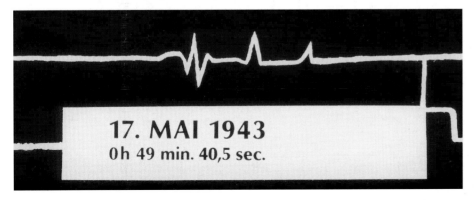

17. MAI 1943
0h 49 min. 40,5 sec.

The blip on the trace at the Institut für Geophysik at Göttingen. (See also page 154.)

The earliest picture of the broken dam — and Christmas trees — taken at 10 a.m. on Monday.

Shutting the door after the horse — or rather water — had bolted! Barrage balloons were flying above the dam on Tuesday.

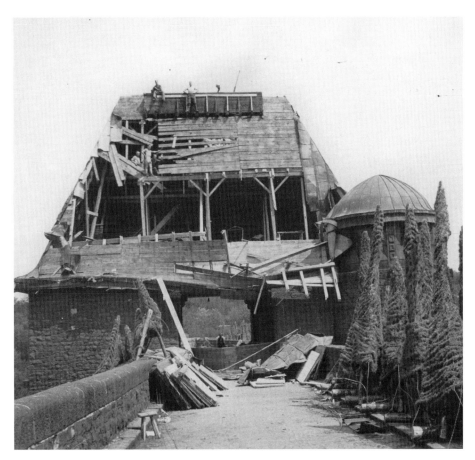

Left: **When Hopgood's mine overshot the dam and exploded on the power house below, the blast wrecked the northern tower. In this picture, taken just as repairs begin, the 2cm flak** gun is visible on the platform on the roof. *Right:* **Evidence of the return fire from the .303 Brownings, loaded with belts containing all tracer for maximum scare effect.**

Back in Britain there was a state of great excitement among the raid's commanders. Once the first two waves were airborne, Harris, Cochrane and Wallis had left Scampton for the headquarters at Grantham and there, in the ops block, they followed the progress of the attack. This was the first time a bomber formation had been in direct contact with its commanders from the target and Wing Commander Wally Dunn, the Signals Officer, decoded and relayed the messages over the loudspeaker. Meanwhile, Wallis paced anxiously up and down, and as each miss was reported he buried his head in his hands. When 'Nigger' came through, Wallis, electrified by the news, jumped to his feet and threw both arms in the air. Officers shook him by the hand and Harris came up and congratulated him. For those present, these were moments that would live with them forever.

Meanwhile, back in Germany, a disaster was unfolding. Karl Schütte was an NCO with the flak battery at the dam: 'On April 16, 1943, I was posted to the 3. Batterie of Flak-Regiment 840 at the Möhne. On the night of the raid we received a telephoned air raid alert from our HQ at Schwansbell Castle near Lünen. It only took a few seconds to get the 2cm guns on the Möhne towers and those in the valley ready to fire.

'Soon a dark object appeared on the horizon and raced at zero feet across the lake towards the centre of the dam. The monster was blazing away at us and it immediately came under our fire. We didn't see its spotlights until it had almost reached the dam because of all the coloured lights from the tracers. I was passing corrections to the aiming gunner but he didn't fire at the spotlights — he fired on his own initiative straight at the bomber and the source of the tracers. The first bomb exploded 50 metres in front of the dam and sent up a huge plume of water. During the second attack I clearly saw our tracers striking home; flames broke out at once and one of the engines was on fire. As the aircraft flew over the dam the flames flickered and got bigger. A great cheer went up, just like when you've scored. Then there was a massive explosion in the valley — the bomb on the burning plane had reduced the power station to ashes. There was such a cloud of smoke that at first we couldn't see what had happened.

'After the direct hit on the power station all the phones went dead and the gun on the south tower was knocked out. The crew ran over to the approach road and reported to Leutnant Widmann. None of the gunners was wounded during the attack and no one from the north tower could help us because after the direct hit on the power station the stairs were damaged and all the ceilings fell in. You could also clearly see the aircraft circling over the trees on the other side of the lake, especially when they had their lights on to draw the flak.

Left: **The power station was blown to pieces and the remains swept away in the huge torrent of 120 million tons of floodwater released. Karl Schütte stands on one of the huge pipes** which once fed the turbines. *Right:* **A 20-ton piece from one of the turbines photographed some 100 metres away. Today this is an exhibit in the Deutsche Museum in Munich.**

'The attack hotted up more and more as they came at us from all directions. Two more huge plumes of water showered down on the dam. During the fourth attack, our gun failed after a premature explosion in the barrel. We bashed away with all our strength trying to clear the jam with a hammer and a metal spike but it was no good. When it came to the fifth attack we did what we'd so often done in training — let loose with our carbines. There was just one flak gun on the road still firing at the aircraft — now they had it all their own way. There was a muffled explosion and when the spray had cleared a bit I had a quick look over the parapet down at the dam wall and shouted: "The wall's had it." The gunners didn't want to believe it at first but the breach got visibly bigger. All I could think was, when it comes to the next attack you'll be down there under that roaring flood. I didn't actually see the bombs bounce off the water as all our attention was on the attacking aircraft and on the tracers.

'As it started to get light between 03.00 and 04.00, another aircraft flew over. The last serviceable gun on the approach road fired at it but in vain. This Lancaster shot up a barn in Günne with its machine guns and set it on fire. Our guns below the dam could only engage the aircraft while they were flying away from us otherwise they might have hit us on our towers. Our 2cm FlaK gun had a range of 2000 metres.'

Another eyewitness, Ferdinand Nölle, the special constable from Günne, recalls: 'During the night of May 16/17, I was on the night watch. Around midnight the sirens went off in the distance. I went over to the power station and helped my friend Clemens Köhler to read the meters. The flak started up outside. I said: "Clemens, get out of the power station and go up to the dam."

'I walked along the dam wall and waited to be relieved by Wilhelm Strotkamp at 00.20. He finally turned up and I asked why he was so late.

'"Yes", he said. "I've been watching the show over on the water side."

'I warned him, "Wilhelm, don't go down into the dam galleries tonight. You'll get drowned if the water comes in." I went to the roadway. After the first miss, there was so much water vapour in the air it was like being in a laundry. Just then another bomb came down and hit the torpedo net. The reel of steel cable holding it unwound at high speed; it couldn't have been fixed properly. I was just about to report to the duty room when some of my friends who'd been watching the raid from behind a thick terrace wall down at the Seehof Restaurant suddenly came running into the duty room shouting: "The wall's gone!"

'The water from one of the explosions poured over the wall and the terraces. Each explosion in the lake was followed by a massive blast. Once I shot three metres across the duty room and bashed my head against a door. It was a good job I was wearing a steel helmet otherwise I'd have smashed my head in. This explosion was worse than anything I'd experienced at Verdun. Strotkamp arrived in the duty room out of breath from below the dam where he'd been on duty. All the windows had been blown out of the duty room and the lights had gone out.

'The phone rang and we both made a grab for it. It was the authorities in Soest asking what was going on at the Möhne. We told them about the breach in the dam and said: "We can't do anything up here. You'd better warn the valley." That took the responsibility away from us. Once the wall had given way you couldn't see down into the Möhne valley below the dam. Everything was blotted out by swathes of mist and all you could hear was the thundering of the water which was now bringing death and destruction to the Möhne and Ruhr valleys. My friend Strotkamp was the only one who actually saw the dam wall shake back and forth like in an earthquake. Then it just opened up like a barn door.'

Unteroffizier Schütte examines the debris littering the floor of the equalising basin.

The remains of the anti-torpedo netting.

A rare photograph taken from the water side shows the patched up south tower. Just 15 million cubic metres of water remain in the reservoir which had been officially opened almost exactly 30 years previously — on July 12, 1913. At the time, a bronze plaque was set into the northern tower to commemorate the building of the dam, which had cost 25 million Goldmarks. The plaque hangs today as a trophy of war in the War Museum in Canberra, Australia (see page 224), the inscription reading (in German): 'In the 25th year of the reign of our Emperor, Wilhelm II, one hundred years after the Fatherland gained its freedom, this Möhne dam entered service. It was erected by the Ruhrtalsperrenverein of Essen as an enduring memorial to the blessed development and creative zeal of these lands of Rhineland-Westphalia. Chairman of the Ruhrtalsperrenverein: Holle, Mayor of the City of Essen.'

Christian Tilenius was specially ordered by the Reichsluftfahrtministerium (Reich Air Ministry) to examine the wreckage of the crashed Lancasters to try to get details of the new weapon. At the same time, he also flew over the dams and took a series of sensational photographs. This one was taken around 6 p.m. on May 18.

Walter Fischer, then a 15-year-old pupil at the grammar school in Soest, recalls: 'Fourteen grammar school boys were lying on their beds in the dormitory of the school's rowing club at Delecke [on the north shore of the reservoir — see map on page 56]. It had been a day of wonderful freedom for them — a day out in the school's fours. Because so many teachers had been called up there was no one in charge at the hostel that evening but the boys didn't feel like going to sleep. On one of the beds a portable gramophone was playing *Lili Marlene*. Seconds later this idyllic scene was shattered; a dull droning sound heralded the arrival of a heavy aircraft. In May 1943 we knew all about the air war and the droning of bombers coming in at high altitude. We also knew the sound of bombs screaming down and the muffled thud of the flak. But this was something quite new.

'During the day, giant herons circled silently and elegantly over Lake Möhne but on this night four-engined bombers were speeding in like arrows — but with a deafening noise — over the spit of land between the Heve basin and the lake. They hopped over the hills and trees and raced towards the dam just a few metres above the mirror-like surface. Every time one of these monsters flew over the lake, the suction from its propellers whisked up a fine spray. It was a fascinating spectacle illuminated from behind by the moon and for fifth-year boys it seemed more like sport than war. We couldn't see the dam itself from Delecke because of the spit of land which juts out with the Haus Delecke restaurant on it. Every time an aircraft appeared, red and green streaks of light went out to meet it — tracers from the 2cm flak guns on the towers of the dam. When these tracer streams hit the aircraft, a strange pattern was formed over the lake. Again and again the bombers flew at the dam wall, blazing away with all guns and churning up great streaks of vapour which were drawn along behind them. It was just as if they planned to touch down on the water. Then behind the spit of land brilliant white plumes of water shot straight up into the air followed shortly afterwards by an explosion. The fifth time there was a muffled thundering explosion. We all thought the dam had been hit.

'We ran over there from Delecke as fast as we could. A hole had been torn in the crest of the dam and you could easily have put a block of flats into it. The water from the Möhne flowed quietly through the breach, but down in the valley it thundered up. The crashing of the water caused the roadway along the top of the dam to vibrate. I thought back to the song that we'd been listening to on our beds in the rowing club when the whole gruesome business began. There's a line in *Lili Marlene* about the swirling fog. But now a fog of doom had descended over the places in the valley which had been hit by the disaster.'

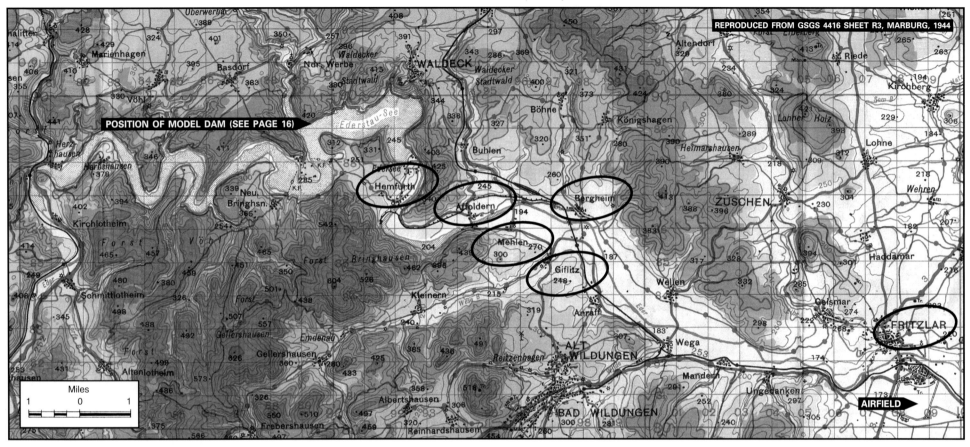

POSITION OF MODEL DAM (SEE PAGE 16)

AIRFIELD

Hidden Target Y: The Eder dam

The remaining five aircraft from the first wave did not encounter any opposition on their way to the Eder reservoir although at first they had great difficulty in identifying the dam itself. The many twists and turns of the valley made navigation difficult and initially Gibson found himself too far to the west. Flight Lieutenant Shannon in AJ-L was also too far west and in fact he mistakenly made a dummy run against the face of a disused quarry near Rehbach which was deceptively similar and lay on the same heading. Shannon was just about to go round for another look when Gibson called him up on the VHF:

'Hello, Cooler aircraft — can you see the target?' Shannon answered faintly, 'I think I'm in the vicinity. I can't see anything. I cannot find the dam.'

'Stand by — I will fire a red Very light — right over the dam.'

'OK — I was a bit south. I'm coming up.'

Soon the Lancasters were circling anti-clockwise over Waldeck Castle which lay north of the dam and the small village of Buhlen. The three heavily-laden Lancasters now faced the problem of flying at 1,000 feet through a gorge by the castle and over the spit of land on the Hammerberg which forms a natural barrier in front of the dam. After this they had to descend to the attack height and then maintain level flight before flying straight at the dam. As soon as the mine had been released, the Lancasters had to be pulled up steeply to avoid the high ground of the Michelskopf opposite.

At around 01.20, Gibson ordered Shannon to attack. AJ-L made three unsuccessful attempts to get into the right approach position but Shannon could not achieve the required height and approach angle so Gibson sent him into a holding pattern and called in Squadron Leader Maudslay in AJ-Z. However, he also failed twice to get into position so Gibson had to order him also to hold off. Then it was Shannon's turn again and, after two more abortive attempts, the bomb-aimer, Flight Sergeant Len Sumpter, was finally able to release the Upkeep but it bounced twice and exploded south of the dam without producing any result. The time was recorded as 01.37 although for some reason the signal 'Goner 79B' was not recorded as received by Grantham until 02.06.

Maudslay then came in again and he released the Upkeep during his second circuit although Gibson saw that it had been dropped too late. It hit the crest of the dam and exploded with a brilliant flash which lit up the whole of the Eder valley like daylight. (Wallis had predicted that this could happen if a bomb struck the dam at too great a velocity.) The explosion came immediately behind Maudslay's Lancaster. Gibson tried in vain to raise him over the VHF and some crew members reported hearing a weak, unnatural, almost disembodied voice. At the time it was believed that Maudslay had crashed after having been caught by the blast but in fact it was not until 02.36 on his return flight that he fell victim to light flak at Emmerich/Klein-Netterden. At 01.57, headquarters at Grantham logged 'Goner 28B' (bomb released, dam overshot, no apparent breach). This was the last time Maudslay's wireless operator contacted headquarters.

WALDECK CASTLE

HAMMERBERG

Time	From	Message
01.45	Group	Flak warning at 51.48 N. 07.12 E transmitted to 3rd Wave.
01.51	G	Called B by W/T.
01.53	G	Called B by W/T.
01.54	G	"Dinghy"
01.55	Group	(Retransmitted on full power by Group H.Q. Aircraft replied "Correct").
01.57	Z	GONER 28B
02.00	N	GONER 710B
02.06	L	GONER 79B
02.10	Group	To 'G'. How many aircraft of first Wave are available for 'C'.
02.11	G	None.

The signals which spelled the end for the Eder dam.

Pilot Officer Les Knight in AJ-N had the only remaining Upkeep and Gibson now ordered him into action. After Knight had finally manoeuvred himself into a suitable position for the release, the bomb bounced three times, struck the dam south of the centre, and exploded. Flying slightly higher and parallel, 1,200 feet away, Gibson had a ringside view of the earthquake-like effect of the explosion. The blast shook the base of the dam and caused it to collapse 'as if a gigantic hand had pushed a hole through cardboard', Gibson wrote later. In the excitement of the moment, Les Knight started to follow the flood wave down the valley until Gibson recalled him and the others. Gibson's wireless operator transmitted the code-word 'Dinghy' at 0154 — the signal that the Eder dam had been breached — whereupon Grantham requested a repeat of the message and further confirmation. Six minutes later the signal, 'Goner 710B' (exploded in contact with dam, large breach) followed from Flight Sergeant Bob Kellow in AJ-N.

Back at No. 5 Group headquarters there was great excitement and Harris immediately asked to be put in touch with the White House in Washington to inform Sir Charles Portal who, at that very moment, was in the process of producing a note to Winston Churchill:

'I understand you wish to be informed about Upkeep, which the Chiefs-of-Staff have agreed should be put into immediate use . . .

'It is most necessary that attacks on the dams (the location of which I would prefer to give you verbally) should be made during this week, when moon and water conditions give the greatest promise of success. By the next favourable moon period the water behind the dams would not be so high, breaching the dams will be more difficult and the effect less.'

Having signed the letter, Portal added a hand-written note:

'Since dictating the above I have received a message from Harris by telephone saying "Upkeep successful on two, possibly three, targets tonight" i.e. night of 16/17th May. Objectives were Möhne and Eder dams + 1 other.'

Two days later, on May 19, Churchill referred to the success of the raid in his address to the US Congress (see page 117).

Left: **Fritz Fisseler, a former salesman, was at home in Nieder-Werbe on leave from his regiment when the Eder dam was attacked. Already alarmed by the explosions, the villagers were further unnerved when they saw the water level in the reservoir falling before their very eyes. Fritz Fisseler jumped on his motor bike and set off with his camera along the road which runs beside the lake. At the time the road had not been cordoned off and he was able to take a crystal-clear shot of the breached dam. However, he was so excited by the dramatic scene that he completely forgot to wind on the film, thus spoiling the remaining exposures! Afraid of a possible police inquiry, Fisseler had the film developed privately by a friend.** *Right:* **Photo taken close to the same spot by Paul Clausius at around 1 p.m. on Monday afternoon — the breach is about 70 metres wide.**

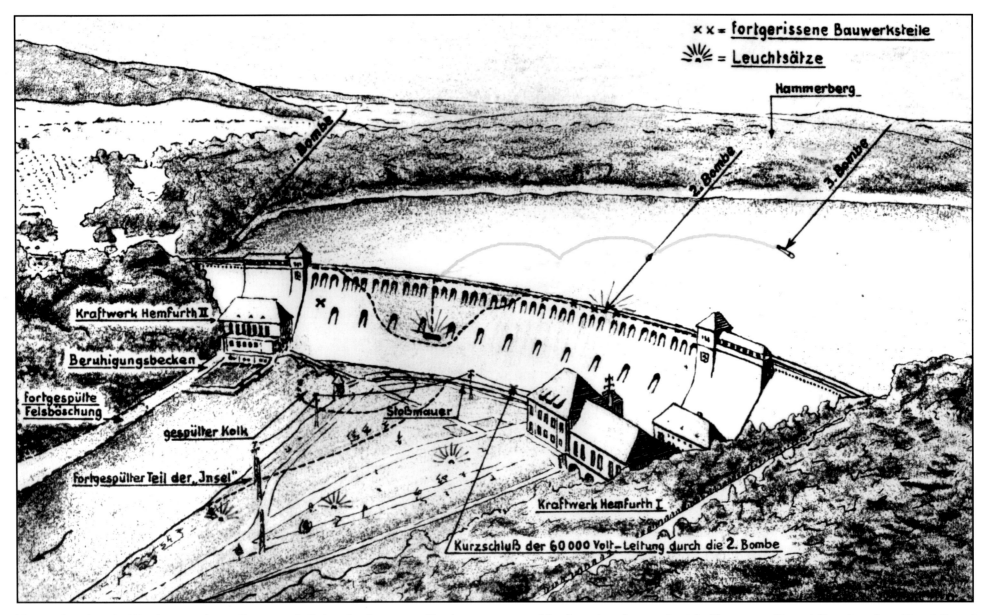

Hammerberg

1. Bombe

2. Bombe

3. Bombe

Kraftwerk Hemfurth II

Beruhigungsbecken

fortgespülte Felsböschung

gespülter Kolk

Stoßmauer

fortgespülter Teil der „Insel"

Kraftwerk Hemfurth I

Kurzschluß der 60 000 Volt-Leitung durch die 2. Bombe

The attack against the Eder dam was shown diagrammatically in a drawing prepared by the Wasser- und Schiffahrtsamt (Water and Navigation Board) of Hannoversch-Münden. Following several unsuccessful runs, Flight Lieutenant Shannon dropped the first Upkeep which exploded near the bank in front of the dam on the Hemfurth II side of the lake. The second mine, released by Squadron Leader Maudslay, hit the crest towards the left-hand side of the dam. Pilot Officer Knight dropped the third and the last remaining weapon. This bounced three times before exploding, blasting some 30,000 tonnes of stone from the wall and leaving a breach approximately 70 metres wide and 22 metres deep. Translation of terms on the drawing: Beruhigungsbecken = Stilling basin. Fortgespülte Felsböschung = Rocky bank washed away. Fortgespülter Teil der "Insel" = Section of "island" washed away. Stoßmauer = Buffer wall. Kraftwerk = Power station. Kurzschluß der 60,000 Volt-Leitung durch die 2. Bombe = Short circuit of the 60,000-volt cable caused by bomb No. 2. Gespülter Kolk = Depression gouged out by the force of the water. Fortgerissene Bauwerksteile = Sections of the structure torn away. Leuchtsätze = Flares.

On the morning of May 17, 24 hours ahead of his British PR rivals, Anton Riediger flying a Fieseler Storch took this photograph of water cascading through the breached dam. Of the 200 million cubic metres of water in the reservoir, some 160 million cubic metres (30 billion gallons) poured out, initially at a rate of 8500 cubic metres (1.8 million gallons) per second, the water excavating a depression in the solid bedrock 10 metres deep and 80 metres across in front of the dam. On the water side, the explosion damaged the turbine inlet valves. Six emergency outlets were slightly damaged and developed leaks from which plumes of water can be seen pouring out. The Hemfurth I power station can be seen on the right of the dam with Hemfurth II on the left.

'In May 1943', recalls Werner Salz, 'I was working as a fitter at the Hemfurth I and Hemfurth II power stations immediately below the dam wall. As was the custom on Sunday evenings in those days, the village youths had gone for a stroll. At around 23.30, as we were coming back over the dam, we met some people who'd been to a civil defence meeting at the Bergmann's house in Hemfurth. At the meeting, villagers who'd raised the matter of the Eder had been told once more that the dam could not be destroyed, nestling as it does between the hills. The reservoir was full to the brim. When the wind blew the waves against the wall, they splashed right over into the valley below.

'I went to bed soon after getting home but around one in the morning, I was rudely awakened by the air raid warning. Immediately after this, aircraft started circling over Hemfurth in a way they'd never done before. I got up and went to the top of a hill above our house. Four-engined aircraft were flying so low between the hills that you could make out the crews in the cockpit in the moonlight. In fact, the air raid warning must have warned everyone that this was the night the Eder dam was going to be attacked. One of the bombers kept flying at the dam with spotlights on. This was not a good sign. At around 01.30, the first heavy bomb fell into the reservoir. When the third explosion occurred, the ground shook. I could feel the shock going through the road. It was then I

realised the dam had been hit. Immediately after this, you could hear the noise of rushing water. All I could think was that our power station had had it. I at once ran back to Hemfurth, where water was already lapping around the houses by the Eder. People were running for their lives; many were looking for their relatives.

'I ran to the dam to see how big the breach in the wall was. It was huge. Masses of water were thundering out — a catastrophe. I was worried about my work mates because there were four men on the night shift. I wondered if they'd drowned. In the grey light of dawn, you could see two men flashing lights on the roof of the control room at Hemfurth I power station. One of the fitters had escaped by going up some stairs to the power station. My two other work mates were fetched down in the morning with ladders from the other side of the control room roof. The fourth, Jakob Kurtze, a machinist from Geismar, couldn't be found. He probably took shelter in the cellar and was washed out when the water forced its way in. It was not until August, when they were working with excavators in the turbine exit channel of Hemfurth I, that they found his body under a mass of gravel.'

A view of the dam taken from the Michelskopf hill. At 8 a.m. on May 16, the water-level indicator had recorded a height of 244.96 metres above the national datum level, thus showing the contents of the reservoir to be 200.20 million cubic metres. The water level was 4cm below the overflow point with a reservoir depth of 40 metres. By 9 a.m. on the morning of the 17th, the indicator stood at 234.60 metres and the level had fallen by 10.40 metres although there was still 106 million cubic metres of water left in the reservoir when this photograph was taken. By 10.55 a.m., a further 12 million tonnes of water had poured through the gap leaving the contents of the reservoir at 94.50 million cubic metres. At 5 p.m. there were still 72.40 million cubic metres of water left but this had fallen to some 40 million cubic metres by Wednesday morning, May 19. The two power stations remained standing. However, the turbines and electrical equipment were damaged by blast and subsequent flooding.

Squadron Leader Maudslay's Upkeep had exploded over the roadway, almost in the middle of the dam, the blast dislodging heavy stone blocks from the parapet and scattering them some 50 metres from their original positions although the road itself at this point remained almost unscathed. Chunks of flying masonry or bomb splinters damaged the 60,000-volt cable from the Hemfurth I power station causing a short-circuit which blew with a brilliant flash. Behind the wooded mountain ridge lies the village of Hemfurth.

This is the water-level measuring tower which stood in the compensation weir of the Eder dam. The massive tower has been undermined by the force of the water and now lies at an angle. The Meßhängebrücke above Hemfurth, a solidly-built iron suspension bridge, has been swept away and now lies in front of the remains of the road bridge. In the background are badly damaged timber-framed houses and behind them on higher ground, the local church.

The German military authorities had considered the Eder reservoir in the Waldeck region to be safe from air attack — and also indestructible — so there were no active or passive air defences in position on the night of the raid. Apparently undamaged, the sliding gates to the emergency outlets in the dam wall are all in the closed position.

'On the evening in question', recalls Emma Becker, 'I'd been to a civil defence meeting at Herr Bergmann's restaurant. A senior civil defence warden from Korbach assured us most emphatically that the dam would never be hit and added that anyone leaving the cellar during an air raid would be a traitor. So there I was, sitting in my neighbours' (the Kohls) air raid shelter with my two children and the other women and children from the neighbourhood just like with any other air raid warning. All of a sudden, Herr Kohl, who'd been outside, shouted: "Everybody out of the cellar! Get up to Beckers' place on the hill, quick. There's a rushing noise. The dam's been hit."

All 19 of us dashed out of the cellar. I was holding my son's hand. When I got round the back of the house I realised that my daughter, Waltraud, was missing. "She came up the stairs", said my son. Then I ran back into the house and dragged her after me like a sack. Then I saw the first wave coming across the nearby playing field. It was about six metres high and as white as snow. We ran up the hill behind our house, but there was a fence in the way. We lifted the children over and were pulling and tearing at the fence when the floodwater caught up with us. What a miracle! The fence gave way and we were safe. People were calling out: "Get down! They're coming in low! They're shooting!" We ran on soaked to the skin. The Bergmanns opened their door and we were able to get warm.'

The Bürgermeister of Hemfurth, Wilhelm Ochse, had heard the loud explosions and, acting with great presence of mind, he used his private telephone to call the sub-post office at Affoldern as soon as he heard the sound of rushing water in the valley. However, at first he could not get through so he phoned a relation, Herr Heck, a painter and decorator in Affoldern, to give the disaster warning. His son, Heinz, and friend, Heinz Sölzer, then rode around the village on their bicycles giving the flood warning.

Wilhelm Schätte, the postmaster at Affoldern, was standing with his wife and children in front of their house when the telephone rang. Because of all the excitement and commotion in the village, their son and daughter had already set off towards the hill at Buhlen where they would be safe. Meanwhile, the door in the corridor had slammed shut with the key on the inside so Schätte had to use a ladder to climb through an open window into the post office to reach the telephone. Mayor Ochse, told him excitedly: 'The water's on its way down! The Eder dam's been breached! Warn the village and pass the warning on!'

The floods turned the low-lying Hemfurth district into a stony wasteland. Eight houses and six commercial buildings were totally destroyed with a further two houses and four firms severely damaged. In the centre is the house belonging to the Kohls, a farming family, and to the right is the Höhle Farm. The Eder valley was less densely populated than the Möhne and Ruhr valleys — a fact which accounted for the significantly fewer fatalities, 68 people being drowned between the dam and Kassel. Another factor contributing to the low death toll was an unofficial telephone alarm system which saved many lives by warning people in outlying districts before they were swamped.

The flooded Eder valley near Lieschensruh with the little village of Affoldern in the background completely cut off from the outside world. Many villagers were able to clamber to safety up the nearby slopes thanks to the early warnings they received and from there they watched in horror as others struggled desperately against the torrent, clinging to pieces of furniture and timbers from demolished houses. In some places, the topsoil was completely stripped from the landscape and elsewhere the ground was left covered with a rocky scree. The surge produced flood levels nine times higher than anything previously recorded along the valley.

The cold light of dawn found the inhabitants of Mehlen, just over eight kilometres downstream (see map page 72), stunned at the scale of the catastrophe which had overtaken them during the night. Men and women, with a sprinkling of Hitlerjugend, stare in disbelief at the valley of the River Eder, which flooded as far as Kassel over 60 kilometres to the north-east. (It is important to remember that unlike the Möhne, the deluge from the Eder reservoir flowed eastwards, i.e. away from the Ruhr.) The maximum high-water levels produced by the deluge from both reservoirs varied only slightly from one another. Initially, 8,500 cubic metres of water per second flowed through the breach in the Eder dam while the outflow from the Möhne amounted to 8,800 cubic metres per second. However, the duration differed significantly: whereas the Möhne emptied itself within 12 hours, the contents of the Eder (1.4 times greater) continued over a period of 48 hours, the difference being caused by the fact that the breach in the Eder was smaller.

Mehlen was swept by a tidal wave some 12 feet high, the home of the Kötter family — No. 26 Waldecker Strasse *(left)* — being torn apart. 'I'd arrived home from the Russian front the previous evening', relates August Kötter. 'Relatives and friends had come round for the latest news. We were sitting around until midnight when my wife told them to go because I was tired. I went to bed and fell asleep at once because I'd been on the go for ten days. All of a sudden, I was woken by people shouting that the dam had been hit. But I reckoned it wouldn't be that easy because of the flak. Before I'd gone to Russia, the guns were still there. Then I saw colours shooting up like a rainbow. This must have been when a bomb caused a short-circuit at the power station. Anyway the planes flew off and I went back to bed. The children were outside and when my wife came in she was horrified that I'd gone back to bed. I told her not to worry because it was all over. Then people started screaming that the dam had gone and everyone should get up the hill. I grabbed some essentials and suddenly remembered our pig. We didn't want it to drown and thought we'd better get it into the house. I opened the door to the sty and it ran up into the kitchen. You'd have thought it'd done it a hundred times. It must have sensed the danger. Then my wife shouted that the water was rising. I realised there was no time to get away and we'd have to stay put. Fortunately the children had already gone. I looked out and saw the water coming like an avalanche. The wave was over three metres high and went straight up like a wall with foam on top. There was a great crash and the water smashed the front door open. It came up to my chest and I had a job getting to the staircase. The kitchen door got forced open, too, and I could hear the pig making a hell of a row in there. The next wave pushed the window open and the pig was washed out squealing like mad. We ran up floor by floor

until we got to the attic. We stood there listening and I removed some tiles to see what was happening. Our neighbours' house had gone and so had a lot of the others. Then there was the most terrific din — great chunks of debris had demolished our porch. The side of the house caved in, taking half the kitchen with it. There was a tremendous jolt and I'd just grabbed my wife when the front of the house collapsed. We ran back to the attic and listened for any new noises. Pieces of debris kept smashing into us and you could hear crashes and gurgling noises as houses and barns went under. There was just half of our house left. I could see the one behind was still OK because it had been protected by ours, and I decided to use the attic stairs as a raft and try to get across. God knows how I got the staircase free but we tied it to a beam so it couldn't float away. My wife tried to climb down slowly, but the rope slipped through her hands, ripping the flesh. Somehow she managed to grab the stairs. We had a mast for the flag on the Führer's birthday and I lowered it to use as an oar. Our raft was more or less underwater, but I shinned down and was about to get on when it tipped over throwing my wife into the water. I jumped in and grabbed her. I somehow managed to get her back on the stairs, which luckily were still held by the rope. She was paralysed with fear and it took me a while to bundle her through the toilet window. After a bit the water receded, and we were rescued by some army engineers in a boat. The bridge by our house had gone and the water had risen five metres. It was ironic that I'd survived in Russia and nearly got drowned at home. I later discovered that the flak had been withdrawn a few weeks before the raid. Our pig survived. A farmer down the valley had put it into his sty. When my wife called, the pig ran straight over because it recognised her voice.' *Right:* A pathetic sight further down the same street — on the right No. 19.

The railway bridge carrying the Bad Wildungen—Korbach—Brilon line was cut between Giflitz and Bergheim. From the window of her house on higher ground in Bergheim, Frau Elisabeth Schröder watched the bridge go. 'A white roller went crashing into the thing and all of a sudden the railway lines went up in the air amid a shower of sparks. Whole sections of the bridge just collapsed.'

Heinz Wiesemann recalled: 'Here in Lieschensruh, when the planes were flying really low, I could see the pilots clearly in their leather helmets in the cockpit. All of a sudden there was a noise like a chair being scraped over the floor. It never occurred to anyone that the Eder dam had been breached. When I looked out of the window, I saw spray in the distance and called to my mother, "They're sending up fog." Equipment for generating fog had previously been used. My bedroom was at the top of the house on the Affoldern side. I was tired after my night shift and wanted to go to bed; just then I heard screaming outside the window. I said to my mother, "There're some drunks shouting down there. They're on their way back from the station at Buhlen." (Later I found out they were people from Affoldern running away.) Suddenly I heard our neighbour shout: "Heinrich! Get out! I think the water's coming!" My father grabbed a drawer of papers from the dresser in the living room — I was in my PT shirt and shorts — and we ran through the water in the garden and up a nearby hill. Then this great flood-wave came along. It must have been a good four metres high and it was surging from side to side down the valley. Three horses galloped past still harnessed to a manger. Then it got dark and I couldn't see anything because of the fog. You couldn't even see your hand in front of your face.

'We went up the railway embankment towards the station at Buhlen where there were 30 to 40 survivors from Affoldern in a room above the waiting room. Some of them were weeping because they'd lost relations. At 4.30 a.m. I went back home. Our house was sticking up out of the water but still standing although the water reached up to 30cm below my bedroom window on the first floor. Two ducks were swimming through the branches of our big chestnut tree and two massive lime trees from the bridge at Affoldern

were lying behind the house; they were so thick that two men would not have been able to get their arms round them. Army engineers in assault boats were looking for the bodies of those who'd drowned. I saw the body of one old man from Affoldern in a muddy field of rye. His beard was all wet and there were worms crawling around in it. Men from the Organisation Todt sorted out our house and cleaned it. We got a dresser and some chairs as compensation from the government.'

The Diaspora Church of the Nonconformist Protestant Lutherans at Bergheim, which was built in 1912, withstood the flood, largely thanks to the barn which stood in front of it and shielded it from the torrent. Behind and to the right is the water-mill known as the Edermühle, and in front of this the seedbeds belonging to the Lötzer family. All five members of the family survived in their attic from where they were rescued the following morning by army engineers in assault boats. However, neighbours who abandoned their houses were drowned when the floodwaters overtook them. The water at this point rose to a height of two metres.

Christian Tilenius took this shot of the inundated Eder valley at Bergheim (about ten kilometres downstream) where the road bridge (in the foreground) and the railway bridge (see opposite page) have both been washed away. We are looking west, back towards the dam just before 6 p.m. of the day after the attack. The Eder valley villages which suffered most from the flooding were those of Hemfurth, Affoldern, Mehlen, Bergheim, Giflitz, Anraff, Wellen and Wega where the topsoil was all stripped away.

In Bergheim and Affoldern, a completely new disposition of land resulted following the disappearance of all the boundary marks and, in the latter village alone, well over 200 separate legal conveyances were required to bring the previous ownership up to date. Moreover, as some owners or heirs to property were still prisoners of war, it was not until five years after the end of the war that all the property conveyances could be officially recorded at the land registry.

Above: **Waterborne Luftwaffe officers inspect the damage at Fritzlar airfield. The height that the water reached can be seen by the line on the buildings in the photo** *below.*

In Bad Wildungen, the head postmaster, Paul Danzglock, had seen the flash of the explosion over by the Eder dam and shortly afterwards the sound of the detonation reached him. He rushed back to the post office and as he came into the yard heard the telephone ringing. He unlocked the door, ran over to the phone and heard a voice: 'Schätte here from Affoldern. They've hit the dam! The water's already coming down!' Then there was a thump and the line went dead. Danzglock immediately informed the police at Fritzlar and Bad Wildungen, who, although they first refused to believe him, did finally pass on the alarm. Meanwhile, one of the operatives who was on duty at the compensation basin at the Affoldern power station had also arrived at Schätte's post office with a flood warning. Only at the very last moment did he manage to escape to higher ground with the Schättes, but two people behind him drowned in the seething waters.

FRITZLAR AIRFIELD

The spate of water rushing down the Eder valley flooded the low-lying countryside, at one time completely covering the Luftwaffe airfield at Fritzlar, 25 kilometres south-south-west of Kassel. Hangars were flooded, personnel huts demolished and the airfield rendered unserviceable.

Although Fritzlar had received a warning it had not been believed so the flood caused more damage than might have been. The Eder bridge was the only crossing in this part of the valley to withstand the flood.

The damage and destruction spread all the way down the valley . . . past the broken bridges between Wolfershausen and Grifte (above left and right) . . . through Zennern (below left) and Guntershausen (below right). By midnight in the district of Hannoversch-Münden, 94 kilometres below the dam, the water had risen to 8.36 metres. Hameln (the Hamelin of

Pied Piper fame) is 229 kilometres from the seat of the disaster and here the River Weser reached its peak at midday on May 19 with a level of 6.94 metres. In Nienburg on May 20, after travelling a total distance of 362 kilometres, the floodwater had risen by midday to 5.96 metres above normal.

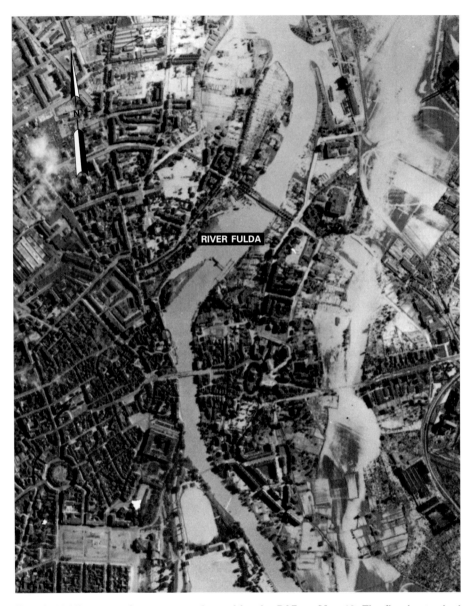

RIVER FULDA

Kassel, 60 kilometres downstream, pictured by the RAF on May 18. The floodwater had reached the city at around 10 a.m. the previous morning with the water level continuing to rise until 3 p.m., and it remained some 13 feet above normal until evening when it began to fall away rapidly. However, as a period of several hours elapsed between the report of the breach in the dam and the arrival of the floodwaters, overnight warnings had already been issued to the areas likely to be affected, thus enabling possessions to be moved from cellars and basements to upper floors. Apart from the damage caused to the military installations and industrial plants, 1,130 houses and 1,220 flats were affected to some extent.

With the Eder reservoir almost empty, by Tuesday the deluge had shrunk to a 'trickle'. This picture was taken from the Michelskopf ridge which the attacking Lancasters had to hop over after launching their mine.

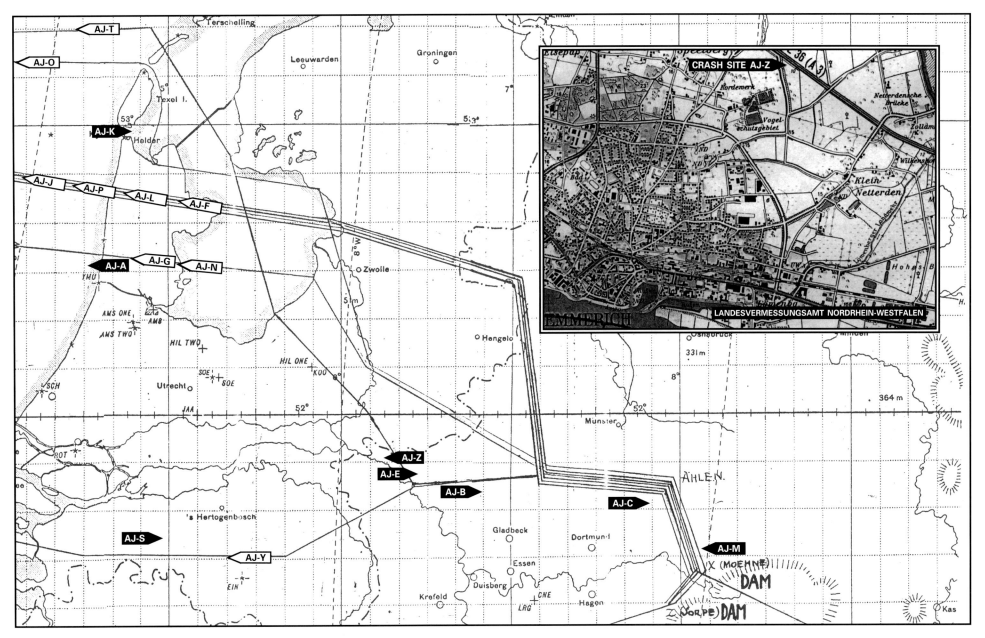

CRASH SITE AJ-Z

LANDESVERMESSUNGSAMT NORDRHEIN-WESTFALEN

Return routes for the nine surviving Lancasters — a contemporary plan from Appendix F of the post-raid report. The crash positions have been added by us but remember that these were not precisely known at the time. From the first wave we have already seen AJ-B come down at Marbeck on the way to the Möhne (pages 54-55) and AJ-M at Ostönnen just after attacking (pages 59-61). Two more inbound aircraft were lost from the second wave: **AJ-K off the Dutch island of Texel (page 92).and AJ-E near the Rhine at Haldern-Herken on the German-Dutch border (pages 92-93). A further two came to grief from the back-up third wave: AJ-C north of Hamm (page 101-105) and AJ-S on the airfield at Gilze-Rijen (page 106). Now, on the way home from the Eder, two Lancasters were shot down: AJ-Z close to Emmerich (inset) and AJ-A on the Dutch coast near IJmuiden (page 91).**

Three more crews lost in the attack are buried in Reichswald Forest War Cemetery with Flight Lieutenant Astell's men of AJ-B (see page 55). Two crews lie side by side, those of Flight Lieutenant Robert Barlow's AJ-E in Row C of Plot 5 (Graves 5-11) and the six men killed in Pilot Officer Warner Ottley's AJ-C in Row F of Plot 31 (Graves 10-15). However, Squadron Leader Henry Maudslay's men in AJ-Z, shot down at Emmerich returning from the Eder, have been split up. All are in Plot 5 but the navigator, Flying Officer Robert Urquhart, the bomb-aimer, Pilot Officer Michael Fuller, and front gunner, Flying Officer William Tytherleigh, are buried collectively (Grave 16-18) in Row B, while the rest of the crew — Warrant Officer Alden Cottam, the wireless operator; Sergeant Norman Burrows, the rear gunner; Squadron Leader Maudslay; and Sergeant John Marriott, the flight engineer — lie in individual graves (1-4) in Row C (above).

Squadron Leader Henry Young (*above left*) **was the fourth Lanc to attack the Möhne and he then continued on to the Eder without a mine as the reserve command aircraft.** *Right:* **On its return to Scampton, AJ-A was brought down as it approached the Dutch coast near IJmuiden — a heavily defended area containing both naval and industrial targets.**

Several German flak units reported firing on a 'Halifax' but the claim could not be accredited to one particular battery. The aircraft crashed off the coast and bodies were washed ashore along several miles of beach between Wijk-aan-Zee (just north of IJmuiden) to Bergen-aan-Zee 20 kilometres further up the coast.

But in the early hours of May 17, the raid was not yet over. At 02.10 Grantham asked Gibson how many aircraft of the first wave were still available for an attack on the Sorpe dam to which Gibson replied: 'None'. Maltby had already left for home after the successful breach of the Möhne and he landed at Scampton unscathed at 03.00. His return along the prescribed exit route had been uneventful apart from some evasive action due to light flak just before Ahlen.

Martin also had a clear run and he touched down at 03.19. Shannon landed at 04.06 having been in the air for a total of six hours and 29 minutes, and Gibson followed nine minutes later after a detour which took him back over the emptying Möhne reservoir and through a known 'hole' in the coastal defences near Egmond. At 04.20, Les Knight's Lancaster also touched down at Scampton. 'Dinghy' Young in AJ-A flew back along exit flight path No. 3, but was shot down near Castricum-aan-Zee to the north of IJmuiden on the Dutch coast at 02.58.

It was ironic that Young was heading for Bergen, where there was a gap in the anti-aircraft defences, for now the crew lie buried in Bergen General Cemetery (*right*), **just a few kilometres from where they came to grief. In life, they flew together but in death the navigator, Flight Sergeant Charles Roberts, and the wireless operator, Sergeant Lawrence Nichols, have been parted from their comrades. They lie buried in Row E (Graves 17 and 28 respectively) of Plot 2 whereas the other six men lie side by side in Row D: Sergeant Gordon Yeo, the front gunner, in Grave 2; Flying Officer Vincent MacCausland, the bomb-aimer (Grave 3); Squadron Leader Young (Grave 4); Sergeant David Horsfall, the flight engineer, in Grave 5; with the rear gunner, Sergeant Wilfred Ibbotson, next to him in Grave 6.**

En route, two Lancasters from the second wave were lost. First, Pilot Officer Vernon Byers (AJ-K) was shot down just before midnight as he crossed the island of Texel. The aircraft crashed in flames just off the southern tip of the island (see page 89). Only the body of the rear gunner, Flight Sergeant James McDowell, was recovered by a fisherman over a month later. (He is now buried in Grave 11 of Row 4 of Plot E at Harlingen on the mainland of the Waddenzee.) The rest of the crew are commemorated on the Runnymede Memorial in Surrey, Pilot Officer Byers on Panel 175; Sergeant Alastair Taylor, the flight engineer, on Panel 166; Flying Officer James Warner, the navigator, on Panel 130; Sergeant John Wilkinson, the wireless operator, on Panel 169; Pilot Officer Arthur Whitaker, the bomb-aimer, on Panel 134; and the front gunner, Sergeant Charles Jarvie, on Panel 154.

Second Wave against the Sorpe Dam

The second wave of Lancasters — those which had taken off before Gibson and were flying the northerly route to the Sorpe dam — did not have much luck. Some 125 miles to the north they crossed the Dutch coast at almost the same time as the first wave in a ruse designed to confuse the defences as to the true intentions of the raiders. Over the island of Texel, Flight Lieutenant John Munro's Lancaster (AJ-W) came under light flak and lost both VHF radio and intercom. Munro therefore decided to abort and landed back at Scampton at half an hour past midnight, the first to return from the operation, but with his Upkeep still on board despite the order not to return with a live mine.

According to Edmund Mantell, one of the gunners at a battery on Texel, Pilot Officer Vernon Byers' Lancaster (AJ-K) was brought down on the coast at around 23.00 by a lucky hit from a 10.5cm flak gun depressed to low elevation. Byers' Lancaster was the first casualty of Operation 'Chastise' but it was not until four weeks later that his mine exploded in the Waddenzee, much to the alarm of some of the island's inhabitants!

The pilot of Lancaster AJ-H, Flying Officer Geoff Rice, also had to break off his mission early. He flew so low over the island of Vlieland that he literally had to hop over the sand dunes. While he was flying low on a south-easterly course there was a sudden massive shudder and his cockpit was engulfed in water as he touched the sea. He instinctively pulled back on the joystick but too late and the bomb was wrenched from its anchorage. Water poured through the empty bomb bay and into the fuselage where Sergeant Steve Burns, the rear gunner, found himself up to his chest in salt water. Rice was therefore also obliged to return to base where he had difficulty landing with the damaged aircraft. Just 20 minutes after Munro touched down, Rice also managed to land.

Johanna Effing witnessed the second crash, that of AJ-E (Flight Lieutenant Barlow), at Haldern-Herken.

Lancaster AJ-E, piloted by Flight Lieutenant Bob Barlow, who had taken off first, intersected the flight path of the first wave near Rees on the Rhine but then he struck the top of an electricity pylon. Johanna Effing heard the Lancaster crash.

'There was a loud bang. When this happened we came out of the cellar at Haldern-Herken and saw the field in front of us blazing fiercely. An aircraft flying from the west had hit the top of a 100,000-volt electricity pylon and crashed into the field. A huge bomb

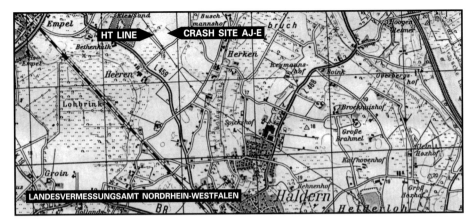

had rolled out 50 metres from where the plane had crashed. Even before it got light, we had a whole crowd of inquisitive people there despite the danger from exploding ammunition. It was not long before the Mayor of Haldern, Herr Lehmann, was on the scene and he climbed onto what was taken to be a large petrol canister. He said, "I'll tell the Chief Administrative Officer that he needn't send us any more petrol coupons for the rest of the war. We've got enough fuel in this tank." When he found out later that he'd been standing on dynamite, he's supposed to have felt quite sick. All the crew were killed and burnt beyond recognition. There were no flak batteries or searchlights here; the plane was just flying too low. The first guards from the scene of the crash came to the house and showed us the valuables which they had found: things like cases, gold rings, watches and a long cylindrical torch. Its owner had scratched all his missions on it — 32 of them. I still remember quite clearly the name "Palermo" and also the names of a lot of other towns. Well, this was a mission he didn't return from.

'The following morning the soldiers who came told us that the crew had been no greenhorns. These soldiers had to search for every smallest piece of the plane — presumably in an attempt to find out how the bomb had been attached. At first, bomb disposal officers couldn't defuse the bomb and we had to open the doors and windows so as to reduce damage in case it exploded while it was being defused. Political prisoners uncovered the bomb and then the bomb disposal officer, Hauptmann Heinz Schweizer, defused it.

'The morning after the bomb had been made safe, I went up to it by myself. It was a monster of a thing — dark green in colour. On one side of it the bomb disposal people had removed a round disc. More than 20 per cent of the bomb was embedded in the ground. Two days later they took it away on a lorry to the weapons' examination depot at Kalkum [after the raid, the Reichsluftfahrtministerium actively fostered research into bouncing bombs — see page 201]. When the field has been harvested, you can still to this day see two depressions where the aircraft crashed into the ground.'

At the weapons examination depot at Kalkum, near Düsseldorf, Hauptmann Heinz Schweizer, who defused the mine explains its workings to senior Nazi Party members. On June 17, Reichsminister Albert Speer, in his capacity as Generalinspekteur für Wasser und Energie, wrote a report on the raid for the Oberbefehlshaber der Luftwaffe, Hermann Göring, with the following preliminary description: 'The cylindrical bomb has no stabilising fins. The diameter is 1270mm and the length is 1530mm. Each rim is secured with 30 bolts and strips of angle iron. The material used for the sides of the cylinder is 12.5mm thick whereas that used for the rims is 10mm thick. A high-explosive charge of some 2600kg is made up of 41.7% trinitroluol, 40.5% hexogen and 17.5% aluminium. The tubes for the three hydrostatic pistols, of the type used in anti-submarine depth-charges, each contain primer charges of 1820kg of Tetryl. The self-destruction charge (intended to prevent an unexploded bomb being recovered if falling on land) consists of 1255kg of Tetryl.' From information gleaned after the recovery of the bomb and the statements of captured aircrew, the Luftwaffe came very close to discovering the bomb's secret. The only unknown factor remained the depth against the wall at which the explosion took place and the necessity for the bomb to explode in contact with the wall.

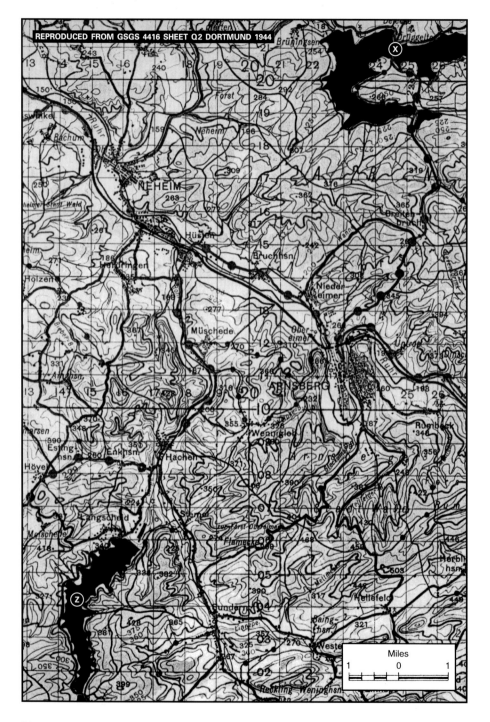

Miles

1   0   1

Four out of the five aircraft in the second wave never made it to the Sorpe. The only Lancaster to reach the dam was AJ-T piloted by the American, Flight Lieutenant Joe McCarthy. He flew at full throttle in the hope of making up the delay caused by the change-over to the reserve aircraft and he reached the target at around 00.45. There was fog around the reservoir but at the dam itself visibility was excellent. On the approach over Langscheid, there were problems avoiding the spire of the village church but McCarthy managed to get below a ridge and fly parallel to the dam. At first, he could not find the prescribed bombing run so in the end he dropped his bomb right on the middle of the dam without any rotation or the help of a spotlight altimeter as the reserve aircraft had not yet been fitted with one. McCarthy landed back at Scampton at 03.23 with one of his tyres punctured by flak.

Josef Kesting, a machinist, gives the following version of events at the dam. 'At around midnight my wife woke me up in our accommodation at the Sorpe power station with the words, "You'd better get up; a plane keeps flying over."

'I had no idea what was going on. I went outside where some work mates were standing in front of the power station. They had received Alert State 3 by telephone. They'd been advised of aircraft approaching Hamm from the Dutch border. Just as I was about to go back inside, a plane flew towards the dam from Langscheid. I saw it fly way below the crest of the dam and over the roadway which runs along the middle; it was less than 100 metres from me. I recognised the English emblem, the rings. I quickly ran into the house and told my wife to get out of the power station. I told her to take the boy and our valuables and go down into the cellar of one of the company flats at the base of the dam below the Brinkschulte inn.

'Shortly after this another plane [actually the same aircraft, McCarthy's AJ-T] appeared, flying parallel to the dam. It dropped an "instrument" like a huge septic tank over the crest and down onto the water side. A few seconds later a column of water thundered 100 metres up and tipped over onto the air side of the dam. Then I thought to myself, tomorrow morning I'll go down to the reservoir and collect the fish in a basket. The column of water cascaded down the dam. I thought the attack was aimed at the power station. In the meantime my boss had arrived at the power station.

'Two hours after this, another plane with spotlights on [this was AJ-F of the third wave] came flying straight at the dam from the water side. It did two circuits of the reservoir and on the second one dropped its bomb, which exploded shortly afterwards. I was in the power station and I didn't see this plane until it was flying over the middle of the dam with its lights on. All the windows in the power station were blown out by the blast, but initially the turbines kept going. Stones from the parapet flew right over into the compensation basin. As I later found out, the bomb struck below the water level; the second one was higher up towards the road and it made deep fissures in the ground.

'When things had calmed down again, Nazi Party leaders came over. They ordered me, in the event of a disaster, to warn those houses at risk below the dam by phone. I knew these telephone numbers by heart just like the Lord's Prayer. They carried out temporary repairs to the dam straight away, and for this they brought bundles of wood and brushwood up to the dam. If there was to be another raid, they planned to stop up the hole with this stuff and seal the leak. The Sorpe dam held, even through the reservoir was completely full. However, they did then reduce the water level a little.

'I had to get out of my accommodation. Flak gunners moved in. We spent a few days with relations in Hagen. They'd already been on one of the Ruhr bridges below the Hohensyburg "waiting for us" — waiting to see which of us would be brought along by the flood! On my way back to the Sorpe dam, I went to buy a ticket to Fröndenberg at the station in Hagen. This was refused on the basis that the Sorpe dam had now been breached, too. I couldn't believe it and phoned the office of the electricity authority in Arnsberg. They confirmed that the Sorpe dam had not been breached. The false alarm about the Sorpe, which set off the panic at the funeral service for the Möhne victims, ran right through the whole Ruhr valley.'

Left: **Target Z — the Sorpe dam with an entirely different method of construction — lay just a few minutes flying time south of the Möhne (Target X).**

AJ-F

AJ-T

This is the only known German photograph showing the damage caused to the Sorpe dam. [1] indicates the point of impact of the mine dropped by Flight Lieutenant Joe McCarthy (AJ-T) — the crater being on the water side, seven to eight metres down the embankment. It is about four to five metres below the surface of the water and some 40 metres from the middle of the dam towards the slope of the southern hill. McCarthy attacked along the length of the dam whereas Flight Sergeant Ken Brown (AJ-F) flew straight at it. His crater [2] is 30 metres away from the other one, five to six metres below the roadway, and some two to three metres below the surface of the water. After the first attack, the turbines in the power station continued to operate but the recording instruments showed that the generators failed at 1.25 a.m. when the flood from the Möhne brought down the 100kv overhead power line at Neheim.

The RAF were soon on the scene to check on the damage and this is the picture that was brought back on Monday morning. On the water side, the two mines damaged the embankment as well as a 120-metre stretch of the paving above the dam's concrete core. The clay around the core was shaken and loosened over a 25-metre stretch and at this level a slight leakage of water occurred through the expansion joints of the drainage system.

However, this eased off when the water level in the reservoir fell from its normal capacity of 70 million cubic metres. The small white blobs, two of which are casting shadows on the embankment, are the barrage balloons, 24 of which were deployed on the morning after the raid and were followed later by anti-aircraft guns and smoke-generators. A torpedo net like the one at the Möhne was also strung across in front of the dam.

Josef Brinkschulte also recalls the attack on the Sorpe: 'During the night of May 16/17, all they had on the Sorpe as a precaution against sabotage was a watchman. The watch consisted of elderly men who did shifts. The first plane flew quite slowly parallel to the dam without any lights. When the bomb had been dropped, the plane flew round the reservoir once more and then turned away to the north-east. They didn't drop any flares near the dam. The second plane came in faster over the water side towards the middle of the dam. When they came for the second time, they turned their lights on and lit up the crest of the dam. Then there was a much heavier explosion than the one from the first bomb, which had hit the dam two hours before. All the tiles came off the roofs of the houses which were about 500 metres below the dam. In the immediate area all the windows got broken. I can still see that massive column of water. The telephones went dead at once. You could easily see the flak and the tracer bullets over towards the Möhne dam after midnight. Shortly after 01.00 I heard the news from an official of the Ruhr Valley Dams Association who'd come over to the Sorpe. He said: "The Möhne's gone".'

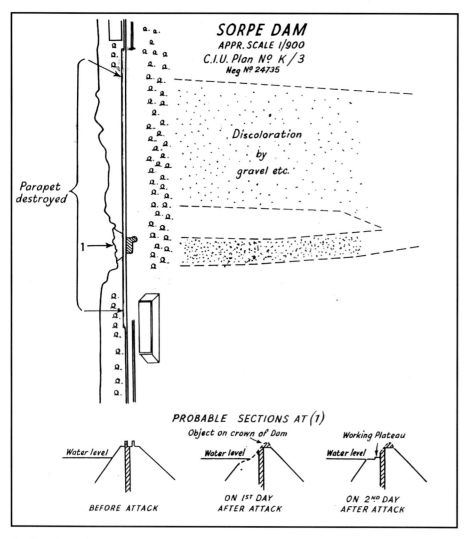

SORPE DAM
APPR. SCALE 1/900
C.I.U. Plan Nº K/3
Neg Nº 24735

Discoloration by gravel etc.

Parapet destroyed

1

PROBABLE SECTIONS AT ①
Object on crown of Dam   *Working Plateau*

Water level   Water level   Water level

BEFORE ATTACK   **ON 1ST DAY AFTER ATTACK**   **ON 2ND DAY AFTER ATTACK**

On May 20, an interpretation report, including the illustration above, was prepared by RAF Medmenham after analysing the photographs taken by No. 542 Squadron on the morning after the raid and also two days later. Six hours after the attack 'the crown of the dam appears damaged over about 200 feet of its length. The upstream parapet which is part of the concrete core and the downsteam parapet have disappeared. The concrete core is visible over some distance and has apparently been exposed to a depth at which it is about 6ft thick . . . Discoloration of the downstream side of the earth dam and on the road indicate that water was splashed over the dam, leaving a wet semi-circle of about 200 feet radius at the time of photography. A 200ft-wide strip of white is seen going from the crown of the dam to the compensating basin and this is probably due to earth, gravel and rubble having been deposited when, following the splash, water was flowing down the face of the dam. The water in the compensating basin is discoloured by mud over two-thirds of the area. . . There is no sign of any of the turbines working.'

The second aircraft seen by Herren Kesting and Brinkschulte was AJ-F with Flight Sergeant Ken Brown at the controls who arrived at the dam at 03.00. Fog had formed in the immediate vicinity but here and there hilltops were sticking up through it. Brown did a circuit which proved difficult because of the church spire and, contrary to the designated plan of attack (which was to fly parallel to the dam), he flew straight at it from the water side. His altimeter showed the right height and the mine was released without any spin, hitting the dam at almost the same spot as McCarthy's weapon, which had exploded two and a half hours earlier. At 03.14 a great plume of water rose from the reservoir and nine minutes later the wireless operator, Sergeant Harry Hewstone, sent the signal 'Goner 78C', which indicated that the Upkeep had been released, exploding in contact with the dam but with no apparent breach.

As Brown flew back, he also went over the Möhne reservoir where the water level had already dropped considerably. A flak gun opened up and there was an exchange of fire between this and the Lancaster's tail gunner, Flight Sergeant Grant MacDonald. On its flight back, the aircraft came under heavy flak near Hamm and again when crossing the Channel coast. When AJ-F landed back at Scampton at 05.33 its fuselage was riddled with holes.

The report goes on to say that 'photographic evidence suggests that there are two points where explosions have taken place. The structure of the dam was not sufficiently damaged to cause complete destruction, and the latest photograph [May 19] shows what may be work in progress on some sort of repair to the concrete core.' *Above:* Gun crew of 4. Zug (Platoon) of 1. Batterie of Flak-Regiment 892 drafted in after the attack as part of the measures to boost the defences at the Sorpe dam. Most of the crew consisted of 15-year-old Luftwaffe auxiliaries.

Another very rare photo, taken from the valley side, shows that the air defence is now putting on a show of strength — though rather too late! Barrage balloons shine at anchor to be launched in the event of an air raid. A 3.7cm anti-aircraft gun also stands ready for action.

Following the 'Chastise' operation, there were 250 dams within the territory controlled by Germany, 25 to 30 of which were given the immediate protection of anti-aircraft guns, smoke-screens, torpedo nets, anti-bouncing bomb deflectors and camouflage.

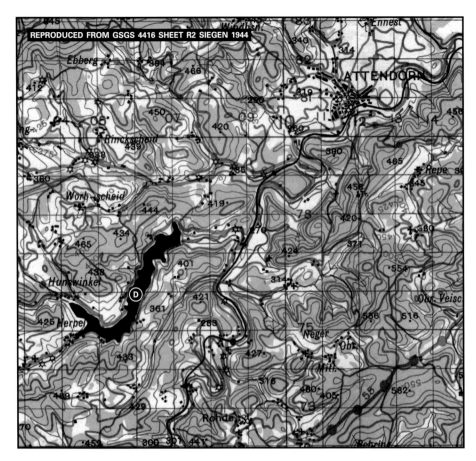

REPRODUCED FROM GSGS 4416 SHEET R2 SIEGEN 1944

The Lister dam — Target D — lies some 30 kilometres south of the Sorpe and was the southernmost dam on the target list. Although assigned to AJ-C en route, it was never attacked as Pilot Officer Warner Ottley was shot down north of Hamm.

Airborne reserve: the Lister, Ennepe and Diemel dams

Two and a half hours after the first and second waves had taken off, the five aircraft of the third wave, which made up an airborne reserve, were on their way to Germany. They followed the same southerly course as that taken by the first wave. Just before Ahlen, Pilot Officer Warner Ottley in Lancaster AJ-C, received the order by W/T to attack the Lister dam. No sooner had this signal been received than the aircraft came under heavy 2cm flak to the north-east of Hamm-Heessen.

Just before take off, Sergeant Fred Tees, who was to have been the Lancaster's front gunner, changed places with the tail gunner, Sergeant Harry Strange — a swap that was to save Tees' life when the aircraft crashed. Later he recalled: 'The inner starboard engine was on fire immediately and long flames leapt past my rear gun position. The hydraulic system failed so the gun turret would not turn any more. At this altitude, there was no escape by parachute, and the more so since my 'chute' was in the fuselage and I could not get at it. Just before the crash the pilot said over the intercom: "I'm sorry, boys, they got us".' After this, Tees remembered no more.

The proposed direction of attack overlaid on a reconnaissance photo of the Lister dam taken by No. 542 Squadron a day later to check for any sign of damage. The Lister was joined with the much larger Bigge lake in 1965.

Auch dieser Viermotorige sah England nicht wieder

Wieder ein viermotoriger Britenbomber, der von einem nächtlichen Ueberfall auf das deutsche Heimatgebiet nicht zurückkehrte und von unserer Flak-Abwehr zum Absturz gebracht wurde. Von der siebenköpfigen Besatzung kamen sechs Mann ums Leben, einer wurde gefangengenommen. (Aufnahme: Westf. Anz., Vos)

'Another four-engined which didn't see England again. This is another four-engined British bomber that did not return home after a night raid on Germany, being brought down by our anti-aircraft guns. Six of the crew of seven were killed; one was captured.' The wreckage of AJ-C lying at Ostbusch in Heessen on the road to Münster. The *Westfälische Anzeiger* published this photograph on its page of local news but did not mention any connection with the raid on the dams. The prisoner was Sergeant Fred Tees.

When the Lancaster crashed at 02.35, the tail section with the rear turret broke away and was flung clear of the immediate range of the Upkeep which exploded somewhat later. Friedrich Kleiböhmer witnessed the crash.

'At the time I was 16 years old and, despite the air raid warning, I went to bed at about 10 p.m. At midnight I was woken up by light flak going off. From the window, I saw a plane flying from north to south; it was about 1000 metres away and was coming under tracer fire. I thought now they've gone mad and they are firing at German planes: you see, at the time English and American planes didn't fly that low. Then I went back to bed.

'A good two hours after this, the flak started up again. Then a four-engined plane came over from the south-east and turned away to the west. It was coming under heavy flak and one engine was on fire. A few seconds later the bomber crashed in the distance at the edge of the woods. Then there was an explosion. Flames blazed up and its ammunition started going off. About 30 seconds later there was a much bigger explosion with an orange-coloured flash. Shortly afterwards, the blast from that explosion — although 3000 metres away — hit me where I was standing at the window and knocked me back into the room. I thought to myself, if you're going to see anything, you'd better go straight away because later on it will all be cordoned off.

Reference :-
DO/6/43

No. 617 Squadron, RAF Station,
Scampton, Lincs.

20th May, 1943.

My Dear Mrs Tees,

It is with deep regret that I write to confirm my telegram advising you that your son, Sergeant F. Tees, is missing as a result of operations on the night of May 16/17th., 1943.

Your son was Front Gunner of an aircraft detailed to carry out an attack against the Möhne Dam. Contact with this aircraft was lost after it took off, and nothing further was heard from it.

It is possible that the crew were able to abandon the aircraft and land safely in enemy territory, in which case news will reach you direct from the International Red Cross Committee within the next six weeks. The captain of your son's aircraft, Pilot Officer Ottley, was an experienced and able pilot, and would, I am sure, do everything possible to ensure the safety of his crew.

Please accept my sincere sympathy during this anxious period of waiting.

I have arranged for your son's personal effects to be taken care of by the Committee of Adjustment Officer at this Station, and these will be forwarded to you through normal channels in due course.

If there is any way in which I can help you, please let me know.

Yours Very Sincerely,

Guy Gibson

Wing Commander,
Commanding, 617 Squadron, RAF.

Mrs. E. Tees,
23, St. James Rd.,
Chichester, Sussex.

On the 18th — after the debriefings — the whole squadron were given leave: three days for the ground crews and seven for the aircrews . . . that is, for the survivors. Gibson remained behind to write to the next of kin of the 56 men who had failed to return.

Three crewmen survived their crashes and we have already seen how Pilot Officer Burcher and Pilot Officer Fraser parachuted to safety from AJ-M (page 59). The third lucky man was Sergeant Tees *(left)*, **miraculously thrown clear of the crashing AJ-C. His escape was even more fortuitous as he had changed places in the rear turret with another man . . . but was it a feeling of guilt that he had survived while a friend had died that led poor Fred to take his own life 38 years later?**

'I hadn't realised that the crash site was so far away. After about a kilometre, I went past my old school. The people were sitting in the cellar and they hadn't noticed anything at all. I carried on and at the edge of the woods I met a school friend so I asked him where the bomber had crashed. He pointed over towards Bockum-Hövel. We were still chatting away when a figure appeared from out of the woods along a track. I jokingly said to my friend that he must be a Tommy. He came up to within five metres of us. When we spoke to him he didn't answer. My friend disappeared back inside the house as he'd realised that the man was English. Then he nipped out by a rear door to phone the police from a neighbour's house. Before he left, he called out to me, "Fritz, that's an Englishman." So I thought to myself I'd better just go up to the man and pretend I am armed by keeping one hand in my jacket pocket. I beckoned him over with my left hand. He immediately put his hands up and said "British" not "English". I took him with me.

'On the way we went past a farmer who gave me a hunting rifle saying this was in case the Englishman did something silly. We went through a deserted area and I was holding him under his left arm because I'd noticed that he couldn't walk properly. I had the hunting rifle on my right shoulder with the barrel at the front and the butt at the rear. As we were going along like this, I thought I'd whistle the song *We're Going to Hang out the Washing on the Siegfried Line* and he immediately started humming along with me. When another English bomber flew over between Heessen and Ahlen, the Englishman looked back after it longingly. At one point as we were going along he got hold of the barrel. I told him to let go and he replied, "OK! OK! OK!"

'We went past two farmhouses which were all in darkness. I didn't want to surprise people at night with an Englishman and so we carried on. At the next farmstead there was a girl I knew leaning out of the window. I called out, "Elli, open up. I've got an Englishman here and he can't walk any further". He sat down on a chair in the kitchen; he was wearing a flying suit. He'd still got some dry leaves in his hair and then I saw his wounds. His hands were badly burned. There were two brown marks on his face but these weren't too bad. His chest was hurting him. I guessed that he'd been thrown out of the plane by the explosion and had hit a tree. I took off his jacket and gave him some water. Then the girl's father came in swearing about how these were the blokes who were destroying everything. The Englishman took no notice and just sat there exhausted. I had a look in his pockets hoping to find a gun or some cigarettes. He hadn't got anything on him apart from a small pointed dagger.

'Half an hour later a policeman arrived in a taxi and I handed the dagger over to him. The policeman was extremely proud to have been able to take an Englishman prisoner. He told the taxi driver to talk to him in the Low German dialect [which is spoken in the north-west of Germany and is akin to English] and to ask how many men there had been in the plane. The Englishman just said one word: "Seven". We all understood that. The policeman said, "There are four of them lying burnt by the plane, this one is the fifth. So there must be two more of them around. Get yourselves armed and make sure you capture them." Then the Englishman got a violent shivering fit; he was shaking really badly. We wrapped him in blankets and sent him off in the taxi.

'I got to the crash site at around four in the morning. A whole lot of blue flames were still shooting up out of the wreckage. The bodies were lying around, one of them impaled on a tree stump through the stomach. Parts of the parachutes on their backs were starting to catch fire. Flak gunners were searching through the wreckage but no one could be bothered to pull the bodies away from the fire.'

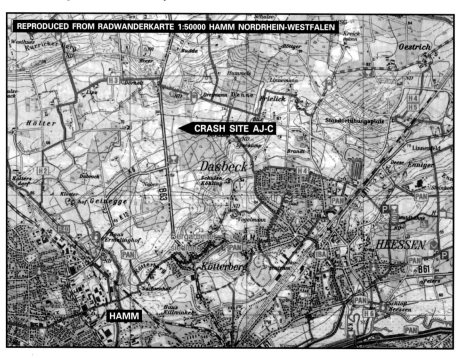

The Lancaster came down in a forest about two kilometres north of Kötterberg.

A memorial was erected on the crash site following an initiative by Bernhard Droste and scouts from the St Marien Church at Heessen and in September 1981 Fred Tees returned to the crash site for the unveiling. In March the following year he committed suicide.

'Guard the peace for war is cruel.' So reads the inscription on the memorial which lies in a wood on the estate of Freiherr von Boeselager.

In May 1943, Hauptmann Malte Schrader was in charge of a 3.7cm flak battery in the Hamm area.

'My unit consisted of several platoons and our job was to defend the railway installations at Hamm. My westerly platoon near Bockum-Hövel reported hearing the noise of aircraft engines coming from the west. As there were no German planes in the air over Hamm we got the order to open fire. In the meantime, some enemy aircraft had already flown over north of Hamm and gone across the Lippe valley. From my command post, I saw a four-engined aircraft flying south-east at roof-top height over the railway installations. We couldn't engage the aircraft because the gun had a safety frame to stop shots hitting the nearby houses. We first had to pull this down and then it took us a while to lower the barrel.

'Sometime after 02.30, No. 1 Platoon reported the first hit on an enemy bomber. Just after this I saw a great fiery glow and moments later there was an explosion. The plane had crashed into a piece of wooded ground near the Hamm-Münster road. I found out that one young Briton had survived the crash. However, before I was able to visit the crash site, I first had to move one of the platoons from my battery over to the Sorpe dam, which had also been attacked during the night. You couldn't get through the Möhne and Ruhr valleys, and so we had to make our way to the Sorpe via the Delecke Bridge and Arnsberg. While we were at the crash site, I found a shredded and bloodstained chart which had come out of the Lancaster; it had a line on it showing the route from the end of the Datteln-Hamm canal to the Möhne and further on to the Eder.

'Back in Hamm later in the morning, I saw the captured airman who was still suffering from shock; he looked pretty timid.'

Above: **A picture taken while the author was filming a documentary about the dams raid. Former Hauptmann Malte Schrader** *(left),* **wartime commander of a flak battery in the Hamm area, holds up the remains of the singed and bloodstained map which he found in the wreckage of Ottley's aircraft.** *Below:* **A clearly discernible flight path had been drawn on the chart from the end of the Datteln-Hamm canal near Uentrop and over the River Möhne to the Eder dam.**

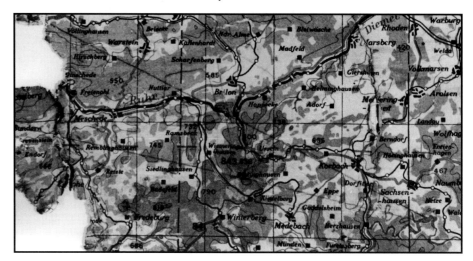

Time	From	Message
02.19	Group	Group called each of the 5 aircraft of the third Wave.
02.21	O	Answered.
02.22	Group	to "O" GILBERT.
	F	Answered
02.24	Group	to "F" DINGHY.
02.25	F	Message received
	Group	to "O" GILBERT
02.26	O	Message received
	Group	Calling "Y"
02.28	Y	Carry on with your message
	Group	to "Y" DINGHY
	Y	Received
	Group	Calling "O"
02.30	O	Carry on with your message
02.31	Group	to "O" GILBERT
	O	Message received
02.32	Group	to "S" DINGHY
02.33	Group	to "S" DINGHY
02.57	L	GONER 79B (Repetition of 02.06 transmission).
03.00	T	GONER 79C
03.23	F	GONER 78C
04.11	O	GONER 58E
04.23	Y	Returning to base unsuccessful (in Bomber Code).

Above: **The only messages received from AJ-C were at 02.30 and 02.31 when Sergeant Jack Guterman acknowledged receipt of the code-word 'GILBERT' which meant divert to the Lister.**

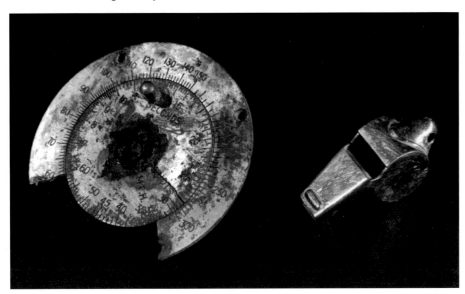

Fifty years later, Werner Ruffing searched the crash site with a metal detector and found the two inner rings from the navigator's time and distance computer and one of the crewmen's signalling whistle for use in case of ditching.

Last resting place for six of the crew: Reichswald War Cemetery. (See also page 90.)

'Nachtjagdgeschwader 2 (Night Fighter Group 2 — NJG2) and one Staffel (squadron) of NJG1 were both based at Gilze-Rijen airfield. I was a Ju 88 wireless operator on the reserve Staffel E/NJG2 which in May had seven aircraft. The Geschwader was on the ground during the night of May 17. Obviously, nuisance raids were expected and the crews were on standby at the airfield waiting to see how the situation would develop. As incoming enemy aircraft had been reported, we had our ears cocked into the night and we heard a plane flying towards the airfield from the west. The flak batteries at the edge of the airfield didn't open fire. I saw a searchlight beam suddenly come on and catch a four-engined plane, which couldn't have been more than 20 metres up. The beam lit it up like daylight. The searchlight was located on a tower between our command post and the hangar and the beam caught the bomber more or less horizontally as it was coming in. The pilot was presumably dazzled and he brought the plane down lower. The bomber grazed across the top of some trees, tearing a great path through the woods before crashing into an empty, rectangular-shaped MT garage which belonged to the airfield's flak defences. If he'd gone on for another 100 metres he would have literally rammed the searchlight tower. The plane caught fire when it crashed and a few seconds later there was a deafening explosion. The blast was so strong that and I and the other aircrews standing about 700 to 800 metres away on the other side of the airfield were almost knocked over.

'When it got light I saw the aircraft. It was a total wreck. All that was left was the rear turret and the tail unit and this was more or less intact. All the crew had been killed. The rear gunner showed no outward signs of injury. He was scantily dressed and had laced-up shoes with holes in the soles; his uniform trousers were thin and worn. No one could find out why the airfield flak hadn't opened fire. It was certainly not every day a plane was brought down by a beam of light like that one was at 2 a.m. on that morning!'

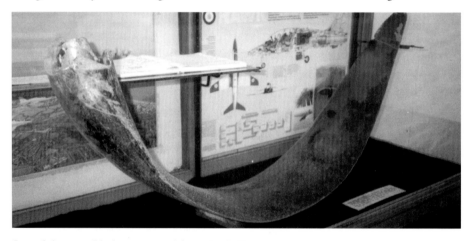

One of the prop blades recovered from AJ-S. Thanks to Dick Breedijk, a No. 617 Squadron aficionado in the Netherlands, it is now on display at Newark Air Museum located on the airfield at Winthorpe, Nottinghamshire.

The last aircraft to take off on Operation 'Chastise' was Lancaster AJ-Y. The pilot, Flight Sergeant Cyril Anderson, encountered heavy flak to the north of the Ruhrgebiet and had navigational problems around the Dülmen lakes. The turning point was obscured by fog and both the front guns had failed. He was supposed to attack the Diemel dam but, as he was off course and could not find his position, at 03.10 he decided to abandon the mission and turn back, especially as he realised he would no longer be able to reach the target before daybreak. He landed back at Scampton at 05.30 and was the second pilot to disobey orders by returning with an Upkeep intact. (Three months later, Sergeant Anderson and his crew failed to return from a mission to Mannhein.)

The Dutch airfield at Gilze-Rijen had been taken over by the Luftwaffe in May 1940. Here it is pictured by No. 542 Squadron on September 5, 1943, although not with any intention of identifying where AJ-S crashed. At the time, all the RAF knew was that 'in the Tilburg area [five miles east of the airfield] at 01.53 hours, it was believed that an aircraft crashed in flames after an explosion occurred in mid-air. This was observed from a distance of 10 miles by F/617 which was flying towards the target at 150 feet and the crashed aircraft was probably S/617 since the only other aircraft missing from this Wave.' We have added the track of AJ-S as it sliced through the trees to crash on the barracks. The crater shows as a white spot.

Lancaster AJ-S with Pilot Officer Lewis Burpee at the controls took off after Ottley but drifted off course over Holland and flew too close to the night fighter base at Gilze-Rijen: he was the second of the reserve force to crash. A Luftwaffe airman, Herbert Scholl, was an eyewitness to what can only be described as a 'shooting down by searchlight'. He later described what happened:

Helmuth Euler seeks out the graves of Pilot Officer Burpee and his crew in Bergen-op-Zoom War Cemetery, 40 kilometres north-west of Antwerp. The remains of four members of the crew — the flight engineer, Sergeant Guy Pegler; the navigator, Sergeant Thomas Jaye; the bomb-aimer Warrant Officer James Arthur; and the front gunner, Sergeant William Long — could not be individually identified so they were buried collectively in Graves 5-7 in Row B of Plot 24. The wireless operator, Pilot Officer Leonard Weller is buried in Plot 27 (Row A, Grave 6) and the rear gunner, Warrant Officer Joseph Brady, in Grave 1 of Row A in Plot 23. *Above:* Pilot Officer Lewis Burpee lies in the same plot but in Row B (Grave 3).

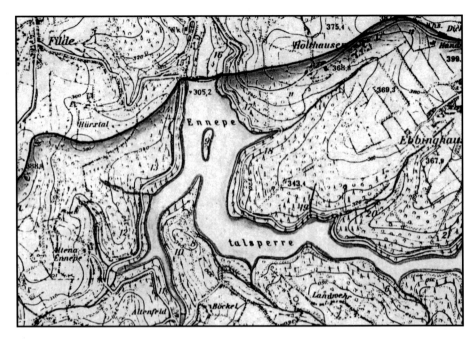

Depending on the level of the water in the reservoir, the 'island' feature in the Ennepe dam *(above)* can change to a spit of land as seen *(right)* by Pilot Officer Bill Townsend on the night of May 16/17, 1943. This picture was taken a day later — again by No. 542 Squadron — to assess any damage.

Confusion: Ennepe or Bever dam?

After the war there were differences of opinion in British aviation circles and amongst war historians generally as to whether Pilot Officer William Townsend in AJ-O had in fact attacked the Ennepe dam or the neighbouring Bever dam. There are discrepancies in RAF records: for example, the Ennepe reservoir is frequently referred to incorrectly as Ennerpe or Ennipe or even Schwelme but Townsend and his navigator, Pilot Officer Lance Howard, always maintained that they had attacked the Ennepe. This is confirmed by their description of the dam's surroundings and the written information submitted to the author about their tactical approach. Townsend's Lancaster was the second aircraft in the flying reserve to attack a dam; it was also the last to do so during Operation 'Chastise'.

One initial difficulty was that the chart showed an island in the lake in front of the dam but in reality this was just a spit of wooded land. (There is no island or spit of land in front of the Bever dam.) The bomb itself caused a further problem, incorrect balancing producing a gyroscopic effect which made the Lancaster shake violently. Also by the time the attack took place, a mantle of fog had descended over the waters of the V-shaped Ennepe reservoir and the trees on the surrounding slopes but after three abortive runs the aircraft achieved the required height over the lake with its spotlights on. AJ-O was dead on course at 355 degrees and the Lancaster approached the dam at a speed of 270 mph. On the fourth approach, the heavy mine was released which, after bouncing twice, sank 150 feet in front of the wall. A few seconds later, at 03.38 (time recorded at the Göttingen seismological station), a spout of water and clay shot 1,000 feet into the air. Townsend then turned for home on a course that took him once more past the Möhne reservoir. Lancaster AJ-O touched down on Scampton's grass runway at 06.13 and, with this landing, Operation 'Chastise' came to an end.

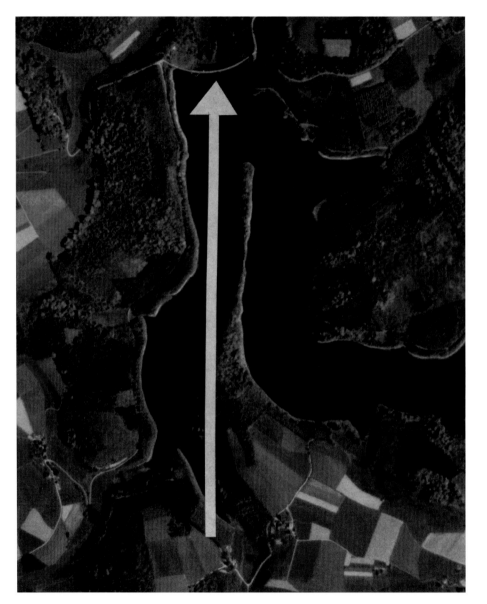

Townsend's Upkeep exploded some 150 feet in front of the dam.

The war diary of the Oberkommando der Wehrmacht for May 1943 includes entries about the raids against the dams which are supplemented with various details — somewhat inaccurate — concerning the number of aircraft, altitude, weapons and readings from radio-location equipment. However, the war diary confirms that the Bever dam (which lies ten kilometres almost due south of the Ennepe — see map pages 4-5 where it is marked [17]) was indeed attacked on the night of May 16/17.

The Bever reservoir was built between 1935 and 1939 in order to regulate the water flow in the River Wupper. It had a predecessor, the 'old Bever reservoir' near Wefelsen which was built between 1896 and 1898. The new dam was of rubble construction, 41.40 metres high, and had an inner core of sheet steel. Its reservoir had a capacity of 27 million cubic metres and, when full, the old dam disappeared under eight metres of water. The redundant dam, which was made of undressed stone, was used at the beginning of the war by the Luftwaffe to test the effects of powerful military explosives and, although damaged at its crest, it retained its overall shape. (It was not until 1959 that it was once more subjected to explosives and demolished.)

Diversionary raids were launched to coincide with the attacks against the dams and the British Daily Summary of Night Operations records the fact that 87 aircraft were in action on the night of May 16/17. Altogether, 55 Lancaster and Wellington bombers were involved in mine-laying operations off the Frisian Islands and the west coast of France while four Wellingtons went on a leaflet-dropping mission to Orléans. In addition to the aircraft committed against the dams, Mosquitos were engaged on nuisance raids: three to Berlin, two to Cologne, two to Düsseldorf, and a further two to Münster. The pilots each reported dropping four 500lb MC bombs on the above-mentioned cities but one Mosquito which should have bombed Berlin attacked Kiel. The 107th air raid on Berlin was recorded at 01.13 while the situation report of the air raid control centre in Düsseldorf shows an alert at 23.15, with the 496th air raid sounding at 23.33. There were several incursions reported of Allied aircraft on an east-south-easterly course at the mouth of the Scheldt and also near Amsterdam. From 00.24, return flights are recorded from the Arnsberg, Berlin, Hanover and Kassel areas.

In Düsseldorf, the air defence log-book has an entry noting the 497th alert at 03.27 with the All Clear being sounded at 04.11. During the course of the night, only two bombs fell on Düsseldorf: one on open countryside near the shooting ranges at Krönerweg in the Unterrath district, and the other within the perimeter of the airfield. In both cases damage to property was minimal.

The Bever dam is situated 35 kilometres from Düsseldorf — barely five minutes flying-time for a Mosquito. Also the two aircraft committed to Cologne that night would have needed but a few minutes to reach the Bever dam so it is possible that it was one of these Mosquitos which dropped a bomb into the reservoir without this having been reported by the pilot at debriefing. The Mosquito pilots claimed to have dropped eight bombs on Düsseldorf — they had also noticed two fires in the city centre — but these reports contradict the city's air raid records.

The following eyewitness account confirms the attack of a twin-engined aircraft on the Bever reservoir. Paul Keiser was a dam watchman.

'I was 38 years old and home on leave. I knew quite a bit about aircraft because in the services I'd seen many planes which had been shot down. On the evening of May 16, 1943, relations from Cologne had come over to visit us to get a break in the country from all the air raid warnings in the city. It had got quite late because of all the lively conversation. The kitchen clock was showing one o'clock when I heard an aircraft. I went out and saw a low-flying aircraft going away from the dam towards the west. It's only a few metres from my house to the Bever dam. Anyway, I stood there on the roadway and again I heard engine noise approaching. From the east, from the direction of Halver, a plane with no lights flew past me about 50 metres high over the northern section of the Bever dam. When he came over for the third time, he dropped a bomb in the lake about 800 metres from the dam wall. It fell 150 metres opposite the Haus Uhlenhorst, that imposing summer residence belonging to the Düsseldorf Gauleiter Florian, who had been there on June 14, 1938 when they held the ceremony to inaugurate the new dam.

'The old damaged wall of the Bever dam was under the water 250 metres further along the flight path from where the bomb went off. The plane went round again and then flew off towards Cologne. You could easily see that it had two engines; the English emblem was on the fuselage and there were big letters which I didn't make a mental note of. I saw the explosion quite clearly, too. The flash and the water went about 20 metres up into the air. It was no higher than the trees on the bank — it was like the way the fizz goes up when you open a bottle of sparkling wine. The bomb didn't bounce at all. You couldn't feel any vibration on the dam, the explosion just went 'phut' in the water.

The controversy over whether AJ-O bombed the correct dam now solved by the eyewitness Paul Keiser who saw a Mosquito drop a 500lb bomb in the reservoir on the same night. [1] The earth wall of the Bever dam. [2] The old dam wall before the reservoir was enlarged. [3] Where the Mosquito dropped its bomb, 800 metres from the new dam, 250 metres from the old dam, and 150 metres from the summer residence [4] of Gauleiter Florian from Düsseldorf. [5] is the point from where Paul Keiser witnessed the attack. Another eyewitness, Helmut Bladt, also saw the circling aircraft at 1 a.m. from point [6].

'Years later, when the reservoir was more or less empty, I had a look around the place where the explosion had taken place and I found a lot of rust patches and some fragments of flattened stuff about as big as a thick piece of walnut shell. When the bomb went off, the plane was halfway to the dam. It didn't have any lights. The moon was shining so brightly that the pilot must have been able to see everything. My wife and Herr Tacke watched the plane approaching from various windows in the house. The following morning we took a boat and went over to the place where the explosion had been. There we used a rake and fished out red bream and perch which had been killed by the blast. Lots of people came over from Hückeswagen to get white fish. The word soon got around that these 'dynamite fish' were there for the asking — food off the ration, you might say. The next day I filled a vegetable bin with fried fish and pickled them in vinegar. I took them with me to my troops. On the leave train to Wilhelmshaven, there were a whole lot of soldiers home from the front drinking French cognac and Russian vodka. It wasn't long before some of them were drunk. Then I opened up my bin and they just fell on it. By the time we got to Bremen the bin was empty. Those chaps back on leave from the front even drank the liquid, too!'

SPECIAL QUESTIONNAIRE

1. What could be seen of the objective during the run up? (With particular reference to the direction of the moon).

2. At what range did you first see the target?

3. (a) Number and height of bounces of "UPKEEP".

    (b) Was "UPKEEP" spun? If so, what R.P.M?

4. Description of explosion, with particular reference to behaviour of the water, height of spout etc.

5. Description of damage to the target.

6. How many runs did you make?

7. Were you obstructed by any other aircraft during your run up?

8. What method of control was used and was it effective?

9. What was the effect of the 100% night tracer carried –

    (a)   On the enemy?

    (b)   On your own gunners?

10. Pilots personal report (criticisms and comments).

Debriefing

As soon as the aircraft had returned, the debriefing took place during which the pilots were asked ten questions but some of the answers made in the excitement of the moment were later to cause confusion. For example, Gibson said that he had seen two breaches in the Möhne dam and Shannon reported that he had blasted a hole nine feet wide in the Eder. Brown's flight engineer maintained that he had seen two breaches alongside each other in the Möhne whereas the front gunner claimed there were three. However, further questioning of the other crew members served to correct these mistakes.

The transmissions from the bombers over the target were so strong that the Chief Signals Officer was able to read them via a GPO telephone line to those sitting in the operations room. Thus, although Gibson's aircraft was flying at an altitude of 100 feet in and out of valleys in the target area, Air-Vice Marshal Cochrane was able to question him and get an answer within the space of a minute.

The balance sheet showing eight Lancasters lost made it clear to Cochrane that on similar operations in the future it would probably be preferable for the aircraft to maintain an altitude of 2,000-3,000 feet on the run in and only descend if night fighters appeared. Such a height would provide an adequate safety margin from machine-gun fire and light flak but be low enough to hinder attacks from enemy night fighters. The aircraft should also be equipped with better navigational aids for low flying at night for the Lancasters returning during the early hours of the morning had considerable difficulty with map reading. The valleys had filled with fog and the landmarks were hard to identify.

Answers to Special Questionnaire. (Arranged in order of attack on each objective).

G/617.   W/C Gibson   GO 939 Time of attack 00.28 hrs.

1.   Saw the whole thing.

2.   3 – 4 miles.

3.   (a) 3. (b) Yes 500

4.   Enormous column of water.

5.   There are two holes in the dam.

6.   One.

7.   No.

8.   V.H.F. (perfect)

9.   (a) Very satisfactory effect against gun positions. (b) No dazzle. Perfect for this job.

10.   River below dam to a distance of about 3 miles was several times its normal size.

      Note on GO 934.

      1st and 3rd hit. 2nd overhit.
      A large hole was definitely knocked in it and a great deal of water was seen flowing out.

P/617   F/Lt. Martin   GO 939 Time of attack 0038 hrs.

1.   Smoke from previous burst obscured objective. Moon on port beam.

2.   From 1½ mile one tower could be seen. Other tower obscured by smoke from last attack.

3.   (a) Not seen. (b) Yes. 480

4.   Spout formation which reached above smoke but height could not be judged.

5.   No visible damage – this aircraft was 3rd to attack.

6.   One.

7.   No.

8.   R/T Good.

9.   Good from gunners point of view.

10.   Very good trip. Numerous searchlight and light flak positions north of the Ruhr against which gunners did wizard work. Rear gunner extinguished two searchlights. Front gunner shot up other flak posts and searchlights. Navigation and map reading wizard. Formation Commander did a great job by diverting the gun fire from target towards himself. Whole crew did their job well.

J/617   F/Lt. Maltby   GO 939 Time of attack 0049 hrs.

1.   All of it including the towers. Would have been easier running into moon instead of from it.

                                              /2.   Saw towers at ....

Watched by Air Chief Marshal Harris and Air Vice-Marshal Cochrane, Gibson's crew are pictured by Flying Officer Bellamy as they are debriefed. Flight Lieutenant Trevor-Roper (killed March 31, 1944) facing on the right. Pilot Officer Spafford can be identified by his bomb-aimer's wing next to Pilot Officer Taerum wearing the 'Canada' flash denoting he is a member of the RCAF. Both men were killed on September 15/16, 1943 in a disastrous attack on the Dortmund-Ems canal. Flight Lieutenant Hutchison and Flight Sergeant Deering of Gibson's crew and Pilot Officer Knight (AJ-N), Sergeant Dennis Powell (AJ-O), Sergeant Daniel Allatson (AJ-F) were also lost on this raid as was No. 617 Squadron's new CO, Squadron Leader George Holden. (Flight Lieutenant Maltby and his crew had all been killed the previous night when an attack against the same target was aborted.)

2. Saw towers at 2,000 feet range.

3. (a) 3. Height not known. (b) Yes.

4. Saw water flung up (harassed by tracer at time).

5. Saw breach in centre of dam before attacking: so went to port and made a contact.

6. One.

7. No. Clear.

8. VHF very good.

9. (a) Not known. (b) No trouble and slightly easier to aim.

10. Found VHF control excellent. In two cases a second aircraft flew alongside the one bombing and machine gunned defences on North side of objective. Good route, flak free and easy to map read.

L/617   F/Lt. Shannon.   GO 934 Time of attack 0139 hrs.

1. Entire target. Moonlight good but would have been better ahead.

2. 3 miles.

3. (a) 2. (b) Yes.

4. Saw enormous spout of water about one minute after attacking. Believed over 1,000 feet high.

5. Made gap about 9 feet wide towards east side. Saw second aircraft overshoot. 3rd aircraft with contact widened gap. Water seen pouring down valley.

6. 3.

7. No.

8. VHF control by No. 1.

9. (a) Not known. (b) Rather dazzling but gunner likes it.

10. Plan worked perfectly. Route extremely good. Shot up a train at COESFELD.

N/617   P/O Knight.   GO 934 Time of attack 0152 hrs.

1. Everything. Moon on starboard beam.

2. 1 mile.

3. (a) Three. Impossible to estimate height. (b) Yes.

4. Spout of water about 800 feet high right on the dam. Explosion must have occurred on contact with dam wall.

5. Large breach in wall of dam about 30 feet below top of dam, leaving top of dam intact. Torrent of water pouring through breach causing tidal wave about 30 feet high seen half a mile down valley from the dam.

6. Two.

7. No.

8. VHF very good.

9. No opposition at target. 100% tracer dazzled gunner but appeared to frighten

/searchlight and gun crews. ....

searchlight and gun crews. Opinion of gunner - ordinary night tracer would have ensured greater accuracy because of reduced dazzle.

10. Routeing excellent. Reports from aircraft ahead re flak found to be very useful. Attack straight forward and as predicted. It was found possible to gain 1,000 feet easily after dropping the Mine. Satisfied that the raid was successful.

T/617   F/Lt. McCarthy.   GO 960 Time of attack 0046 hrs.

1. Everything. Moon on starboard beam.

2. Five miles.

3. N/A. (Line bombing).

4. Half-circular swelling of water with wall of dam as diameter, followed by a spout of water about 1,000 feet high.

5. Crown or causeway of dam crumbled for a distance of about 15 to 20 feet.

6. Ten.

7. No.

8. None. Operating independently.

9. Betrayed position of aircraft to searchlights and light flak on route. No opposition at target and no guns fired.

10. Pilot not in favour of 100% tracer. Cannot say if a big breach in dam was made, but the raid seemed to be successful. Route out good and easily followed (blue) Route return (red I) failed to find pinpoints because of faulty compass, so set course as route out and headed for Zuider Zee.

F/617   F/Sgt. Brown.   GO 960 Time of attack 0314 hrs.

1. Everything. Moon on starboard beam.

2. 500 yards.

3. (a) N/A. (Line bombed) (b) N/A.

4. Missile dropped about 10 feet away from dam about two-thirds of way across. Semi-circular swelling of water against dam wall followed by spout of water about 1,000 feet high.

5. Crumbling of crown of dam for about distance of 300 feet.

6. Ten.

7. No.

8. No control - Independent attack.

9. Very dazzling. Ordinary night tracer preferred. Appeared to have considerable effect on accuracy of searchlights.

10. Routeing good. Raid on this target seemed to be successful. Difficult to attack because of hills and trees on both banks. Went to have a look at GO 939. Flight engineer saw two large breaches close together between the two targets. Each breach was about a quarter width of space between the two towers. Water was pouring through both gaps, shooting well out before falling in two powerful jets. The valley seemed to be well covered with water. Report confirmed by air bomber. Front gunner reports a third breach beyond the tower on the N.E. end of dam. Breach about half the size of other

/two. Water pouring ....

two. Water pouring through.

O/617.   F/Sgt. Townsend.   GO 935   Time of attack 0337 hrs.

1. Sighted by profile of hills. Running into moon in half light reflected on mist and water.

2. ¾ mile approximately.

3. (a) One. Explosion occurred approximately 30 seconds after release. (b) Yes.

4. High column of dirt and water. Circle afterwards meeting dam.

5. No sign of damage.

6. Three.

7. No.

8. None.

9. (a) Has a good deterrent effect on flak. (b) No trouble with dazzle or stoppages and very encouraging to crew.

10. The island shown in centre of lake on target map is actually joined to the spit. Did three dummy runs and circled several times having difficulty with drifting mist and dazzle from moon. Considered timing was too late as we were still over Germany in daylight. Kept the aircraft right on the deck and cruised at about 240, this appeared to fox the defences. Had a look at MOEHNE DAM on way in and could not find it for some time. Found sheet of water about 7 miles long and extending to four miles wide up valleys with dam in middle. Roofs of houses could be seen sticking up above the water which was flowing very fast.

Y/617.   F/Sgt. Anderson.

1. to 8. N/A.

9. Very satisfactory — no dazzle and continuous line very helpful and apparently scaring the enemy.

10. Unable to find lakes near DULMEN. Mist in valleys made recognition difficult and above five minutes before DULMEN we were forced off our track by searchlights being at that time unable to shoot at them owing to stoppages in rear turret. Realised we could not reach target in time so turned back at 03.10 hours bringing the mine back.

Following the debriefings, a preliminary report was issued on May 27, 1943 for the personal use of the Chief of Air Staff 'without waiting for a more detailed report which is now in course of preparation by Bomber Command'. A rider was attached concerning the security measures adopted: 'In view of the highly secret nature of the operation, special security measures were taken. At the 2nd Ad Hoc Committee Meeting at the Air Ministry on the 2nd April, 1943, special attention was given to the security aspect of the operation, and security measures including issue of special passes for witnesses of the trials and visits to the works, code-names for the operation, special cover plans, directions for the Press representative, etc. were issued.' *Right:* Page 4 of the CAS's report gave this breakdown for the attack — note that the Ennepe dam is incorrectly referred to as the Schwelm.

Summary of Operations

8. Detailed 19

   Took Off 19

   Primary 10

   Alternative 1

   Abortive 3

   Missing ... ... 8 (3 of which are believed to have attacked)

Mohne Dam ... ... 5 attacked

Eder Dam ... ... 3 attacked

Sorpe Dam ... ... 2 attacked

Schwelm Dam ... ... 1 attacked

Believed Cause of Abortives and Missing Aircraft

9. **Abortives:**   **Cause**

   1 Lancaster   –   Enemy Action

   1 Lancaster   –   Collision with sea on way to target.

   1 Lancaster   –   Returned early.

   Missing:

   1 Lancaster   –   Flak on way to target.

   1 Lancaster   •   Flak when attacking the Mohne Dam.

   1 Lancaster   –   Believed damaged by store after attacking the Eder Dam.

   5 Lancasters   –   Unknown.

The Daily Telegraph
and Morning Post

No. 27,435   LONDON, TUESDAY, MAY 18, 1943   Printed in LONDON and MANCHESTER   PRICE 1½d.

R.A.F. BLOW UP THREE KEY DAMS IN GERMANY

DEVASTATION SWEEPS DOWN RUHR VALLEY

BRIDGES AND POWER PLANTS ENGULFED

ADVANCING FLOODS STILL SPREADING FAST

With one single blow the R.A.F. has precipitated what may prove to be the greatest industrial disaster yet inflicted on Germany in this war.

A force of Lancasters, loaded with mines and with crews specially trained for the task, early yesterday morning attacked and destroyed the great dams on the Mohne and Sorpe rivers, tributaries of the Ruhr, and also the dam on the Eder River.

To-day walls of water sweeping down the Ruhr and Eder valleys are carrying everything before them.

The Air Ministry announced last night that a partial reconnaissance of the Ruhr Valley and the district near the Eder dam shows that the floods are spreading fast.

"The waters are sweeping down the Ruhr Valley," it stated. "Railways and road bridges are broken down. Hydro-electrical power stations are destroyed or damaged, a railway marshalling yard is under water.

"The floods from the breached Eder dam are

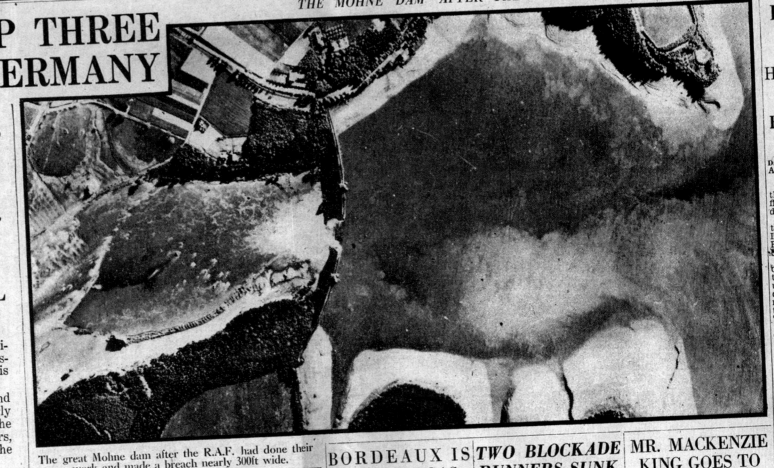

THE MOHNE DAM AFTER THE R.A.F. RAID

The great Mohne dam after the R.A.F. had done their work and made a breach nearly 300ft wide.

PILOT SEES BREACH IN DAM BY MOONLIGHT

SUCCESS AT FOURTH ATTEMPT

The full official account of the raid on the dams in South-West Germany was given by the Air Ministry last night in the following statement:

For many weeks picked Lancaster crews had been training for one operation. They worked in secrecy on a bomber station which, as far as possible, was cut off from any contact with the

BORDEAUX IS WITHOUT GAS OR WATER

LIBERATORS POUND U-BOAT BASES

The U-boat bases at Bordeaux, Lorient and Kereman, all on the Atlantic coast of France, were the targets for a large number of American bombers in daylight yesterday. Four heavy and 10 medium bombers are missing.

Vichy radio stated last night that 148 people were killed and 228 injured at Bordeaux. Reports said that the town was

TWO BLOCKADE RUNNERS SUNK IN ATLANTIC

SCUTTLED BY NAZI CREWS

Cruiser patrols of the Royal Navy have intercepted two more blockade runners bound for Germany and heavily laden with cargoes from the Far East. The enemy vessels scuttled themselves after interception.

An Admiralty communiqué stated last night that one of them, the German armed ship Silvaplana, 4,793 tons, carried a

MR. MACKENZIE KING GOES TO WASHINGTON

FROM OUR OWN CORRESPONDENT
WASHINGTON, Monday.

Mr. Mackenzie King, the Canadian Prime Minister, left Ottawa to-day for Washington for conferences with Mr. Churchill and Mr. Roosevelt.

Mr. Churchill and the President resumed their talks at the White House to-day. In accordance with Mr. Roosevelt's request to the Press to "put the lid on" news of these discussions over the week-end, nothing further can be said about the Prime Minister's appointments during the past two days.

According to reports from London

Congratulations in Britain

The first official news of the previous night's operation was given by the Secretary of State for Air, Sir Archibald Sinclair, when he spoke at a ceremony on Monday marking Norwegian Constitution Day (commemorating independence from Sweden in 1814) at the Royal Albert Hall attended by King Haakon VII of Norway and the Crown Prince.

'I have got news — great news — for you to day', Sir Archibald declared enthusiastically. 'Bomber Command — the javelin in our armoury — struck last night a heavy blow of a new kind at the sources of German war power.

'The two greatest dams in Germany, the one containing 134,000,000 tons of water and the other 202,000,000 tons were breached by bombers despatched by Air Chief Marshal Harris. The walls of the Möhne and Eder dams were broken and the water descended the valleys of the Ruhr and the Eder in huge waves.

'The operation was one of extraordinary difficulty and hazard. It is a trenchant blow for the victory of the Allies.'

The first Air Ministry communiqué, issued shortly after Sir Archibald's speech, announced: 'In the early hours of this morning, a force of Lancasters attacked with mines the dams at the Möhne and Sorpe reservoirs. These control two-thirds of the water storage capacity of the Ruhr basin. Reconnaissance later established that the Möhne dam had been breached over a length of 100 yards and that the power station below had been swept away by the resulting floods.

'The Eder dam, which controls the headwaters of the Weser and Fulda valleys and operates several power stations, was also attacked and was reported as breached. Photographs show the river below in full flood. The attacks were pressed home from a very low level with great determination and coolness in the face of fierce resistance.'

This was followed with a more extensive report which was issued to the Press on Monday evening in time for publication in Tuesday morning's nationals.

Meanwhile, behind the scenes, a flurry of letters and telegrams were being despatched between the leading players, one of the first being Sir Arthur Harris's congratulations to No. 5 Group:

'Please convey to all concerned my warmest congratulations on the brilliantly successful execution of last night's operations. To the aircrews I would say that their keenness and thoroughness in training and their skill and determination in pressing home their attacks will for ever be an inspiration to the Royal Air Force. In this memorable operation they have won a major victory in the battle of the Ruhr, the effects of which will last until the Boche is swept away in the flood of final disaster.'

MESSAGE FORM

Office Serial No.

Call and Preface	IN		No. of Groups	Office Date Stamp
	OUT		**GR**	

(Above this line is for Signals use only.)

TO* HEADQUARTERS BOMBER COMMAND

FROM* AIR MINISTRY, WHITEHALL.

Originator's Number	Date	In reply to	Number and Date
H 740	17/5.		

(Write horizontally)

FOLLOWING FOR COMMANDER-IN-CHIEF FROM SECRETARY OF STATE.

BEGINS: THE WAR CABINET HAVE INSTRUCTED ME TO CONVEY TO YOU

AND TO ALL WHO SHARED IN THE PREPARATION AND EXECUTION OF LAST

NIGHT'S OPERATIONS, AND PARTICULARLY TO WING COMMANDER GIBSON

AND HIS SQUADRON, THEIR CONGRATULATIONS ON THE GREAT SUCCESS

ACHIEVED.   THIS ATTACK, PRESSED HOME IN THE FACE OF STRONG

RESISTANCE, IS A TESTIMONY ALIKE TO THE TACTICAL RESOURCE AND

ENERGY OF THOSE WHO PLANNED IT, TO THE GALLANTRY AND DETERMINATION

OF THE AIRCREWS AND TO THE EXCELLENCE OF BRITISH DESIGN AND

WORKMANSHIP.   THE WAR CABINET HAVE NOTED WITH SATISFACTION THE

DAMAGE DONE TO GERMAN WAR POWER.   ENDS.

ARCHIBALD SINCLAIR.

One of the first official telegrams was from the War Cabinet (via the Secretary of State for Air) to Bomber Command headquarters.

TELEGRAM FROM AIR CHIEF VICE MARSHAL SIR ARTHUR HARRIS.

PERSONAL PRIORITY FOR MR. B.N. WALLIS

BUT FOR YOUR KNOWLEDGE SKILL AND PERSISTENCE,   OFTEN IN THE FACE OF DISCOURAGEMENT AND DISAPPOINTMENT,   IN THE DESIGN PRODUCTION AND SERVICING OF THE EQUIPMENT USED IN THE DESTRUCTION OF THE DAMS THE EFFORTS OF OUR GALLANT CREWS WOULD HAVE BEEN IN VAIN.   WE IN BOMBER COMMAND IN PARTICULAR AND THE UNITED NATIONS AS A WHOLE OWE EVERYTHING TO YOU IN THE FIRST PLACE FOR THE OUTSTANDING SUCCESS ACHIEVED.

BOMBER COMMAND

In spite of his initial critical attitude to the bouncing bomb, Sir Arthur Harris was quick to heap his praise on Barnes Wallis.

KEEP YOUR MOVEMENTS SECRET.

A.C.F.

W.A. DIVISION

R.A.F.
May 20th.   Scampton.

My Dear Mr Wallis,

Now that the floods are subsiding and the tumult dying down (wait for the Scampe) I've at last found time to drop you a line.

I'm afraid I'm not much of a letter writer but I would like to say just this. The weapon, that you gave us to deliver worked like a dream and you have earned the thanks of the civilized world.

All my pilots and I are honoured that we had the opportunity to take part in the last great experiment which has crowned all your theories.

And now, I think you need a holiday,

Best Regards to Nanty Shots and Mandy

Yours Sincerely,
Guy Gibson

WRITE ON BOTH SIDES.   IT'S A WARTIME ECONOMY.

Sir Ralph Cochrane joined in the congratulations over the effectiveness of the new weapon: 'Headquarters, No. 5 Group, 17th May, 1943. Dear Wallis, Before reaching the end of this somewhat long but exciting day I feel I must write to tell you how much I admire the perseverance which brought you the astounding success which was achieved last night. Without your determination to ensure that a method which you knew to be technically sound was given a fair trial we should not have been able to deliver the blow which struck Germany last night . . . Yours sincerely, R. A. Cochrane. PS. Since writing this I have heard the result of the full photographic cover. What a disaster!' *Above:* Before he left to go on leave, Gibson penned his personal 'thank you' to Wallis.

MOST SECRET

ALCOVE NO. 266

COPY NO 13

T.O.O. 171610Z

Date: 17th May, 1943

MOST IMMEDIATE

Personal and Secret for Prime Minister from Secretary of State for air.

P.R.U. reports confirm success of upkeep. Photos this morning show 200 foot breach in Mohne Dam, disappearance of Power Station and widespread floods reaching to Dortmund. While Eder Dam not yet photographed Power Station one mile down stream has been under water and very bad flooding has clearly taken place. Main storage lake of reservoir appears drained. Sorpe Dam being of different construction not expected to be breached but crest damaged for 200 feet. Water flowing over, seepage hoped for. Surprise was achieved and weapon functioned admirably but attack involved very accurate and low flying and our losses were 8 missing out of 19 Lancasters despatched. Wing Commander Gibson directed the operations by R/T and, after dropping his weapon, flew around shooting at the flak. He returned unscathed.

T.O.O. 171610Z

Meanwhile, in Washington, Churchill was at the 'Trident' conference when the news was telegraphed through from Sir Archibald Sinclair, the message timed at 16.10 Zebra time, i.e. 4.10 p.m. Greenwich Mean Time which was then two hours behind British Double Summer Time.

Churchill spent the following day in preparing his address to be delivered to the United States Congress on the 19th. He began speaking shortly after mid-day, his 50-minute speech being relayed to the BBC in London for a live broadcast. The Prime Minister included a piece about the raid: 'You have just read of the destruction of the great dams which feed the canals and provide power to the enemy's munition works. That was a gallant operation costing eight out of the 19 Lancaster bombers employed but it will play a very far-reaching part in German military output. It is our settled policy, the settled policy of our two staffs of war-making authorities — to make it impossible for Germany to carry on any form of war industry on a large or concentrated scale, either in Germany, in Italy, or in the enemy-occupied countries. [Cheers]. Wherever these centres exist, or are developed, they will be destroyed and the munitions population will be dispersed. If they don't like what is coming to them, let them disperse beforehand on their own. [Cheers] This process will continue ceaselessly, with ever-increasing weight and intensity, until the German and Italian peoples abandon or destroy the monstrous tyrannies which they have incubated and reared in their midst. [Cheers] In the meanwhile, our air offensive is forcing Germany to withdraw an ever larger proportion of its war-making capacity from the fighting fronts in order to provide protection against the air attacks. Hundreds of fighter aircraft, thousands of anti-aircraft cannon, and many hundreds of thousands of men, together with a vast share in the output of the war factories, have already been assigned to this purely defensive function. All this is at the expense of the enemy's power of new aggression or after the enemy's power to resume the initiative. Surveying the whole aspect of the air war, we cannot doubt that it is a major factor in the process of victory.'

Death Valley. This is Neheim nearly ten kilometres downstream from the Möhne dam. In the background to the left is the Wiedenberg hill onto which hundreds of Ukrainian women escaped from their labour camp by wading through the waters of the Möhne river. In the foreground, rubble and debris are being cleared from the Werler Strasse.

In the small hamlet of Himmelpforten, just three kilometres below the dam, stood the Porta Coeli convent chapel built over 700 years previously from the grey stone of the valley. It had long been used by the order of Cistercian nuns and both church and convent had survived wars, looting and pillage, only to fall victim to the catastrophic floods on the night of May 16/17, 1943. Art treasures adorned the walls and altars of its baroque interior, parts of which dated from Gothic times. *Left:* This photograph of a woman decorating the altar was taken one day before the disaster. A 16-year-old boy, Werner Hellmann, saw the church collapse from a distance of 200 metres: 'I was on the bank at Köster and I could clearly see the weathervane on top of the steeple sticking up out of that thundering flood which by then had reached its highest point. After a while the steeple tipped over to one side and went under. The bell gave out a single, dull clang.' *Above:* A working party of soldiers takes a breather among the debris at Himmelpforten. The raging river has already carved a new course for itself which they have bridged to enable them to search for the treasures from the church. Items were found as far away as Schwerte, 40 kilometres to the west. What pieces were recovered have now been incorporated in the new parish church of St Bernhard Himmelpforten in Niederense on a slope out of reach of any further floods.

Death Valley

As the Möhne dam gave way, a giant wall of water shot through the breach into the valley, which now echoed to a muffled rumbling. Within barely a minute the flood had engulfed the first buildings — the rifle club and three hydro-electric power stations in Günne — and claimed the first victims. There were already 30 deaths in the village, some of the bodies being carried down as far as Fröndenberg 30 kilometres away. The avalanche of water — over 30 feet high in some narrow sections of what became known as the 'Todestal' or Death Valley — sped towards unsuspecting villages and towns, smashing all that lay in its path, the roaring of the water reverberating from the wooded slopes. Karl-Heinz Dohle from Niederense witnessed the destruction of the Himmelpforten monastery in Niederense:

'I was standing in the garden with my father. We were looking at those great birds of destruction flying low over the village towards the dam wall and blazing away with tracer bullets. After a few explosions, we heard a thundering and rushing noise from the east.

A feeling of unease — morbid curiosity — impelled us to Kösters Ufer, a hill above the Himmelpforten monastery buildings. Through the valley, a crashing wave bore down on the baroque Porta Coeli chapel just as if the Niagara Falls had been unleashed. The chapel was 700 years old, a simply beautiful work of art erected to the glory of God by the devout Westphalian Cistercians as their "Gateway to Heaven". In no time at all, the church was underwater — all you could see was the tower sticking up out of the foaming water. The spire held out against the thundering surge for about ten minutes, then it tipped over to the west and went under with one last muffled clang of the bell. It was eerie seeing that mass of water in the moonlight at such close quarters. Uprooted trees were being carried along by the surging water.

'The following morning I saw the devastation caused by the catastrophe. Himmelpforten had simply ceased to exist. Joseph Berkenkopf, the priest, was drowned in the air raid shelter. Some of the trees on the road into Günne had railway lines wrapped round them like corkscrews. The flotsam had stripped away all the bark; they were standing there like white ghosts.'

119

The flood waters reached Adolf Nölle's inn at Günne at 00.50, one minute after the Möhne dam had been breached. The waves were up to eight metres in height and caused serious damage to the building but Nölle kept his nerve and guided the household out of the cellar and into the loft where they sheltered behind a massive chimney breast while they waited to be rescued. All the furniture was lost, save for the wall clock in the bar and, although it has been repaired many times, it always stops at ten to one — the time when the water rose to its maximum level in the inn.

Twenty minutes after the dam had given way, a tidal wave some 30 feet high reached the unsuspecting town of Neheim. Here many people were drowned in their cellars where they had gone to shelter from the air raid. Some of them managed to struggle through the torrent, from floor to floor and, smashing holes in the roof, to cling to chimneys but, even then, there was sometimes no escape. The force of the water ripped even well-built houses from their foundations, this roof section having been carried away and dumped almost undamaged in what had now become Neheim's Valley of Death where the dead lay strewn amid the detritus.

Frau Elisabeth Lingenhöfer also has vivid memories of that night: 'I was living in a timber-framed house right by the River Möhne at Niederense. I'd only been in there a fortnight and I'd just got the curtains up. That Saturday evening we'd been over to the Apollo cinema in Neheim on our bikes to see one of the first colour films, *Die goldene Stadt* (The Golden City). In the film someone gets killed in a bog. When we got home I was going to write a letter to my husband, who was in the forces, but my sister-in-law thought we'd better go to bed. Just at that moment these great aeroplanes came roaring over the village. Explosions and shooting echoed over from the distance. I got my three children out of bed; first of all we went down into the cellar. All of a sudden, we heard a muffled roaring and a crashing noise. We got out of the cellar straightaway and just after this it was full of foaming water. There was a raging sea of water all round the house. I could probably have got through myself but never with the three children so we dashed up to the first floor and shouted for help from the windows. We called the neighbours but it was no good at all.

'The water rose higher and higher so we went up to the second floor and from there to the loft but the water came up there, too. The children were crying and clinging on to me; some of the other people from the house were praying. I started to knock the tiles out and climbed through the laths onto the roof. The women passed the children through after me. I got rid of all the tiles right up to the gable and exposed the laths. Then the others from the house climbed through too.

From the Wiedenberg hill, people from Neheim look out aghast at the expanse of water which has cut their town in half.

'With the children in front of me I sat on the ridge of the roof; I had one leg over one side and the other leg over the other. When I think about it now, it's a miracle how we managed it. All the joints in the house were groaning and creaking and it was rocking from side to side. Tree trunks were crashing through the half-timbered sides of the house. I just clung desperately to the roof hoping that if it gave way I'd be able to swim off with the children. The lightning conductor had got stretched out from all the pulling. The water carried a little timber-framed house past us towards Neheim and in a window on a table in one of the rooms there was a candle giving off a peculiar kind of light. Tree trunks from the saw-mill kept crashing down in front of the house; dead cows were carried along past the roof. Then planes came round quite low with lights on. At first we thought they were going to rescue us. But when they started shooting, we ducked down on the roof so the airmen couldn't see us.

'While I was sitting up there on the ridge with the flood going past, I couldn't help thinking about the film. I thought, it's all over; we're all going down into the bog together, just like in the film a few hours earlier. At last the water started to go down. I put my youngest daughter to sleep in a wash tub in the loft. I got colic pains from the stress of it all, and had to lie down in the loft, too. It was more difficult getting down from the roof than it had been getting up there as the entire staircase had gone. My little daughter woke up and was hungry.

'Towards morning the water level dropped. Firemen and neighbours got us down from the roof with ladders; we'd been hanging on up there for over seven hours. Great piles of mud had wrecked the flats but at least we were still alive. The water had risen to over eight metres. All the furniture had been washed out through the doors and windows. First of all they looked after us in the houses on higher ground on the Steetsberg. I wouldn't want to live in a valley below a dam any more. I can't escape the fear; it's always with me. I wouldn't want to go through that again.'

A view of the Werler Strasse in Neheim looking towards the Totenberg. In the centre of the picture all that can be seen are the remains of some foundations while on the mud-covered street people stand discussing the catastrophe. After heavy raids, relief operations were initiated by the government in order to improve public morale, and welfare provisions for the homeless in the form of emergency rations normally included cigarettes and chocolate. In this case, for a period of three days, the entire population received a special issue of real coffee, spirits and confectionery. One pensioner holds a bottle of schnapps — one of the 5,000 handed out by Deputy Gauleiter Albert Hoffmann as presents to the Neheim salvage workers. Because of the lack of cooking facilities, three field-kitchens were also despatched to Neheim from Münster.

At Neheim-Hüsten, Norbert Kampmann's tobacconist's shop was at No. 6 Hauptstrasse near the parish church of St Johannes Baptist. Just after 1 o'clock in the morning, he received an agitated call from his brother-in-law who lived on the Steetsberg in Niederense: 'The Möhne's coming down. Raise the alarm and get out of there.' Herr Kampmann at once ran across the road to the police station situated opposite in the town hall and informed the person on duty about the call. 'That can't be right', the man responded unconcernedly, 'we'd have known about it a long time ago. If that'd been the case, we'd have received an official call.'

The police station in Neheim received other calls from people advising them that the Möhne dam had been breached but the callers were brushed off curtly with the comment: 'Don't come with that old story again'. And then the phone was put down. Thus valuable time was lost which could have been used to send a provisional warning to lower-lying parts of the town which were at risk and where people were in their shelters blissfully unaware of the new danger bearing down on them. When the official message about the breach in the dam finally came through from the District Government at Arnsberg, it was too late to sound the alarm. (It was only after the disaster that flood-warning plans for the towns and villages at risk were set up with escape routes and audible warnings.)

One consequence of the flood was that for a while Neheim became a town cut in two. A concrete bridge, an iron bridge and several footbridges had been swept away so army engineers set up a ferry service near the Werler Strasse using rubber inflatables. Shortly after this, a temporary wooden footbridge, almost 100 metres in length, was set up across valley below the Wiedenberg hill. During the weeks and months that followed, more than 3,000 workers were engaged clearing away rubble and re-establishing some semblance of order. Both the Möhne and Ruhr rivers had to be diverted back into their old beds.

Hermann Kaiser, another Neheim resident and the 13-year-old son of the well-known lighting manufacturer, described his rescue:

'As a rule we only went down into the air raid shelter when we got a warning from the switchboard at our firm. Just like every other large firm in Neheim, it had a direct telephone connection with the Air Raid Warning HQ in Dortmund. When a message was received from there saying that enemy planes were approaching the area, there was always enough time to go to the shelter. We were woken up before midnight and then went into the cellar, which was situated — as was the way then — three-quarters below ground. The shelter itself was in the centre of the house and so it had added protection from more walls and the ceiling had been strengthened with thick planks and supporting pillars. There were camp beds ready so the children could go back to sleep.

'Because it was Mother's Day, my parents had gone over to grandmother's place at Stolberg in the Rhineland. In the air raid shelter with myself and my sisters aged 10, 15 and 20 was the housemaid and our Russian cook, Anna. She had a bright and airy room with big windows next to the playroom and the ironing room in the cellar. Anna had been in the household with us from the start — from the very first day the Russian women came to Neheim. At first she'd come in the mornings and go in the evenings. Then my mother got round my father so that she'd be allowed to live in the house with us. She was a very good cook and often used to make Russian dishes for us. Because of this we'd even got hold of two baby lambs. We often noticed that she was terribly homesick and really sad about the death of her husband, who'd been in the Soviet Navy. His photograph was on her bedside table. Many a night she'd cry and open the window. She did this on the night before the disaster. On the Saturday she'd told us again that she wouldn't be able to stand it much longer; something or other would happen. Kaiser's night watchman also came past our house on his rounds at 10 p.m. and found her crying in a heart-rending way. He asked her why she was crying and she replied: "I'll be back with my husband again tonight".

'You could hear the detonations of the bombs at the Möhne. Later, when the explosions and the noise from the aircraft over the town had died down, Anna went to her room and shut herself in. She always went to bed early. Just then the telephone rang upstairs. Our housemaid went up but came straight back down and said, "There's something going on outside. I think they're dropping incendiaries. There's a terrible splashing and rattling noise." Suddenly our then driver and gardener, Josef Greis, came bursting into the cellar shouting out, "Get out! Get out! Everyone out of here — NOW!"

'At first we had no idea what had happened. He hammered on Anna's door, and he shouted, too, but she didn't open up. Perhaps she was afraid of the noise and all the commotion outside. Herr Greis tried everything to get her out of the house. At first all I could think of was the incendiaries; I grabbed my little briefcase where I kept my underwear and a shirt. We ran out of the house in a panic. I had my briefcase over my head, supposing that stuff was coming down from above. Our house was right by the millrace. In front, in the bright moonlight, I saw something silvery — something splashing on the ground. I still thought it was incendiaries going off. Then we ran up between our factory buildings towards the Ringstrasse where hundreds of people had found safety. On the way, the water was already surging over the rails of the Ruhr-Lippe railway.

'With my parents away, that's how Herr Greis came to save us and we owe him our lives. He only lived about 100 metres away. When there was an air raid warning, he checked to see if we'd gone into the shelter. As a matter of principle, my father didn't go down into the cellar: he just stayed in bed. If my parents had been at home, my mother would first have had to go up into the house to wake him so we would all have been waiting in the cellar like good little children, and valuable escape time would have been lost.

'The flood wave came very fast; it was a matter of minutes. There was a young woman working for the Bahnschulte family; she lost her parents even though they were only ten metres behind her when she came out of the cellar. She escaped with her life but they were drowned right there on the road behind her. I ran with my brothers and sisters to the highest point on the Neheim Kopf just wearing our pyjamas, night-dresses or dressing gowns. Fear had driven us right up there. On the Ringstrasse, people said to us, "Don't go up any further. Come into the house."

'From the hill I saw great stretches of water in the Möhne valley as wide as the Mississippi. They went rolling down the valley and off into the night making a noise like 25 express trains. The next morning they found Anna drowned in the laundry room . . . she'd been washed in there from her bedroom. It seemed that she'd made no attempt to get away.'

All that was left of the large detached residence belonging to the Kaiser family. The parents were away but Josef Greis, the gardener (who was also the chauffeur to the director of the Kaiser lighting factory) managed to save the children from the house in the nick of time, but Anna, the Russian cook, was too frightened to leave and was drowned.

Dozens of houses were carried away, the Kaiser residence being the only building in the valley to withstand the massive force of the water. A huge section of solid rock, 18 metres long by 5 metres high, was even carved out of the Wiedenberg hill and, where the valley is at its narrowest point between Niederense and Neheim, marks on trees indicated that the water reached a record height of 15 metres (over 45 feet). Amid the chaos, troops tried to recover the bodies quickly lest the warm May weather should spark off an epidemic. Tide marks on the houses in the background are a reminder of the level reached by the flood waters. Meanwhile at the embarkation point, people are waiting to be ferried across.

Soldiers search for bodies in the wreckage which has been washed up along the sides of the valley. Police, who had been seconded in from the surrounding area, kept watch on the Ruhr bridges and public throughfares for only the inhabitants of Neheim and people working there were allowed into the town upon production of an identity card. The SA was responsible for public order and the Hitler Youth was drafted in to help clear up. Red Cross nurses had the task of washing the bodies that were recovered.

Ferdi Dröge, a 16-year-old apprentice at a plumbing and installation firm in the Möhne-Strasse at Neheim, lived ten kilometres from the dam.

'At night, if there was an air raid warning, I had to take my two cases and go with the boss's wife to the shelter at the Hillebrand lighting firm nearby while my employer was on stand-by with the fire brigade. This night, as soon as we got out on the street, we saw the tracers going up over by the Möhne dam. We guessed at once that it was an attack but no one thought things would turn out as they did. There were already 150 to 200 people from the neighbourhood sitting in the works' shelter as they reckoned their own shelter at the training workshop was not safe enough because it only had a wooden roof. There was nothing special about the Hillebrand shelter but everyone had his favourite corner. As usual we all sat on planks and beer barrels eating snacks and playing cards. After 15 or 20 minutes Johannes Kessler ran into the shelter in quite a state and shouted out: "The Möhne's had it." We realised at once that he meant the dam. I thought to myself, water is pouring out so you'd better take a short cut down to the little bridge over the Möhne and see if the stream is twice as high as usual, say, chest deep.

'People got out of that shelter in no time at all. On my way to the bridge I suddenly heard terrible screams, and behind me the people who had just left the shelter began to shout too. The screams came from up the valley from the area of the Russian women's camp. I'd seen these women and girls every day from the workshop window because hundreds of Ukrainian and Polish women were working in factories in the town. Then all of a sudden I saw this wave surging down. It looked like a black block of flats with terraces; it was full of trees, pieces of wood and animals. That pitch-black wall of water coming towards me was at least 12 metres high; in it, and looking as if they were stacked on top of each other, were sections of wooden huts and people screaming. Dotted around in among those whirling bits of wood were little lights which went out in the spray. I was no more than 200 metres from the leading edge of that wave.

'I ran back up the Möhne-Strasse faster than I'd ever run in my life. At about the same time the flood roared past me in the valley and into the transformer station. This caused a short circuit and a colossal flash lit up the valley. The water then came on across the Möhne-Strasse and we all ran uphill along the Friedensstrasse. Halfway up we stopped and followed the tragedy down in the valley — the crashing, the roaring, the smashing and the death cries. Seen from the side, the first giant wave looked like steps. Each wall of water rose up above the one in front as the torrent thrust its way down the valley. In front of the Totenberg, houses twisted and disappeared into the flood. I saw a smashed-up hut and through the spray I could make out some shadowy figures on it. Then it crashed into the buildings of the Brökelmann firm and fell to bits. The cries stopped.

'Next morning, when the water had subsided, the valley looked as if a mower had been through it. Hundreds of dead Russian women were lying scattered amongst pieces of debris, lumps of mud, cupboards, suitcases and personal belongings — a picture of abject misery. Six months later, when the rubbish was cleared away, workmen found more bodies of female Russian forced labourers.

'The Red Cross set up field-kitchens at the roadside in the disaster zone and served goulash. Nurses handed out food and sandwiches to those who'd suffered in the flood until they were able to look after themselves again. They cursed the British bombers. There was a lot of surreptitious griping and whispering about the minimal flak defences on the dam. Even before the disaster, people had been asking what had happened to the barrage balloons on the dam wall; why the number of flak guns had been reduced and why the lake was so full. The fact that there were only a few small guns up on the towers and on the wall had spread like wildfire through Neheim even before the raid. Later there were no official statements from the authorities or the Party.'

Those bodies of the foreign workers that were immediately recovered were taken away in lorries for burial without coffins in two mass graves at the cemetery. Meanwhile the pews in the nave of St Johannes Baptist Church were stacked to one side so that the German dead could be laid out for identification. At the same time, carpenters from the surrounding area hurriedly began making dozens of coffins for the German victims. But, as the clear-up continued, human remains were still being found in Neheim three months later.

Thursday, May 20, 10 a.m. The funeral for the German victims thus far recovered is under-way at the Neheim cemetery in the Möhne-Strasse. Party members, representatives of the armed services and the authorities, the fire brigade and the Hitlerjugend have taken up positions by the 53 coffins. Relatives stand in the background. Speeches from Bannführer Klosterhoff and Deputy Gauleiter Vetter spoke of an uncompromising and unshakeable belief in victory. The Party funeral ended with the singing of patriotic songs. Then, just as the religious funeral service was about to begin, an alarm from the Sorpe dam caused panic to break out at the cemetery and in the town. The *Westfälische Landeszeitung — Rote Erde* published an illustrated report of the funeral but remained silent about the alarm — which proved to be false — and the ensuing panic.

Father Joseph Hellmann was the parish priest at Neheim. 'Our church, St Johannes Baptist, was set up as a mortuary with the pews in the nave removed to make room for 200 coffins. Soon after this, the bodies were brought in by soldiers who had been detached to the town. Men, women and children — every age group from babes in arms to the very old — were laid out side by side in the church for identification. In many cases this was possible from notebooks, identity cards, rings and other items which had also been recovered. However, some bodies which had been mutilated by injuries and the effects of water had to be recorded as "unidentified". It was terrible to see the bodies — many had their hands twisted and their faces contorted with fear but some looked peaceful as if they were asleep. Others had embarked on their journey to eternity holding a crucifix or a rosary. Relatives came to see their departed loved ones for the last time. Over 400 female foreign workers had already been laid to rest in mass graves. Then came the French, including a Catholic priest who had been responsible for the spiritual welfare of his countrymen, followed by the Belgians, the Dutch and finally our own Germans.'

The first burial of the Neheim flood victims took place on Thursday, May 20, the service being conducted by Dr Friedrich Rintelen, Generalvikar of Paderborn and on May 24, he sent the following letter to the Reich Minister of the Interior, Dr Frick, in Berlin:

'The undersigned feels obliged to bring the following matters to your attention. In the town of Neheim, which suffered so greatly in the disaster caused by the destruction of the Möhne dam, the Catholic church had been prepared for the laying out of the victims. The majority of the undecorated, and for the most part makeshift, coffins had been furnished with a plain wooden cross. On the order of some authority unknown to me, these crosses were suddenly removed one day. The devoutly Catholic population of Neheim, especially the relatives of the victims, were most deeply incensed by this action. Their indignation was expressed with such force that it became necessary to replace the crosses.

'During the course of discussions regarding the funeral of the victims, it was initially proposed that the ceremony of State and Party should take place at the cemetery on the morning of May 20. The services of the two Christian denominations were to take place during the afternoon. It was finally agreed that the official ceremony should be at 10.00, with the religious rites to follow at the graves. The state ceremony was due to be completed by approximately 11.45. As representative of the Archbishop of Paderborn, I proposed to conduct the religious rites myself. Together with the participating clergy, I went to the cemetery early to spare the bereaved relatives any unnecessary waiting. As we arrived, the proceedings were just concluding with the singing of the Party and national anthems.

'When the various Party groups had left the cemetery and the coffins had been placed in the mass graves, the large assembly of bereaved relatives gathered around the graves. I started to read a short extract from the Gospel. Just as I had reached the end of the final sentence, the sirens went off signalling an air raid warning. At this point I brought the funeral service to a speedy conclusion. Just then a truck with some lads in it raced along the road in front of the cemetery. They were yelling: "Water! The Sorpe dam!" Their waving made it clear that everyone should flee the cemetery slope and seek refuge in the hills. With a cry of horror, the nervous, overwrought and terrified gathering of many hundreds scattered. Some rushed up the cemetery slope and disappeared into the nearby woods; others ran home to their children and sick. As the cemetery stands on high ground, and the local clergy confirmed it was in absolutely no danger from the Sorpe, I initially remained at the graveside so as not to exacerbate the anxiety. Shortly afterwards the siren went off again, but it did not sound the all clear. (If it had done so the congregation could possibly have reassembled around the graves.) In the event, the siren signalled the air raid warning.

'We then left the cemetery and proceeded to the town where there had also been scenes of dreadful panic. For example, people had gone to the hospital shouting that the water was on its way down and that the patients should be carried up to the attic. People fled to the hills in their masses. Those remaining explained to us on the street that it had only been a practice alarm. This had also been announced over a loudspeaker. I was naturally most indignant and at once went to the town hall with the parish priest in order to ascertain if it had indeed been just a practice — a practice carried out at all times just as the funeral service was due to begin.

'At the town hall, I met the Chief Administrative Officer for the district of Arnsberg, who told me that it had not been a practice. The danger from air raids had been extreme and the alarm had indeed been genuine. When I requested that he find out who had sanctioned the alarm, he telephoned the air raid control centre. Just at that moment the door opened and the District President of Arnsberg [Lothar Eickhoff — see pages 171-175] stormed into the room with the words, "An outrageous scandal!" At this point he saw us for what we were. We were introduced by the Chief Administrative Officer. I explained the reason for my presence at the town hall whereupon the District President told me that a dispatch rider had brought news that the Sorpe dam had been breached. As a result the alarm was sounded; the state of general panic had been exacerbated by the ringing of church bells. However, it was certain that nothing had happened to the Sorpe dam.

'Further to the above, I would make the following observation: at the start of the funeral service, and following instructions from the parish priest, the sexton tolled the death-knell for three minutes. There then followed the alarm, and the news spread through Neheim that the Sorpe dam had been breached. Someone rushed up to the sexton and told him that he should sound the alarm by ringing all the bells. Quite understandably this is what he proceeded to do. Given the general state of turmoil, one cannot hold it against a simple sexton if, following an unauthorised sounding of sirens by a responsible authority, he should yield to pressure for the alarm peal to be rung.

'Moreover, the most foolish course of action when there is danger of flooding would be to make people go into the cellars by sounding an air raid warning. The local police have retrospectively imposed a ban on the ringing of bells on those grounds. Ringing will in future take place only as a warning if the Sorpe dam is breached. In the interest of government authority, I consider it necessary to report the events in Neheim. I request, Herr Reichsminister, that an immediate and thorough investigation be instigated with the view to severely punishing, if appropriate, those responsible. I would also express the hope that you will see fit to repeal the ban on the ringing of bells.'

When Dr Rintelen received a response from the Interior Ministry it simply stated that the events had been investigated and that no one could be held to blame. 'In future', the reply stated, 'the Generalvikar should not trouble senior government departments with such complaints, but instead address them to the subordinate authorities.'

On May 13, 1943, three days before the raid, an RAF reconnaissance aircraft overflying the Möhne dam took a series of exposures including this one which has just caught the edge of Neheim. It shows the forced workers' huts lying between the river and the Obergraben on what amounts to an island below the Wiedenberg hill. Further to the right lies the lone 'French hut' beside the Möhne-Strasse. The bend in the river is easily recognisable from the trees that run alongside it. At bottom left is the cemetery where the funeral took place.

By far the largest loss of life occurred when the nearby camp housing female forced labourers was swept away.

From the start of the war, the Labour and Health and Safety Inspectorates, acting under orders from the Reichsarbeitsministerium, (Reich Labour Ministry) systematically combed all branches of the economy seeking manpower for the armed forces. When all the reserves had been exhausted, firms not engaged in essential war work were shut down. Factories were merged in the interest of greater efficiency, women were employed, and the industrial working week was increased to 60 hours. When these possibilities had also been exhausted, foreign labour was employed on a massive scale. With an ever-deteriorating situation at the fronts, intensifying air raids on the cities, and a decrease in nutrition for the civilian population, such labour was needed to fill shortfalls in industry, mining and agriculture. Millions of prisoners of war and foreign workers — the latter mainly drafted in against their will — were procured to work in the Reich and its sphere of influence. As the number of foreign civilians volunteering for work proved insufficient, a solution was sought in so-called procurement squads, and after 1942 these started rounding up labour in the east for deportation to Germany.

The movement of forced workers was organised by the Reichsbahn (German State Railway) while labour exchanges were responsible for allocating the foreign workers, or 'Fremdarbeiter' as they were euphemistically called, to individual firms. As German workers were withdrawn, armament plants informed the relevant labour exchanges of their manpower requirements. The labour exchanges then allocated foreign workers to firms which were responsible for their board and lodging. On this basis, over 1,200 female foreign workers from the Ukraine and Poland had arrived at the railway station at Soest up to the early summer of 1943. Their destination was the camp at Neheim set up by the armament company Wohn- und Verpflegungslager eGmbH, and run for them by the Deutsche Arbeitsfront (the Nazi labour organisation).

'I was at this camp and was employed at the Kleki works', says Darja Michajlowna Moros now living in the Ukraine. 'I remember that we were woken up during the night by an alarm. There were lots of these alarms, and we were basically fed up with them. Because of this we really didn't want to get up. However, on the night in question it was a warning which saved our lives. We ran out of the huts just as we were. There were lots of us and we couldn't all get through the gate. The camp was surrounded by a high barbed-wire fence. There would have been even more casualties if a guard hadn't saved us. His Christian name was Robert but I can't remember his surname. All I can remember is that he was very old and had a limp. He cut through the wire with a pair of pliers and made gaps for us. He shouted "Schnell! Schnell!" urging us all to hurry up the hill and out of reach of the water.

'I lived in a hut with ten women from my village and we all survived. They now all live in different villages. Herr Robert saved our lives but when the great wave arrived he couldn't save himself and he drowned. The water came up very fast and swept people's legs from under them. Anyone who fell went under; and all this was going on in the dark. In the morning there was a great lake where the huts had been — and the bodies of all those who'd drowned. They were pulling bodies out of the water for a week and they took them away in lorries to mass graves on the other side of town. We stayed up on the hill above the River Möhne until the morning, soaked through, half naked and freezing cold. Then they took us survivors to a farmer and he gave us something to eat. Everyone got a piece of bread and a mug of milk. Afterwards they sent us all back to work in the same factories.'

'My mother, Elena Wolkowa, was born in the city of Tomsk in Siberia', recalls Erika Hoffmeister, 'but from the age of four she lived in what was then Stalino, in the Ukraine. In April 1942, she was deported to Germany as a forced worker. In fact she didn't really need to go; she put herself forward in place of her elder sister who had two children. And so it was that she ended up with another sister at the hutted camp in Neheim which was situated in fields by the River Möhne. My father, Karl Josef Stüppardt, got to know her when he was a guard at this camp. She and the other girls used to get homesick and would run away — once they even got as far as Oeventrop. Many a time my father had to bring her back but he always saw to it that she wasn't punished. He'd fallen in love with Elena,

WIEDENBERG

LAGER-BARACKEN

FRANZOSEN-BARACKE

FRIEDHOF

Five days after the British photograph was taken, Death Valley was captured on film for archive purposes by a German photo-reconnaissance flight at 11 a.m. on May 18. The valley between the wooded Wiedenberg hill at the top and the Möhne-Strasse below is under water — it appears as a grey strip running through the centre. The huts occupied by the foreign workers have been totally smashed and swept away with the exception of the single French hut which stands on higher ground at the edge of the valley.

129

A Russian woman searches through the mud outside a wrecked armaments factory near the barracks of the Wohn- und Verpflegungslager eGmbH which vanished.

even though any relationship with the forced workers was strictly forbidden. As a result they would meet secretly. My father's sister co-operated by arranging visits to the hairdresser where Elena was treated as a deaf mute so as not to give herself away. My mother could speak only a few words of German and it was the same for my father with Russian. They even managed to go to the cinema together in Neheim, right in the middle of the war, and as a film fan she learnt her German in the cinema. While she was at the camp she saw some films three times. She went shopping in the village with my aunt, who did the talking for her.

'My father told me how big-wigs would sometimes visit the camp. On such occasions, the girls had to make the place look really smart. It was amazing — considering the limited resources available to them — how the Ukrainian girls managed to deck the place out. They had to wave flowers when visitors came to the camp. The food was better then, too. Once there was an inspection by General Andrei Vlassov, a Soviet officer who had been taken prisoner by the Germans. This was probably done for propaganda purposes. At the beginning of 1945 he formed a "Russian Liberation Army" from Russian prisoners of war which consisted of two divisions for Hitler's Germany. In May 1945 Vlassov and his men were taken prisoner by the Americans, who sent them back to the Soviet Union. Vlassov himself was executed in Moscow on August 1, 1946.

'While we were out on Sunday walks', says Erika, 'my father would tell me about his experiences at the camp with my mother. He showed me where my mother's hut had been and decades later you could still see the foundations and the concrete outline of the toilet blocks. On that particular night, my father heard a terrible explosion. When this happened he took his alsatian and went for a walk around the wire to find out exactly what was going on. Shortly after this it felt as if a storm was brewing up but then it suddenly occurred to him that the Möhne dam could have been hit. He quickly ran to the first huts,

opened them up and shouted: "Everyone out! The Möhne dam's been hit! The water's coming down!"

'Many of the women in the huts didn't take his warning seriously. They said it couldn't be right and stayed in bed. Others ran through the gate towards the Möhne-Strasse. The water was surging around their feet and they kept running uphill. He told me that my mother had ran out through the open camp gate in her slip with an overcoat over her shoulders yet the water had already caught her by the time she reached the Hillebrand works. The women who survived were first accommodated at the Gildenhaus (Guildhall) and later they were sent to a camp behind the main railway station. My father kept in touch with his Elena but, because he'd helped the foreign women, he was detained at the Neheim police station and punished.'

'The end of the war saw a happy ending for my mother and father when they were married on June 16, 1945 at St Johannes Baptist. This was one of the first post-war marriages in Neheim, perhaps the very first German-Russian marriage in the whole of Germany. My mother wore my sister-in-law's wedding dress with a long train. The church was overflowing and all the former Russian prisoners sang from the gallery of the organ loft.

Elena Wolkowa pictured at the camp on May 31, 1942 holding a German child (Elisabeth Schulte) together with a young Russian girl, Tamara.

After the raid, the Health and Safety Inspectorate in Soest made the following statement in a letter to the District President in Arnsberg on May 26, 1943:

'The large camp for Eastern workers for the factories at Neheim has ceased to exist. According to information from management, the camp was set up at a cost of 1 million RM. It has also been pointed out that during consultations within the firms, the question frequently arose as to whether this camp did not lie in an area liable to flooding by the River Möhne. The choice of this site for the camp was certainly unsuitable, especially as it was a long way on foot to some of the Neheim firms. Furthermore, the drainage of the area and problems of access complicated matters further. I assume that the idea of a camp will not arise again because for many other reasons the conditions remain unfavourable. There were frequent complaints about insufficient food and poor supervision of the Eastern workers. In addition to this, difficulties arose from the fact that the workers were employed at different factories and therefore made comparisons regarding work and treatment.'

ЗДЕСЬ ПОКОЯТСЯ
479 РАБОЧИХ ИЗ РОССИИ И ПОЛЬШИ
ПОГИБШИХ 17.5.1943 ПРИ МЁНЗЕЕ — КАТАСТРОФЕ

TU SPOCZYWA
479 POLAKOW I ROSIANOW
KTORZY DNIA 17.5.43 R.
ZGINELI TRAGICZNA SMIERCIA PODCZAS MONSEEKATASTROFY

The bodies of 479 unidentified women lie in this mass grave at the Neheim cemetery. All were forced workers from the Soviet Union and Poland, the burial registers of Neheim recording the names of 529 (497 female and 32 male) unnamed 'Ostarbeiter' and 'Ostarbeiterinnen' (male and female Eastern workers) as they were then called. Subsequent burials comprised 59 French prisoners of war including a Catholic priest involved in pastoral care, Henri Plaquerent from Rouen; nine Belgian prisoners of war; 14 Dutch civilian workers and 49 unnamed persons. While the German losses were lamented and glorified in the local newspapers of the day, foreign deaths were recorded simply as a statistics by the authorities. After the war some of the Dutch, Belgian and French bodies were exhumed and taken back to their homelands. Over 250 female forced workers still remain unaccounted for to this day.

André Guillon, a former French prisoner of war, from Poitiers, has the following memories of that night:

'At the time I was working at Brökelmanns, an aluminium firm in Neheim. At first we lived in a cellar under the kitchen but this later became an air raid shelter for foreign workers because after 1943 more and more bombers came over. We were a mixed bunch — Germans, French, Belgians and Dutch — and we were all pleased to go down into this shelter. When there was an air raid, everyone could decide for himself whether to stay in the factory, go to the shelter, or out onto the Werler Strasse and look for cover outside. The government was short of troops and so they'd reduced the number of guards and we could move around much as we liked in the factory. We lived in a hut about two kilometres from the Brökelmann works, near the Möhne-Strasse over towards the dam.

The sole surviving barrack hut which housed the French POWs undergoing repair with debris remaining piled up against the fence.

'On that dreadful night we first heard the noise of aircraft and then a strange sound like an express train. After a warning call, all the prisoners — about 100 — rushed the guard-house. The German guards at once decided to open up the huts and the camp gate. The water crashed through into the hut very fast. My friend and I were the last two to get out and we were very lucky indeed as the door swung outwards so we had a job to open it against the pressure of the water. Many of our friends escaped by climbing onto the roof while others swam to the bank. Only one Frenchman got drowned. One hut nearby with around 90 Russian women in it rocked about for a moment like Noah's Ark on the foaming waves and then just shattered and sank.

'I thought the dam broke in two stages because the first wave that came down to Neheim was nine metres high and this was followed by a second one six metres high. All those people who'd gone to shelter at the Brökelmann aluminium works got drowned. The door of the air raid shelter was not locked or blocked but I remember that it opened inwards so all those on the night shift who'd chosen to go inside were pushed back by the pressure of the water.

'The next morning we had to line up facing the factory while the Germans searched for the victims. When the cellar had been pumped out, I went down and saw my dead friends hanging there squashed between the heating pipes and the ceiling. They'd climbed up there in a desperate search for air. I couldn't find anyone who'd actually seen the terrible things that had gone on in that shelter. About 60 bodies were laid out without coffins opposite the factory. Later they were taken away in a truck, but I never knew where.

'They gave me a shovel and I helped to put the bed of the River Möhne back to rights. While we were doing this, we kept finding bodies, mainly of Russian women. After the disaster the Germans let us have civilian clothes sent from France and we were allowed to move freely around Neheim, which we couldn't do before the catastrophe. Also, after the tragedy, we were no longer guarded.'

Another eyewitness in Neheim was Willy Kaufmann: 'There was an air raid warning on. From the houses on the Wiedenberg where I lived I saw these peculiar mushroom-shaped clouds rising up over a wood on the horizon towards the Möhne dam. A bit later neighbours heard a roaring and rumbling noise in the distance rather like trains but they didn't attach any importance to it. Suddenly this loud shrieking echoed through the night — a signal to us that something terrible must have happened. I immediately got the feeling — especially because I'd seen those mushroom clouds — that the Möhne dam had been hit. It engulfed the Russian camp between the river and the millrace. I told my wife to get a pillow and the little boy; I'd get the air raid pack from the cellar and the kitbag with the kind of valuables that everyone took with them when there was a raid. Outside, the commotion and the rushing noise got louder and louder. There was already water underfoot when I left the cellar. Then I ran fast up the road, uphill. I called out to my wife: "Further up! Further up!"

'I saw the houses in our neighbourhood collapse — they made a horrible cracking noise, just like you get when a dentist wrenches out a tooth. We had to hold one of our neighbours back because he wanted to get back inside his collapsing house to save his relatives. Fortunately they'd got out by another route across the Werler Strasse and then up to the Totenberg; in all the confusion he hadn't noticed this. The Volkshalle was also totally wrecked but the French prisoners of war managed to escape the same way up the hill. You could hear the noise of the water for at least a quarter of an hour before it got down to Neheim. I saw the electricity pylons in the valley bend over and go under with a flash. Two motor boats from the lake that had somehow survived the drop through the breach in the dam were racing through between the houses. They were elegantly swimming along with the current through the whirlpools. Sometimes it seemed as though they'd be dashed to pieces against one of the houses that were still standing but, just before, they turned abruptly away and floated along with the current until they got stranded somewhere.

'Our house stayed up, but the staircase was gone; the water stood 20cm above the ground-floor windows. The whole roof of a building came thrusting down with the current towards a house which was still standing. We thought it would smash into it and carry it away but in the end the roof ran aground.'

The overgrown foundations of the Russian barrack huts still visible 40 years later.

On May 18, 1943, Luftgaubildstelle VI (Luftgau Photographic Section 6) ordered Oberstleutnant von Groote to carry out a photo reconnaissance of the course of the Möhne floods. The photographs were taken to the scale of 1:8000 from a height of 1600 metres with a large-format camera. The first exposure was taken at 11 a.m. — 34 hours after the attack. The coverage stretched from the Möhne reservoir to the city of Essen, the light grey strip indicating the 120-kilometre trail of destruction. [1] The breached Möhne — the seat of the disaster. The 120,000 kVA power station immediately under the dam has completely disappeared and the southern power station is irreparably damaged. When the extent of the breach was realised, the sluice gates at the far, eastern end of the reservoir (out of the picture to the right) were closed to prevent the water reserves in the Wamel Basin from being lost as well. [2] Two bends in the valley south-east of Niederense [3]. [4] Site of the Porta Coeli church. *Below right:* [5] The built-up area of Neheim where the swollen Möhne [6] flows into the River Ruhr [7] where the bridge [8] has withstood the backed-up floodwaters.

[9] The watercourse, known locally as the Mühlen or Obergraben, which supplied water to several firms and fed the hydro-electric turbines of the Brökelmann electrical company and which once flowed out of the Möhne below the Wiedenberg hill [10], has been completely filled with gravel and stones. *Below left:* [11] The spot known as 'Im Ohl' where a bank of several hundred thousand cubic metres of rubbish and stones is now blocking the valley. This impeded the flow of water thereby causing stretches of the lower Möhne valley to remain submerged. [12] The badly damaged bridge across the Ruhr near Haus Füchten (a stately home).

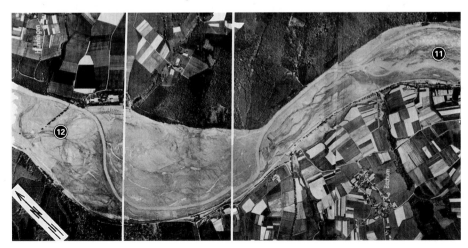

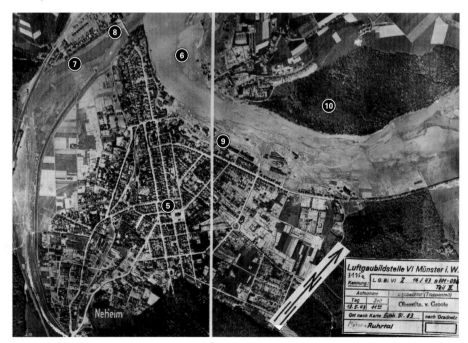

Along this whole section of the Ruhr valley between Echthausen [13] and Warmen [14] the floodwaters destroyed railway lines and bridges as well as waterworks and power stations. The water also washed away the topsoil and deposited mud and debris over everything in its path. Above Echthausen, where the Ruhr curves round at its northernmost point, while the basic structure of the large waterworks has survived, the weirs and machinery have been destroyed and their settlement tanks have silted up. At Wickede [15], the weirs of the Soest waterworks and the municipal power station have disappeared. Twenty-two kilometres downstream from the Möhne dam, a section of the Wickede railway bridge [16] lies in the bed of the River Ruhr. The line between the Ruhrgebiet and Kassel remained cut at this point for weeks, something not picked up by the British photo-reconnaissance interpreters. Large areas of Wickede are underwater. *Below:* The ruined road bridge [17] on the B63 from Wickede to Menden.

Hermann Kerstholt, a patient at a military hospital in Arnsberg, was spending the weekend at Wickede.

'On Mothers' Day, my eldest children and I went to Echthausen to see my mother-in-law, who lived on higher ground in the village. I stayed there the night and was woken up by a violent tremor. The timber-framed house was shaking in every joint and it seemed to heave. I got up and found my sister-in-law on the landing. She said, "Hermann, what on earth's going on? Those planes are flying very low."

"Yes, I can hear them, too", I replied. I suddenly felt very uneasy indeed and went to the window from where I had a good night view over the Ruhr valley. About half an hour later, I heard a strange noise. I thought the planes had hit a train in the Ruhr valley. There was a noise like you get when you run off water, and this got much louder. Then I made out what looked like a grey wall — a foaming flood rolling down the valley. Floating along on the top were sections of huts with people on them signalling with lamps. There were also steady lights moving around, and sometimes lights flared up and went out like you get when you strike a match and throw it down. When I saw the water carrying the huts down from Neheim, I immediately thought of my relations sitting downstream at Wickede in their comfortable air raid shelter. Whenever there was an air raid, they would go straight down there.

'I ran quickly to my uncle's house (Herr Rasche, the mayor) in Echthausen, who had a telephone and phoned through to Wickede and told them to leave the shelter as fast as possible and get to where they'd be safe from the flood. I was going to run down to Wickede from Echthausen straightaway but that was impossible because all the bridges had gone. The Ruhr valley was deep in surging floodwater and the bridge to Menden had gone too. I reached Wickede by going over the hills at the edge of the forest. There was a great stretch of water as far as the eye could see but not a soul in sight so I went back to Echthausen feeling really worried. I kept wondering whether my relations had managed to escape. The telephone lines to Wickede were dead but, in the event, my relations had survived.'

Despite its weight, this train (44215) was derailed in the station at Wickede.

Railway wagons were washed away and deposited outside the local cinema!

'We'd been rudely awakened by the alarm', recalls Karl Brockmeier, 'and then after a while there was an eerie feeling outside. We called the Quenters, our neighbours, but there was no answer. We later found out they'd already left the house after receiving a telephoned warning. I ran downstairs and opened the front door only to see the floodwater coming towards me. We ran up to the attic carrying our baby and from the window we saw the seething water. The situation was desperate. I climbed onto the roof of the adjacent workshop, which belonged to the Quenter firm, and tried to get help. And then came our dramatic rescue.

'My daughter — she was 12 years old at the time — had previously found a long piece of rope in the road. She'd taken it to school because the teacher was going to find out who it belonged to but he'd told her to keep it. This rope turned out to be our salvation. Terrified as we were, I tied the rope around the chimney and threw it over to our neighbours' window, the Rennebaums. They quickly attached their end and I did a tight-rope act, sliding three metres above the seething water with my daughter in front of me. My wife waited in the attic with the baby while I was trying to get help at the Rennebaums. But then the chimney gave way and the whole of the Quenter's house got swept away by the water. Their roof was carried over and got stuck on the roof of the metalwork building. My wife and baby were in the roof timbers and they got carried off with it. She was injured by falling tiles and the baby was in such a state from all the blood that we really feared for his life and it was a further six hours before they were rescued.

'I found an odd pair of boots in the mud and was the first to go into the Henke's house where I saw the mother and her four children lying dead in the mud. Herr Bauer was standing at the corner of Ringstrasse and Hauptstrasse cursing this nice present which the Führer had given us. This was reported to the Gestapo and they took him off to the police station for questioning.

'A few days later there was another full-scale alarm when the Sorpe dam was supposed to have been hit but fortunately this turned out to be a false alarm. It was a good eight days before we could start looking for our belongings. We found our sewing machine in the hedge at Koch's chain factory. I carried on looking — but it was a pointless task — and when we got back the sewing machine had already gone. They looked after us at the inn which was run by the Arndt family. We saw all the people who'd drowned. I got my Communion picture back sometime later. It was dated 1913 and had been washed down as far as Fröndenberg. It was all that was left of our household possessions.'

The centre of destruction in the small town of Wickede. The water steamrollered its way through the town, sweeping all in its path. The photograph was taken on the corner of Hauptstrasse and Ringstrasse near the place where today the memorial stands dedicated to those who lost their lives in the flood.

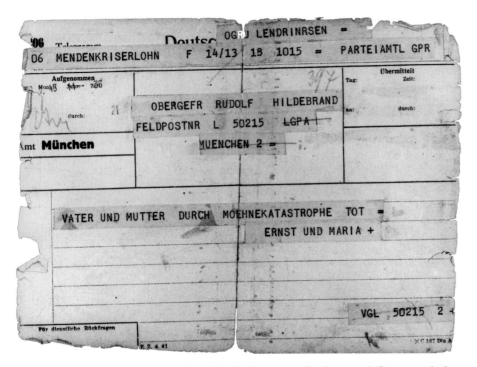

'Flood disaster due to enemy action. Family house totally destroyed. Parents missing. Return at once', said the first telegram sent to Obergefreiter Rudolf Hillebrand serving with the Afrika Korps near Tunis. Two days later came the second telegram *(above)* with tragic news from Ernst and Maria: 'Father and mother killed in Möhne disaster'.

The identification of the dead proved extremely difficult in Wickede as some of them had been washed downstream from Neheim and Günne. Other bodies were still being found months later as far away as the Essen area. A dossier was prepared containing information about where each corpse had been found with a description of personal possessions.

'At the time I was 16 years old and lived in the Ringstrasse at Wickede with my mother, grandmother and two brothers', remembers Hanna Maria Kampschulte. 'My father was in the forces. Following the air raid warning and the explosions — you could really feel the blast from one of them — we children had gone back to bed and were expecting the All Clear. But mother couldn't settle down and went from one window to another listening into the night. At around twenty to two, she woke us up saying, "There's an awful rushing noise outside and it's getting foggy even though there's a full moon. Get up at once. I'm sure they've hit the Möhne dam."

'I ran over to the window and saw water pouring round all the houses just like a huge grey lindworm. I shouted, "Water! Water!" and woke my brother and grandmother, who at the age of 82 had no idea at all what was going on. We went up into the attic. Mother took little Udo up there and we both went back down again to get some things from the wardrobes. When we went down for the second time, the water had already reached the top floor and was gushing out through the windows. All five of us cowered in the attic; little Udo was crying bitterly because he was tired and didn't understand what was happening to him. Down below we could hear the terrible noise of rushing water and a clattering; but this was being drowned out by cries for help. Mother took Udo on her lap, hugged him and said to us, "We're all going to die together. We're all going to drown; no one will be able to help us!" My brother, Willi, looked through the skylight and shouted that the Meier's house next door had already gone. There would have been seven people in there — father, mother and five little children. I pulled him away from the window and just then I saw the Gerdes' big pear tree opposite tear away the whole front of their house. For a while the house stood there — sliced through from the roof right down to

the level of the water. You could see them crouching on the floor, praying in the candle-light. Then a massive wave came along and they tumbled over each other on the floor. That big house and all the people just sank into the water like a vanishing spectre.

'We all held on to each other praying, sobbing and crying. Then there was a slight jerk and we started to sink. Before we knew what was happening, water started lapping around our feet. Then my mother said, "Hannchen, you can swim, and Willi will have to try. Perhaps you can save yourselves. Whatever will daddy do without us!" The floor pushed us up against the roof timbers and we got stuck. I reached up above my head and felt the laths and the tiles. With a final effort I pushed some tiles out, squeezed my head through and then I could breathe again. The roof was being carried along by the current. I clambered up and pushed some clothes through the hole in the hope someone would grab them. I took some more tiles off but I couldn't see anyone.

'The roof which had saved me gradually disintegrated until it finally fell apart completely and sank. A section of flooring which came floating past became my next raft. All around me were doors, bit of furniture, barrels, boxes and cows — some dead and some still mooing. And in amongst all of this were dead and injured people. When my piece of flooring fell apart I grabbed hold of a door and climbed onto it. I suddenly heard cries for help in the mist and shouted out, "Who's there?" It was our neighbour, Franz Lohage, who had his mother and a Fraulein Neurath with him. They were being carried off in different directions. Then I bumped into a weir and fell into a whirlpool which was two or three metres deep. When this happened, I lost my door. I struggled and struggled but there was no escaping. Amongst all the debris was a broken telegraph pole and this came towards me. I tried to grab it, but it was turning and difficult to hold on to. Nevertheless

Left: **On Friday, May 21, a large group of mourners assembled on the Platz der Wurag in Wickede. The coffins, bedecked with wreaths, have been placed between four columns.**
Right: **Before the cortège moved off to the cemetery, Kreisleiter Ernst addressed the mourners: 'After three and a half years of war, the homeland and the armed forces stand together in closed ranks. The enemy knows this too and is therefore trying to bring the homeland down with his contemptible terror raids. With the raid on the Möhne dam he murdered** peaceful, sleeping people — men, women and children. We convey our deepest sympathy to the relatives of the dead for their grave misfortune. Through their sacrifice for the coming victory they have paid a great toll in human life. The enemy will encounter courageous and stout hearts here in the homeland, too, if he attacks this community of people who stand together unshakeably united in their absolute and unreserved trust in the Führer.' The unidentified were buried in a mass grave. In all, 118 of the town's inhabitants were drowned.**

I did get out of the whirlpool with the help of this twisting piece of wood. A wardrobe, a bedstead and then another door saved me after this. I went down the Löhn on the door towards a row of houses. There were lights in the windows and people reached out to help me. The door and I hit the first house; my raft started to spin taking me with it and then I hit another house. I crashed into it again and again. It all seemed absolutely hopeless. The people at the windows even tried throwing a rope down to me but it was no good. Then I went over a railway embankment, and came out of the main current into a stretch of calm water where I got stuck in a row of dead willows near the road to Fröndenburg — I had been swept nearly ten kilometres from Wickede by the torrent.

'I was hoarse from all the shouting. I climbed up into a willow. All the debris was piling up higher and higher in front of me. And then I saw a cow that had somehow survived. All night long this cow tried to climb up to me with its front legs, and it started licking my feet. Every time it moved, the trees creaked and groaned and bent over more and more. I was afraid they wouldn't stand the strain. I took some of my clothes off so I'd be able to move more easily if I had to jump back into the water. I also wanted to cover my feet and stop the cow coming up. I was coated in mud and clay and freezing cold. I was totally exhausted and it was as much as I could do to call for help. No one replied.

'Things gradually quietened down and it began to get light and as dawn broke the water started to subside. I thought I could hear voices in the distance and I called for help again. Someone tried to keep my spirits up from the bank saying that as soon as the water dropped a bit more they would come and rescue me. At around eight o'clock, I saw a man up to his shoulders in water feeling his way over to the tree which had saved my life. He picked me up in his strong arms and carried me over to dry land. He was from Frohnhausen and was home on leave; he was later killed in the war. I was taken to a farmer's house where they washed me, gave me some dry clothes and put me in bed to get warm. But I couldn't sleep and went back to have another look at the place where I'd been rescued. On the railway embankment they'd collected a whole lot of drowned people; they'd been horribly knocked about. Among them were some neighbours. The bodies were taken to the hospital yard at Fröndenberg to be cleaned up and identified. At lunchtime, I heard about three other people from my neighbourhood who'd been rescued and I went over to see them. We hugged and were glad to see each other. In the afternoon we went back to Wickede but there was a great mass of stones where our house had been — just mud and muck. I went to my uncle and aunt's house. When I went in they thought they'd seen a ghost — I must have looked like one in my black clothes which belonged to the farmer's grandmother — nothing else fitted me!

'My father arrived home on leave the next day — a sad reunion because I was all he had left. We borrowed some bicycles and rode over to Fröndenberg to try to find our next of kin and identify them. They'd already found my grandmother, my mother and Udo. They were lying amongst the other bodies laid out in long rows in the mortuary and in the hospital yard. Simple pine coffins had been prepared. They put mother with Udo in her arms in one coffin; granny was in the next one.

'We didn't find Willi. My father had presumably picked him out from a photograph but in the meantime he'd been buried in Fröndenberg with the unidentified dead. Father really wanted to bring him back to Wickede to be with the rest of the family so he went to the cemetery at Fröndenberg with some of his colleagues. Unfortunately they'd numbered the photographs and the coffins, not the actual graves, and after opening four graves without finding Willi, my father gave up.'

The destruction of the railway bridge at Wickede caused the most serious interruption to one of the main stretches of the German Reichsbahn network, the line leading from the Ruhrgebiet to Kassel. The stone abutment piers had been torn apart and a mass of twisted

girders and rails, derailed engines and rolling stock were evidence of the awesome power of the water. Long stretches of embankment and track between Wickede and Neheim had been torn up and washed away.

As the route was a major supply line between the Ruhr and the Eastern Front, the repair of the bridge was given top priority and army engineers were immediately drafted in to begin building a new bridge. Kompanie 2A of Eisenbahn-Pionier-Bataillon I based at Fürstenwalde, near Berlin, were detached to Wickede and they arrived to begin work at 5 a.m. on May 24.

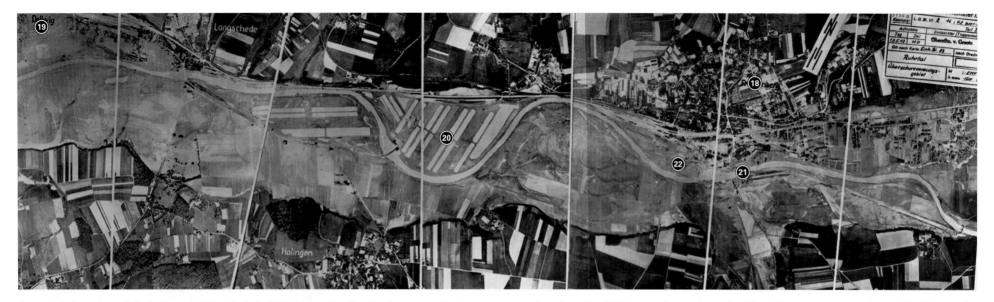

An aerial view from Fröndenberg [18] to Dellwig [19] where the floodwaters spread out across the full width of the Ruhr valley. This section of the valley was of particular interest to the British photo-reconnaissance interpreters and aerial photographs of the Frönden-berg-Bösperde region were splashed across the pages of the world's press. Easily recognisable are the reservoirs [20] in the loop of the river near Fröndenberg which provided drinking water. Initially the damage to the water supply industry seemed enormous — the Möhne reservoir was, after all, the mainstay for the entire Westphalian industrial region to the east of the Rhine with its some four and a half million inhabitants. However, the requirements of the Ruhr coalfields during the summer of 1943 were met by calling upon other deposits. Water was drawn from the River Lippe; more was pumped back from the Rhine to the lower reaches of the Ruhr, and further reserves were obtained from the Sorpe reservoir. The sewage treatments works in the Ruhr valley were also badly affected and there was considerable damage to the pumping station and the new sewage works at Frön-denberg. In the picture, the old works are buried under gravel; the feeder channel is destroyed; the bed of the River Ruhr has shifted, and masses of earth from the flood embankment of the new sewage works have been washed over to the far bank. The flood-waters have also destroyed the hutted camp [22] where Russian prisoners of war were housed, claiming the lives of 30 prisoners and four guards.

Fröndenberg was a total disaster area and Helene Schulte wrote to her brother in Berlin on May 30 describing the general mood in the town:

'Dear Adolf. I don't even feel like talking about what happened, but since you asked I'm writing briefly to tell you (in fact eight closely-typed pages!). I still can't get over how any country could go about things in such a slap-dash way. Experts must surely have known the danger and been able to work out how high the water would rise. If they'd done this, people could have been told what to do. The waters reached us two hours after the Möhne dam had been breached. And what a lot could have been done during that time. People and livestock need not have been lost and so much property could have been saved. All that was needed was a sense of responsibility and a bit of organisation. So here we are amongst the rubble, having escaped death by the skin of our teeth and hardly able to bear the stench of decay. There are cracks in the Sorpe dam too, and so that may be another thing to delight us at some future date. We're sitting on a powder keg, and wake up with a start every time we hear a shout or someone running. From time to time the sirens fail and then men ride through the streets on bicycles blowing horns and shouting that there's an air raid warning. Sometimes you just hear the horns and then I think of the water. The man with the horn doesn't dare go into the danger zone. This alarm business is particularly nerve-racking at night. If that wasn't enough, during the first weeks those people whose cellars were full of water ran around like hunted animals and all streamed up to the air raid shelters at houses on higher ground.

'At about a quarter to three on the night of the raid, we heard the sirens of the emergency services in the far distance. At the same time we heard a noise like goods trains being shunted. Then things started happening thick and fast; it was just a matter of sec-onds. From over by the River Ruhr we could hear people shouting, "Get back, the water's coming." When the water arrived, it didn't come up through the cellar like with normal floods. Instead it came roaring through the streets and smashed its way into the houses. The cellar filled up more or less at once, but we brought some oil paintings and a child from there. When we got back up, we were soaked through. Then the electricity failed and all the lights went out. Luckily we had a candle handy and we put it on the attic stairs to give us some emergency lighting.

'As the water rose, all we could think was that the whole house would be overwhelmed by the flood and that we wouldn't live to see the morning. If you hadn't seen it, you could-n't imagine what a monstrous thing that raging and ever-rising torrent was. The moon was shining so you could see everything quite clearly. I kept shining a torch down the stairs to see how long it would be before the water reached us. The high-water mark was six cen-timetres below the level of the first-floor ceiling. We sat upstairs wet through and exhausted among all the wreckage; all we had was one small candle, but we were happy enough that the water had stopped rising. We shared out cognac from a flask and even gave some to the child because it was chilled to the bone. Then we blew out the candle and hung out of the window. However, our problems were not yet over because our house was the first in the row and everything came straight at us: bits of bridges, fences, walls from weekend chalets complete with doors and window frames, sections of cowsheds and so on. We kept thinking the house would collapse but it held. More than 160 bodies were washed down to Fröndenberg. Most were identified by their next of kin, who'd come try-ing to find them, but it was impossible to identify 26 of them. These were buried at Frön-denberg after they'd been photographed.

The road bridge, [21] on the aerial photograph opposite, from Fröndenberg to Menden (in the foreground) was swept away as was the heavy girder railway bridge beyond.

The steel section of the double-track railway bridge was ripped in two and carried almost 100 metres from its foundations to the south bank of the river.

'The situation here was less severe than in the narrower Ruhr valleys further upstream. The stricken area presents a picture of devastation. Gardens have been washed away, trees ripped out and mounds of the most incredible stuff deposited. There are 2,000 servicemen here as well as people from the Reichsarbeitsdienst (Reich Labour Service), the SA and 800 men from the Organisation Todt. The Women's Organisation, the Bund Deutscher Mädel (League of German Girls) and girls' schools from Unna, Hamm and Iserlohn arrived to provide domestic help. The soldiers who've been on permanent duty in the bombed cities have run out of sympathy for the fate of individuals. However, they do say that although they've seen plenty in Essen, Dortmund and other places, water is worse than fire. My fingers were all bleeding and swollen from where I'd been scratching around in the mud looking for our papers and things in the cellar. Our files were floating around down there, and most of them fell apart after their soaking. The savings books were later found by chance in a field.

'It wasn't until Friday evening that we got drinking water again; we just sat there every day in all that mud and muck. In the morning I just spat on my hands and wiped my face. Due to the lack of water, the sanitary conditions were quite indescribable; then there was the psychological pressure — a wrecked flat — with hunger, thirst, no cooking facilities, no lights, no dishes; and to cap it all, not a kind word from anyone. Johanna was the only one to come. They brought hot coffee — real coffee — along the streets but not along ours, the one nearest to the river. When I complained, they sent a truck along with some of the real coffee. In the meantime, there were special rations — but what's the good of asparagus if you've got no means of cooking it. It was only thanks to a couple of soldiers — one from Cologne with his dialect and dry sense of humour and another from Detmold — that my low spirits were lifted somewhat. They were so willing and understanding.

'However, the worst thing was during the cleaning up. It nearly gave me a heart attack. We'd just collected the muddy clothes from the cellar when the following happened. At around midday, when the soldiers had gone off to get their food, a piercing shriek echoed through the streets. "Flood! Get out of the houses and up to the Sümberg!" I couldn't take it in. In a flash all the staff had done a bunk; just one nice young girl hung on and took the dirty clothes upstairs for me so they didn't all float off again. I couldn't have cared less. I was sick to death of it all. But patrols went through all the houses and I was forced to leave. The story was that the Sorpe had been hit. An hour later, they let us come back — a false alarm! Can you imagine anything like it? Fancy giving people here a shock like that. Our nerves were already at breaking point. The false alarm originated from Neheim where they'd arranged that if there was to be another dam disaster they would ring the church bells. (There would have been no point in doing that here. Our beautiful bells, which had been spared during the First World War owing to their distinctive tone, had long since gone to be melted down for the arms drive.) By the way, we could have made a fish dish because there were certainly plenty of fish lying around in the flat.

'Now I've probably told you enough and will close. I've made a carbon copy of this letter and in the future I'll give it to anyone who wants to know what happened. I don't want to say any more. I've borrowed this typewriter from the office, but I can't keep it any longer. You mustn't think I've exaggerated any of this; on the contrary. It's just not possible to describe the terror of it all. Down below in the house everything is in such a mess, but up here we've got a brilliant view — from the bedroom you can see right over to Schwitten because all the trees have gone.

Lots of love, Helene'

With both means of crossing the river gone, people have gathered on the far bank on the left to be ferried across the Ruhr by boat.

The funeral service for the Fröndenberg victims took place on Saturday, May 22, at the war memorial below the cemetery. No crosses adorned the coffins which had been placed on gun carriages beneath the flags and standards of the Third Reich. In their speeches, regional and district officials did their best to channel the sorrow of the bereaved into feelings of hate and revenge. Such mass funerals provided the authorities with an opportunity for propaganda and the public were exhorted to remain steadfast. The victims were then carried to their final resting place to the beat of muffled drums, priests and family members following at the rear of the cortège.

Some 45 kilometres further downstream from the dam lies Schwerte where the warning came at 3 a.m. although the reason was not given as Party officials wanted to avoid a panic, hoping that the current would lose its strength by the time the water spread out on the broad flatlands of the Ruhr valley. But when the flood reached the town at 5.15 a.m. it was still very strong and houses were swallowed up in seconds. In the event, the floodwater took four hours to pass through the town. [24] Geisecke. [25] Rheinen.

Some 45 kilometres further downstream lies Schwerte where Elfriede Pitzer was living.

'There was a full-scale alert in progress which lasted all night. At some time during the night the volunteer fire brigade moved into the Mühlenstrasse under Chief Fire Officer Kathol, who was in charge at that time. It seems the alarm had been raised at the fire station. There was some talk of flooding but you couldn't get anything definite. My mother, Auguste Grewe, asked the fire officer once more but he calmed her saying, "It's not as bad as all that, grandma. Even if the flood water does come up, we'll be here to help." In spite of these comforting words, my mother got me to dress my paralysed sister, Hanna, who slept in the back bedroom of the downstairs flat, and bring her up. A fireman helped to carry her. Just as I was about to go back downstairs with him, we were caught on the staircase by the water which was rushing in. A fireman who'd been standing in front of our house probably saw the wave at the lower end of the Mühlenstrasse. He came charging up our stairs leaving the front door open. This must have happened just as we were putting Hanna onto a table in my flat. I didn't see the other fireman until he was already in the attic. I thought my mother must have gone up there, too; she was not among those who'd escaped. So she must have still been in her flat. Partly because of the open front door, the water forced its way into the ground floor, thus making it impossible for my mother to get to the stairs, which would have saved her. The emergency services rescued us later with a rowing boat which they put up against the back windows of the top flat. When the water started to recede, the body of my mother was recovered from the flat below. Thus my mother, Auguste Grewe, at the age of 78 had become a victim of this senseless disaster.'

Speaking later of the recovery operation, Walter Schuhmacher said that 'we approached the rear of the Grewe's house in a rowing boat. The current was strong. We moored the boat temporarily at the corner of the shed and looked in through the window of the downstairs flat. There was a bed floating around in the room and we poked it with our oars. All of a sudden, a hand came out from under the bedstead. Once we had made quite sure the woman was dead, we looped our rope around the hand and towed the body over to the bank.'

Operations underway on Monday morning in Schwerte to rescue people trapped on roofs and upper floors. *Left:* French POWs on the roof of their billet. *Below:* Siegfried, the dark brown gelding, is led to safety by 17-year-old Günter Swolana in the flooded Hellpoth-Strasse. When the waves rolled in, the horse was tethered in a stable belonging to the Havers family behind the inn, Im Reiche des Wassers. Terrified by the swiftly rising water, the animal broke free and climbed onto bales of straw and remained there until released in the morning. The occupants of the Nierhoff store watch from their open windows.

The spectacular railway viaduct at Herdecke on the section of line between Hagen and Dortmund became operational in 1879. It carried the double-track railway line 314 metres across the River Ruhr and had 11 columns each 31.5 metres in height. Over the years, this famous landmark had survived many a knock as floods swept down the valley.

However, this time, the force of the 120 million cubic metres of water from the breached dam, 56 kilometres away, succeeded in pushing over the fifth column from the Herdecke bank sending the two arched sections on either side, each one some 20 metres wide, crashing into the waters below.

Ulrich Hake, who was at that time employed by the Reichsarbeitsdienst, was returning to his unit in Lippstadt.

'As per the timetable, passenger train No. 1435 to Dortmund South left Platform 5 of the main station at Hagen at 13.30 on May 17, 1943. I was sitting in one of the carriages looking out of the window as the train travelled at about 20 kph in a wide curve over the Herdecke viaduct. All of a sudden, one of the columns collapsed and the tracks were left hanging across the gap. I wrenched the door open and jumped head over heels out of the moving train and down the gravel embankment. One of the female ticket inspectors also jumped out and the train stopped almost at once. Passengers had pulled the emergency brake. The train came to a halt a third of the way along the track leading to the viaduct. The staff let the passengers get out of the leading carriages and they slowly walked back past the train to the start of the viaduct. The train remained in that position for about an hour while the staff discussed what to do. Finally the engine pulled the carriages back along that section of track really slowly so that the viaduct, which was still shaking, should not be subjected to any further vibration. When we had all got back on, the train reversed to the main railway station at Hagen. I reached my destination, Lippstadt, by a roundabout route and got into trouble from my superiors because I was late. Even today, I still get an uneasy feeling when I go over the Herdecke viaduct.'

This was the scene confronting the driver of Train 1435 as he approached the viaduct. The train had left Hagen railway station for Dortmund-Süd punctually at 13.30 and narrowly escaped disaster when the driver managed to bring the train to a halt just before the abyss. Some daring souls, undeterred by the boiling waters below, are reputed to have clambered across to the Herdecke side with their suitcases!

That night, Wilhelm Duhme was on duty and going about his duties as a track inspector.

'The viaduct was vibrating because of the pressure from the mass of water. I was on my tour of inspection and had just passed the place where the break later occurred when one of the columns collapsed. I immediately ran towards the oncoming passenger train from Hagen which had just stopped on the viaduct. The driver had probably received the order to drive slowly and seen the viaduct collapse.'

Lotte Buerstätte was a schoolgirl travelling on the train and recalls that 'the train had been going along at walking pace for a long time. It was overcrowded and I remember that it was very long. We schoolgirls didn't know what had happened during the night. Our fellow passengers seemed very uneasy and all of a sudden we saw an appallingly horrific scene outside — an immense, seething mass of water roaring and gurgling along. It was filled with trees, roofs and animals. Then a scream went through the compartment. Through the train window we saw the masonry from one of the columns of the viaduct crash into the raging waters. Spray splashed right up, the train stopped, and we jumped out of the compartment. We just ran and ran along the embankment towards Vorhalle.'

On May 19, British photo-reconnaissance aircraft took this shot of the shattered Herdecke viaduct and King George VI showed particular interest in a stereoscopic image of this picture when he visited Scampton on May 27 (see page 167). Viewed in three dimensions, the perspective of the railway lines hanging between the columns coupled with the shadow cast by the viaduct must have conveyed a vivid impression of the force of the disaster which had befallen the Ruhr valley.

Four Nazi officials contemplate the damage below the Hohensyburg near Westhofen where the flood has covered the entire width of the Ruhr valley. To the right of the picture can be seen part of a large shed belonging to the Brüninghaus steelworks. On the ridge in the background is the Vincke Tower.

In the Ruhr valley, between Dellwig and Rheinen, the main casualty was the Dortmund waterworks which suffered when 74,500 square metres of filter beds and a water catchment area of 690,000 square metres were silted up. Workers from the Organisation Todt, the Reichsarbeitsdienst, and the water company itself removed mud from the affected areas. A 200-metre section of the railway line to Ergste was also destroyed and the basins of the waterworks disappeared under water.

Downstream from Neheim to Schwerte, the width of the flood wave in the valley varied from 800 to 1200 metres. From Schwerte to Baldeneysee, the waters similarly extended to a width of between 400 and 1200 metres. In low-lying areas of the valley along the 150-kilometre stretch from the Möhne dam to the confluence of the Ruhr with the Rhine, the water extended to a width of five kilometres in places.

Near Westhofen, a suburb of Schwerte, close to where the River Lenne flows into the Ruhr, is the Hengstey Lake where the foundations of the four-track railway bridge were damaged by erosion of the river bed. For some days after the disaster, this bridge provided the only crossing point over the Möhne and Ruhr rivers between the dam and Hagen. Coking plants around Dortmund and Hamm were forced to shut down because of a shortage of water and this in turn led to problems with gas supplies. For a period of several days, the output from coking plants in the Ruhrgebiet was halved, thus necessitating drastic cut-backs.

The barrages of the Ruhr Valley Dams Association at the Hengstey Lake, and at Stiftsmühle between Hengstey and Harkortsee, were also silted up or suffered damage when their embankments were washed away. As soon as it was realised that the Möhne dam had been breached, the contents of the Hengstey and Harkort Lakes (some 6.1 million cubic metres of water) were released, thus enabling at least part of the Möhne floodwaters to be absorbed by these two reservoirs.

The power station at Herdecke, (some 60 kilometres downstream from the dam) with an output of 132,000kW was, at the time, a key element in the network of the Rheinisch-Westfälisches Elektrizitätswerk. The machine rooms were left under some two metres of water thus causing electricity supplies to be interrupted for 14 days. The power station at Harkortsee was similarly affected.

In the upper Ruhr valley, the flood wave could not be measured because the instruments for recording water levels had not been designed for such magnitudes. The following times with associated high-water levels and peak flows were logged on May 17, 1943: Witten 10.30, 6.98m, 3000 cubic metres per second; Hattingen Railway Bridge 14.00, 6.30m, 2600 cubic metres per second; Horst 16.00, 7.12m, 2500 cubic metres per second, Spillenburg 16.30, 6.40m, 2400 cubic metres per second; Mülheim 22.45, 5.47m, 1800 cubic metres per second.

In Witten, the Bernhardsglück factory buildings and parts of the town's steelworks were under water, together with eight accommodation huts for workers; the local waterworks were flooded and in the town 200 people made homeless.

As soon as the police radio message was received in Herbede, houses in the Ruhr valley were cleared and the miners brought up from the nearby coalmine belonging to the Bergbau-AG Lothringen. Although the area around the pit was flooded, the shaft itself was protected with sandbags and remained dry.

The wall of water that raced through the valley destroyed no fewer than 178 filter beds, including the primary beds of all the waterworks in the valley — a total area of 1,000,000 square metres, and the Organisation Todt was faced with the immediate task of clearing an area of 8,000,000 square metres. The Reichsarbeitsdienst had the task of restoring the embankments and dykes of the various waterworks and by August 27, 97 filter beds were already operational with a further 20 provisionally ready. Of the 890,000 square metres of land which had been polluted with sewage, by that date 168,000 square metres had been dealt with and a further 190,000 square metres were receiving the attention of the Organisation Todt.

It was only below the Baldeney Lake near Essen, some 120 kilometres downstream from the dam, that water levels failed to reach the record highs of the St Catherine's Day floods of 1890. As the lake had been drained in 1941 to prevent it being used as a landmark by aircraft heading for Essen, it was possible for a substantial amount of water to be diverted into the empty lake which had a capacity of nine million cubic metres. All the lower-lying areas of the Ruhr valley between this point and Mülheim were flooded to widths varying between 900 and 1200 metres.

The flooded Ruhr valley between Witten-Heven and Herbede.

At Gelsenkirchen, the waterworks at Altendorf-Steele with its 32 filter beds, covering a total surface area of 242,000 square metres, were totally covered in mud and parts of the town of Steele were submerged. On May 18, the Essen regional newspaper announced that all drinking water must be boiled and an identical warning appeared in the Dortmund press a few days later. The floods continued down as far as Duisberg-Ruhrort on the Rhine where the water level rose by 1.5 metres.

There was even concern within the Nazi judiciary over the Möhne disaster. At 11.00 on May 17, Herr Hans Semler, President of the Superior Provincial Court in Hamm, acting with the approval of the Chief Public Prosecutor of the Reichsjustizministerium (Reich Justice Ministry) in Berlin, telephoned for the immediate transfer of 1,200 so called 'Nacht und Nebel' prisoners from penal establishments in the Ruhrgebiet. (These prisoners were those arrested under the 'Night and Fog Decree' dating from December 7, 1941, under which 'persons endangering German security' who were not to be executed immediately were to be seized and vanish without trace into the night and fog.) Semler added that the air raids of the previous night had destroyed the Möhne and Eder dams and heavy incendiary raids were now anticipated. He said that the enemy had lately taken to using large aerial mines like the one which had fallen on Bochum, and these could destroy prison walls thus giving the inmates an opportunity to escape.

RAF Bomber Command subsequently decided to capitalise on the lack of water for fire-fighting and launched a follow-up attack against the city of Dortmund — the largest raid in the 'Battle of the Ruhr' which had begun in March. During the night of May 23/24, between 00.57 and 01.56, 724 bombers dropped 2,042 tonnes of HE and incendiary bombs on the city. Pilots reported widespread fires, with smoke rising to 10,000 feet, but the fire services did not encounter any particular difficulties due to a shortage of water. The anti-aircraft defences were overwhelmed by the attack which was centred on the main railway station but 38 British aircraft were lost to flak and night fighters.

Above: **Ninety kilometres west of the dam, the deluge still had the force to sweep locomotives from the rails.** *Below:* **The wrecked railway bridge near Hirsel in the lower Ruhr valley.**

Led by Generaloberst Hubert Weise (nicknamed 'Poison Dwarf'), a group of high-ranking officers arrive to inspect the damage to the Möhne dam on May 18. This picture was taken from the top of the northern tower. *Inset:* The official communiqué issued on behalf of Hitler's headquarters by the Oberkommando der Wehrmacht on May 17.

The general public in Germany were told nothing specific about the disaster which had befallen the Ruhrgebiet. On May 19, local newspapers printed an authorised press release with different headlines but all emphasising a racial element: 'Attack on the dams — inspired by Jews', 'The Jewish attack against the dams' and 'Jewish crimes reach monstrous proportions'.

Reaction in Germany

On May 17, 1943 at 2 p.m., the Grossdeutsche Rundfunk broadcast the official war communiqué with its customary initial announcement before the news. 'Aus dem Führerhauptquartier' (From the Headquarters of the Führer). 'Das Oberkommando der Wehrmacht gibt bekannt' (A bulletin from the Supreme Command of the Armed Forces): 'Successful combat activity is reported from the area of Welikije Luki. In various other sectors of the Eastern Front, surprise attacks by German patrols have overrun and destroyed enemy positions, taking prisoners and capturing equipment. Scattered attacks by Soviet troops have been repulsed, at times in co-operation with the Luftwaffe. During the course of planned strikes on enemy supply lines in the southern and central sectors of the Eastern Front, key railway stations and a number of freight trains of all types were yesterday attacked again by German military aircraft and destroyed.'

Following this long-winded catalogue of insignificant successes on the Eastern Front, the radio went on to report the raids against the dams but its understated words and veiled references played down the attacks. 'The territory of the Reich was penetrated last night by light enemy air formations, which dropped a small number of HE bombs in various places. Two dams were damaged, the ensuing rush of water causing heavy losses among the civilian population. Eight of the attacking aircraft were shot down, nine other enemy aircraft were destroyed over the occupied western areas, including one by the army.'

The German public learned nothing more — not even the names of the dams were mentioned. The authorities did not permit foreign correspondents into the areas affected by the catastrophe on the grounds that since the British had declared the dams to be military targets, accordingly, they formed part of the restricted area. Yet by casting a mantle of silence the Nazi leadership provided material for the rumour to run rife and a shock wave reverberated through the German population — a shock wave that caused perhaps more damage than the floods themselves.

According to the 'confidential bulletins' that were spoon-fed to the regional press offices every day, 'No mention at all must be made of the bombing of the dams'. However, on May 19, the Deutsche Nachrichtenbüro (German News Agency) was forced to concede the truth. Following the laconic reference in the OKW bulletin, regional papers now reported the catastrophe in their circulation areas where it could not be kept secret and, in any case, the death notices of whole families had made the misery public knowledge.

'With regard to the air raid on the dams, the Deutsche Nachrichtenbüro has learned that losses among the civilian population are not as high as had first been assumed. According to official estimates so far, the number of casualties amounts to 370 German dead; 341 prisoners of war of various nationalities have also lost their lives.' This was more or less true as it would have been impossible to give exact figures just two days after the raid and, even today, the exact number of victims is impossible to establish, but it could well exceed 1,400 as the bodies of many of the missing were never found.

Above: **Karl Schütte:** 'Early in the morning, the first senior officer, General Schmidt from Luftgau VI in Münster, landed in a Fieseler Storch to inspect the damage. The officer in charge of our six-gun battery, Leutnant Jörg Widmann, was immediately decorated with the Iron Cross, Second Class. In the afternoon all of us gunners had to parade and, together with six of my pals, I was awarded the Iron Cross, Second Class. We were amazed: after all, the thing which we were supposed to be defending had been destroyed. But apparently our superiors saw things differently. At 20.00 on the evening of May 17, Albert Speer, the Armament Minister, came with a large staff to carry out his own inspection of the damage. Generaloberst Weise, Commander in Chief of Air Defence, inspected the breached dam on May 18. There was another visit on June 9, this time by Dr Wilhelm Frick, the Reich Interior Minister. We had always regarded a posting to the Möhne as a cushy number and called it "the Flak Sanatorium" but Leutnant Widmann would always say: "Listen boys. You really have no idea at all of your responsibility and exactly what depends on the Möhne dam. It supplies all the factories in the Ruhrgebiet". After the raid the whole thing was made into a fortress.' (Note how a white 'kill' ring has already been painted around the barrel of the 2cm FlaK on the northernmost tower.)

News of the destruction of the dams must have come as a bombshell to government circles in Berlin. This is revealed by the confidential entry for May 18 in the diary of the Minister for Propaganda, Joseph Goebbels, although again it, too, suffers from a lack of information and consequently contains many errors. Dr Goebbels noted: 'The English came in with 30 – 40 aircraft across a wide front at altitudes varying between 50 and 300 metres and returned at 3,000 to 5,000 metres. Among others, the Eder, Möhne and Sorpe dams were attacked and badly hit. The enemy aircraft used searchlights to illuminate the Eder and circled overhead for a long time. Then two torpedoes were fired into the reservoir, which was full to the brim, ripping the dam open and leaving a deep breach 40 metres wide. The mass of water gushed out with great force over the surrounding area. Thirty villages were flooded. In some cases these have completely disappeared but in other cases people have managed to save themselves by climbing onto the roofs. A rescue operation has not yet been possible as even the army engineers cannot get there because of the current. We must expect many casualties together with a great loss of livestock.

The battery commander, Leutnant Jörg Widmann, pictured after the award ceremony on Monday afternoon, beside the gun which helped bring down Hopgood's AJ-M.

ORDER OF THE DAY

During the night of May 16/17, 1943, the Möhne dam was attacked at low level by four enemy aircraft which pressed home a series of closely bunched and repeated attacks. The two platoons of 3/840 which were deployed at the Möhne dam under the command of Leutnant Widmann displayed outstanding courage and soldierly fulfilment of duty while engaging the aircraft in the face of repeated attacks and remaining undeterred by the bombs which fell near them. A barrage of accurate fire was kept up until their gun barrels glowed red-hot and resulted, despite the strong armour of the aircraft, in the shooting down of two of them. I express particular recognition to Leutnant Widmann and his gun crews for their exemplary dedication and outstanding performance.

On the day after the raid, Leutnant Widmann and six members of 3/840 were awarded the Iron Cross, Second Class for outstanding bravery.

The above order is to be promulgated before the paraded personnel of all batteries.

OBERST SOUCHON, MAY 17, 1943

Above: **Karl Schütte (right) was the only gunner to survive the war and 25 years later the author interviewed him in front of the rebuilt dam** *(below).* **Now in the uniform of the Bundeswehr, he wears his Iron Cross, Second Class ribbon beside the First Class awarded for service at the front in Italy.**

The Gruppenbefehl for the award incorrectly states that two aircraft were shot down and of course five aircraft made bombing runs, not four. After the award ceremony, the head of the administrative region, Kreisleiter Ernst, issued invitations for a battery celebration at Haus Kleis restaurant in Delecke for which girls from the Bund Deutscher Mädel (League of German Girls) in Körbecke were brought over for the dance.

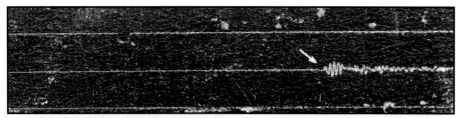

[1] 00:27:29.8 Uhr DSZ

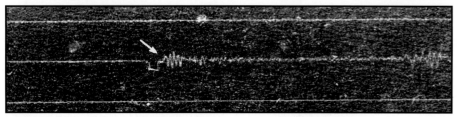

[2] 00:38:04.1 Uhr DSZ

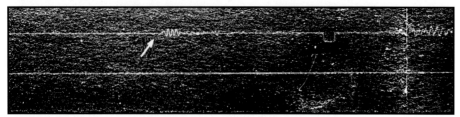

[3] 00:43:51.4 Uhr DSZ

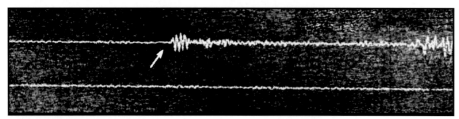

[4] 00:49:29.5 Uhr DSZ

GEOPHYSIKALISCHEN INSTITUT GÖTTINGEN

	Time (DSZ)	Pilot	Period	Maximum Deflection
		Möhne dam		
[1]	00.27:29.8	Gibson	40,8 sec	0,6 mm
[2]	00.38:04.1	Martin	14,9 sec	0,8 mm
[3]	00.43:51.4	Young	2,6 sec	0,2 mm
[4]	00.49:29.5	Maltby	40,5 sec	0,8 mm (Destruction)
		Eder dam		
[5]	01.37:28.1	Shannon	34,0 sec	0,4 mm
[6]	01.50:53.9	Knight	57,0 sec	0,2 mm (Destruction)
		Ennepe dam		
[7]	03.38:	Townsend	Faint mark only	

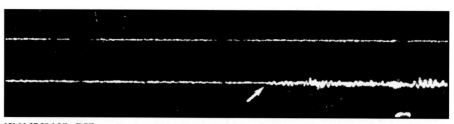

[5] 01:37:28.1 Uhr DSZ

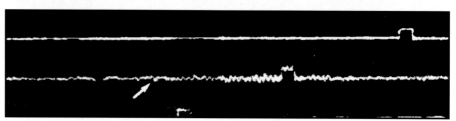

[6] 01:50:53.9 Uhr DSZ

Using the same equipment as is employed to register earthquakes, the seismographs left permanently running at the Geophysical Institute at Göttingen unwittingly recorded the shock-waves of the exploding mines. Of the eleven Upkeeps dropped, four did not register: Hopgood's on the Möhne power station at 00.33; McCarthy's direct hit on the Sorpe at 00.45; Maudslay's which exploded over the Eder at 01.43, and Brown's hit on the Sorpe at 03.14. This is because the explosions occurred either above water or were deadened by the earth embankment of the Sorpe so that less pressure was exerted on the underground rock formations which transmit the shock waves. These illustrations (enlarged) were recently reconstructed by students at the Institute. The arrows show the beginning of each shock wave which, in the case of the Möhne dam 130 kilometres away, took around 20 seconds to reach the instrumentation at a wave running time of 6.5 km/sec. (All times are German Summer Time (DSZ), the same as British Double Summer Time in force in May 1943.)

The Eder was closer at 75 kilometres so for that dam one must only subtract 11½ seconds for the time the shock wave took to reach Göttingen. Thus the actual explosions can now be timed exactly down to a tenth of a second: [1] 00:27:09.8 DSZ. [2] 00:37:44.1 DSZ. [3] 00:43:31.4 DSZ. [4] 00:49:09.5 DSZ. [5] 01:37:16.6 DSZ. [6] 01:50:42.4 DSZ.

This will also be accompanied by a failure of the harvest. The power station has been damaged and the loss of electrical power is still being assessed. Aircraft also attacked the Möhne dam with torpedoes from the water side causing a breach and sweeping away the power station. Severe damage has been caused to water supplies to the Ruhrgebiet, including both drinking water and water for the fire services. There has also been a major loss of electrical power. In the case of the Sorpe, the dam was also damaged and the surrounding area badly flooded. As the telephone lines are all down no further details are available at present.'

Dr Wilhelm Frick (centre), the Minister of the Interior, flanked on his left by the District President from Arnsberg, Lothar Eickhoff, and on his right by Deputy Gauleiter and Reichsverteidigungskommissar Albert Hoffmann of South Westphalia, on the inspection tour of the Möhne dam on June 9. (In May 1945 Frick was arrested by the Allies and put on trial at Nuremberg charged with war crimes. Found guilty of three out of the four charges — waging a war of aggression; the violation of the laws of war; and crimes against humanity, which included persecution and extermination — he was executed in October 1946.)

LOG OF THE KASSEL AIR DEFENCE WARNING HQ

01.11	Report that Möhne dam has been hit.
01.12	Observation post at Waldeck reports a low-flying enemy aircraft.
01.14	Information passed to police.
01.15	Enemy aircraft over Eder reservoir.
01.17	Waldeck reports red flares dropped.
01.20	Waldeck reports single red parachute flare dropped; probable attack on dam.
01.25	Red parachute flare over Eder reservoir.
01.30	Four four-engined aircraft circling low over Eder reservoir.
01.32	Aircraft over Eder reservoir.
01.36	Waldeck, aircraft circling over reservoir.
01.41	Situation unchanged.
01.43	Two four-engined aircraft over Eder reservoir.
01.45	Smoke rising over dam wall [Maudslay's miss?].
01.53	Two four-engined aircraft circling over reservoir.
02.04	Four-engined aircraft in Waldeck area.
02.05	Light over dam.
02.18	Enemy aircraft leaving area of Eder reservoir and heading away north-west.
02.35	One enemy aircraft circling over Marburg/Lahn area [Maudslay?].
02.36	Warning control Bad Wildungen from observation post at Mauserwerk Waldeck: Affoldern under water, houses collapsing.
02.42	Eder dam hit.
03.14	Situation in alert area calming, slight enemy activity to the west of Arnsberg-Münster.

LUFTSCHÜTZWARNKOMMANDO KASSEL
MAY 16/17, 1943.

Following an entry about the war in Serbia, Propaganda Minister Goebbels noted further: 'Last night's air raid has inflicted great damage on us. The attack by British aircraft on our dams was highly successful. The Führer is extremely angry and impatient over the Luftwaffe's lack of preparedness. Initially, dramatic reports came in from the affected Gaus but during the course of the day the effects of the raid are turning out to be less serious than had previously been thought. For a time the talk was of many thousands of victims. Damage to production was more than normal. Gauleiters in all the Gaus containing dams which have not been attacked are naturally most concerned, since the air defences there are quite inadequate. Reports from the Gaus which have been affected by the floods speak for themselves. Unfortunately some people in the ministries are in the habit of panicking, especially Berndt, who bombards me all day long with telephone calls, none of which reveal anything factual.' [Alfred Berndt was a young newspaperman who enjoyed a meteoric career under Goebbels and was one of his most trusted lieutenants.]

'Naturally London is making a meal of its success. Some English photo reconnaissance aircraft have already ascertained that the raid on the dams was successful. In any case, this is what we are admitting in the OKW bulletin. It is only of some consolation that London had three air raid warnings last night. All we did was to carry out nuisance raids on the British capital without managing to cause any particular damage. As far as the air war is concerned the English are now well ahead. They exaggerate in a most irritating way but they can justifiably claim a considerable success. They are promising further heavy raids and are talking about an intensification of the air war. This will certainly give us something to worry about during the weeks and months to come.'

On May 19 Goebbels' private diary adds: 'The English and Americans talk of little else but the air war. Their successful attack on the German dams has caused a great sensation in both London and Washington. They are naturally fully aware of what they have achieved by this attack. Bettany, the former Reuter correspondent in Berlin, has claimed that the plan for the attack was the idea of a Jew who had emigrated from Berlin. I am having this statement summarised into a short bulletin for publication within the territory of the Reich, especially in the areas that suffered the disaster. One sees here how dangerous the Jews are and how right we are to put them behind bars. [This report from Reuters was false.] As can be expected the Americans are sensationalising the extensive flooding of the surrounding area in the wildest possible way. The consequences are certainly quite devastating for our armament industry. Thank God the number of dead is not as high as was at first feared. The English and Americans are already talking of 10,000 dead. In fact the number stands at between 1,000 and 2,000. As far as this whole raid is concerned the fact that the English were so well informed convinces me that treachery was afoot even within the Reich itself. Furthermore after the raid they had such precise intelligence about the damage they had inflicted, it is hard to believe this was obtained solely from photo reconnaissance.'

After some entries about conduct of the war, Propaganda Minister Goebbels went on to write further about the catastrophe: 'The devastation which has been caused to the dams does not seem to be quite as great at we had first expected. However, it is nonetheless sufficient to cause considerable difficulties for our industries along the Ruhr and Rhine. Initially the talk was of between 5,000 and 7,000 dead, but it now emerges there

Gemeinsamer Kampf aller gegen die Hochwassernot

Das Möhne- und Ruhrtal zeigte nach dem Britenangriff unbeugsamen Widerstandswillen

Ueberall, wo Notstand eintrat, wurde mit den im Augenblick zur Verfügung stehenden Mitteln tatkräftig eingegriffen. Nicht zuletzt setzten sich auch unsere Jungen (Bild links zeigt einen Löschzug der HJ beim Auspumpen eines Kellers), und unsere Frauen (Bild rechts zeigt Mitglieder der NS-Frauenschaft bei Reinigungsarbeiten von Flußschlamm) hervorragend ein.

Aus dem Ruhrtal. In den frühen Morgenstunden des Montag und dem weiteren Verlauf des Tages hat die Bevölkerung des Möhne- und Ruhrtales schwer unter den Folgen des britischen Angriffs auf die Möhne-Talsperre zu leiden gehabt und dem britischen Luftterror eine große Anzahl Menschenleben zum Opfer gebracht. Insbesondere an den Stellen der Flußläufe, an denen das Wasser sich staute, erhielten die Fluten durch Rückschwall besondere Wucht und rissen Wohnstätten und Hofgebäude mit sich fort. Vielfach wurde auch das Vieh auf den Uferweiden vom strömenden Wasser überrascht und mitgerissen.

Sofort nach dem Bekanntwerden der schweren Prüfung der Bevölkerung setzten Partei und Staat alle verfügbaren Hilfsmaßnahmen für die Betroffenen und Bedrohten ein. Mit den Gliederungen der Partei und den Männern und Maiden des Reichsarbeitsdienstes kämpften Wehrmachtabteilungen gegen die Wasserschäden an. Die Partei nahm sich an den Schadensstellen und in den schnell hergerichteten Betreuungsstätten der Obdachlosen an und umsorgte sie mit allem, was in der plötzlich hereingebrochenen Not und in der Bedrängnis des Augenblicks getan und herangeschafft werden konnte. Mit ihnen zusammen bewiesen die nicht betroffenen Volksgenossen eine einmütige Solidarität und setzten

Wo Volksgenossen ihr Heim verloren hatten, waren bald die Feldküchen der Wehrmacht und des NSKK zur Stelle.

Aufnahmen: Schley.

sich mit Aufbietung aller Kräfte für den Nachbarn und sein Hab und Gut ein. Aus allen umliegenden Städten und Dörfern eilten alarmierte Hilfskräfte — Politische Leiter, Stürme der SA, Gefolgschaften der HJ, Mädelgruppen, NSKK-Fahrbereitschaften — nach den Anweisungen der Befehlsstellen strahlenmäßig zu den heimgesuchten Stellen des Ruhrtales und reihten sich tatkräftig in die örtlichen Hilfsmaßnahmen ein.

Wie in den vom Bombenterror heimgesuchten Industriestädten unseres Gaues zeigten auch die Volksgenossen in den Bergen an der Ruhr im Augenblick der Not äußerste Tatkraft und entschlossene Hilfsbereitschaft, die in unzähligen Fällen bis zum Einsatz des eigenen Lebens gingen. In der Stunde der Not hat die Volksgemeinschaft zusammengestanden und eine geschlossene Front gebildet. Was noch getan werden kann, um die Not zu lindern, wird getan werden. Die Toten, die dem britischen Luftterror zum Opfer fielen, werden uns für alle Zeiten unvergängliche Zeugen des Kampfes sein, den das ganze deutsche Volk um sein Leben kämpft und den es gewinnen muß, wenn wir immer, mag der Feind seine Ziele suchen, wo er will, so entschlossen und unerschütterlich zueinander stehen wie in diesen Tagen der Prüfung und der Kameradschaft.

156

Translation of the official press release which appeared in the Neheim edition of the *Westfälische Landeszeitung — Rote Erde* on May 19 (opposite).

were only around 700 in all, of whom about half were Russian prisoners of war. Those reports from Berndt which gave me such headaches on the first day now turn out to have been totally exaggerated. It is obvious that Berndt got his information from the BBC. Once again we see how impractical and irrational it is to pass on such alarmist reports to the upper echelons of leadership. First of all they impose terrible burdens and secondly they are in most cases incorrect. I am issuing a short statement about the loss of life caused by the dams' raid. The main reason for this is that the English and Americans are making a great sensation out of it all and are going on about thousands of dead and how the damage is hardly repairable. Our communiqué will probably throw cold water on all these fantasies.'

On May 20 Dr Goebbels recorded in his diary: 'Speer phoned me this evening and gave me a report about the dams. [Albert Speer was then the Minister for Armaments and Munitions and in charge of the overall direction of the war economy.] He flew over there straightaway and had a look at the damage. Thank God it is not as bad as Speer had also

first assumed. He has taken a series of far-reaching measures, in particular transferring a large contingent of workers from the Atlantic Wall to clear away the damage. In all, this amounts to 6,000 to 7,000 men who are already on their way and will soon be at work. Speer hopes we can be on the way towards starting production again by the beginning of next week. By the end of next week everything should be going flat out again. Speer is a real genius when it comes to organisation. He does not allow himself to be taken aback and fazed by serious misfortunes; he always takes the appropriate measures and does not shrink from dictatorial rulings when they are relevant. The Führer has given him total power and he has made full use of it.'

The secret situation reports of the Sicherheitsdienst, the intelligence branch of the SS (known as the SD), also dealt with the dams' raids in their 'Meldungen aus dem Reich' (Reports from the Reich). One of the tasks of the SD was to maintain an inland intelligence service at the Reichssicherheitshauptamt (Reich Central Security Office) for the purpose of researching civilian morale across a wide social spectrum. They were also required to report on the effects of government measures. From numerous individual reports from the judiciary, administration, economy, culture and informers, the Institute for Research into Public Opinion drew up its 'Morale and Situation Reports' much like Mass Observation did in Britain. Report No. 385 dated May 24, 1943 stated in its 'General Section' from information which had been received:

'The attack on the dams' — the instigators were Jews'. The headline in the May 19 edition of the *Soester Anzeiger*. The same bulletin was published in six local newspapers.

'Of all the military events, it is the present development of the air war which is most frequently discussed with great concern by all sections of the population. The results of the attacks on the Möhne and Eder dams, the magnitude of which is often grossly exaggerated, have gone around the Reich by word of mouth and spread like wildfire. This has tended to terrify people, especially as the loss of life was given as high in the official war communiqué. In the early days especially, the wildest rumours were circulating amongst wide sections of the population, for example the talk was of 10,000 – 30,000 deaths. When the official casualty figures were announced things calmed down somewhat although they were met by great distrust in many places. They are however regarded as a benchmark, judged by which the rumoured figures must have been too high. Broad sections of the population believe the stories that are going around about the havoc caused by the torrents of water and the economic damage brought about by the water and the loss of electricity. In all this they see proof of a "cold-blooded planning of the air war by the enemy". The raid on the dams has proved that we can be severely hit from the air by relatively modest means. In many cases the damage caused by an attack on the dams has proved itself to be greater than that achieved by the terror attacks on the Ruhrgebiet. Many of our fellow citizens are seeking an explanation as to how such an attack could have been possible at all; they fear that defending the dams with flak and balloons was not enough.'

Of the 13 Australians who took part, eight of the survivors are pictured. L-R: Flight Lieutenant Robert Hay (AJ-P), Pilot Officer Lance Howard (AJ-O), Flight Lieutenant David Shannon (AJ-L), Flight Lieutenant Jack Leggo (AJ-P), Pilot Officer Frederick Spafford (AJ-G), Flight Lieutenant Harold Martin (AJ-P), Pilot Officer Leslie Knight (AJ-N) and Flight Sergeant Bob Kellow (AJ-N). Missing from this photo are the two Australians on AJ-E who lost their lives, Flight Lieutenant Robert Barlow, the pilot, and his wireless operator, Flying Officer Charles Williams. Also, Pilot Officer Anthony Burcher, the rear gunner of Hopgood's AJ-M who survived the crash to become a prisoner of war. Two other Aussies late on parade are Pilot Officer Bert Foxlee and Flight Sergeant Thomas Simpson, the gunners on AJ-P.

Awards

'All Lancaster aircrews which returned from the raid on the German Dams on 16/17th May, 1943 were today presented to the King and Queen by Wing Commander Guy Gibson, VC, DSO and Bar, DFC and Bar. The presentations were made in front of the Lancaster in which Wing Commander Gibson led the attack. Their Majesties spoke to each officer and NCO in the Squadron and the Queen also inspected a parade of WAAF on the Station, many of whom helped in the raid.

'Accompanied by Air Vice-Marshal R. A. Cochrane, CB , CBE, AFC, (Air Officer Commanding the Group); Group Captain J. N. H. Whitworth, DSO, DFC (Station Commander); Wing Commander F. C. Hopcroft, DFC (Commander of another Lancaster squadron); Mr Wallis, Scientific Adviser; and many of the Officers who took part in the raid, their Majesties had lunch in the Officers' Mess. After coffee, the King especially congratulated Flight Lieutenant David Shannon, from Bridgwater, S. Australia. For Flight Lieutenant Shannon, whose efforts secured the final breaching of the Eder dam, it was a double celebration — the award of the DSO and his 21st birthday.

'The King and Queen were shown complete models of the Dams which the crews had studied before the attack. Booms, platforms and power stations were clearly shown and Wing Commander Gibson explained the plan of attack. Their Majesties examined also through lenses stereoscopic pictures of the flooding of the valleys. The power house and marshalling yard 15 miles downstream from the breach were shown before and after flooding. Kassel was shown with the floods filling the Tiergarten and making a path of water straight across the important factory area. Another photograph over which the King paused showed Herdecke Viaduct with the railway lines hanging free over the river.

'Two draft coats of arms for the Squadron were submitted to his Majesty by Wing Commander Gibson. Both of them were drawn on the Station. One showed a hammer parting the chains on the wrists of Europe. The motto was "Alter the map". The second suggestion showed a breached Dam in the centre with the motto "Après moi le déluge". No decision was taken and the King suggested the expert advice should be sought of the Chester Herald.'

PRESS STATEMENT FOR RELEASE AFTER 08.30 HOURS, MAY 28, 1943

Twenty-nine Canadians took part in the operation of whom 13 were killed and one taken prisoner. These are the 16 that came back. Back row, L-R: Sergeant Stefan Oancia (AJ-F); Sergeant Frederick Sutherland and Sergeant Harry O'Brien (AJ-N); Flight Sergeant Ken Brown (AJ-F); Flight Sergeant Harvey Weeks (AJ-W); Flight Sergeant John Thrasher (AJ-H); Flight Sergeant George Deering (AJ-G); Sergeant William Radcliffe, Flight Sergeant Don McLean and Flight Lieutenant Joseph McCarthy (AJ-T); Flight Sergeant Grant MacDonald (AJ-F). Front row, L-R: Sergeant Percy Pigeon (AJ-W); Pilot Officer Torger Taerum (AJ-G); Flying Officer Danny Walker (AJ-L), Sergeant Chester Gowrie (AJ-H); Flying Officer David Rodger (AJ-T).

The 13 Canadians lost on the operation were: Flying Officer Kenneth Earnshaw, navigator on AJ-M; Flying Officer Vincent MacCausland, the bomb-aimer on AJ-A; Flying Officer Robert Urquhart, the navigator on AJ-Z and Warrant Officer Alden Cottam, the wireless operator; Pilot Officer Floyd Wile and Flight Sergeant Francis Garbas, the navigator and front gunner with AJ-B; Flying Officer Harvey Glinz, the front gunner on AJ-E; Pilot Officer Vernon Byers, pilot of AJ-K, and his rear gunner, Flight Sergeant James McDowell; and Pilot Officer Lewis Burpee, the pilot of AJ-S, with his bomb-aimer and rear gunner, Warrant Officers Class 2 James Arthur and Joseph Brady. Pilot Officer Jim Fraser, the bomb-aimer on AJ-M, also does not appear as he was made a prisoner of war.

Most Humbly submitted to Your Majesty by Your Majesty's Most Humble and Most Devoted Servant,

App^d. GRI

THAT Your Majesty may be graciously pleased to confer the Victoria Cross on Acting Wing Commander Guy Penrose GIBSON, D.S.O., D.F.C., (39438), Reserve of Air Force Officers, No.617 Squadron, Bomber Command, in the following circumstances;-

This officer served as a night bomber pilot at the beginning of the war and quickly established a reputation as an outstanding operational pilot. In addition to taking the fullest possible share in all normal operations, he made single-handed attacks during his "rest" nights on such highly defended objectives as the German battleship "Tirpitz", then completing in Wilhelmshaven.

When his tour of operational duty was concluded, he asked for a further operational posting and went to a night-fighter unit instead of being posted for instructional duties. In the course of his second operational tour, he destroyed at least three enemy bombers and contributed much to the raising and development of new night-fighter formations.

After a short period in a training unit, he again volunteered for operational duties and returned to night bombers. Both as an operational pilot and as leader of his squadron, he achieved outstandingly successful results and his personal courage knew no bounds. Berlin, Cologne, Danzig, Gdynia, Genoa, Le Creusot, Milan, Nuremberg and Stuttgart were among the targets he attacked by day and by night.

On the conclusion of his third operational tour, Wing Commander Gibson pressed strongly to be allowed to remain on operations and he was selected to command a squadron then forming for special tasks. Under his inspiring leadership, this squadron has now executed one of the most devastating attacks of the war - the breaching of the Moehne and Eder dams.

/The ...

Air Ministry

22nd May, 1943.

In recommending Gibson for the award of the Victoria Cross, his immediate boss, Air Vice-Marshal Cochrane, highlighted the fact that 'the task was fraught with danger and difficulty. Wing Commander Gibson personally made the initial attack on the Möhne dam. Descending to within a few feet of the water and taking the full brunt of the anti-aircraft defences, he launched his projectiles with great accuracy. Afterwards he circled very low for 30 minutes, drawing the enemy fire on himself in order to leave as free a run as possible to the following aircraft which were attacking the dam in turn.'

"	14	"	P.		P/O WHITWORTH. D.S.O. D.F.C.	FULL DRESS REHEARSAL ON UPPINGHAM LAKE AND COLCHESTER RES. COMPLETELY SUCCESSFULL.											3.05	
"	16	LANCASTER	G.	SELF	SGT PULFORD P/O DEERING FLt TREVOR ROPER FLt HUTCHISON P/O SPAFFORD P/O TAERUM.	LED ATTACK ON MÖHNE AN EDER DAMS. SUCCESSFUL.											6.40	

	(1)	(2)	(3)	(4)	(5)	(6)	(7)	(8)	(9)	(10)	(11)	(12)	(13)
	50.25	431.50	3.10	8.50	4.20	577.40	16.00	–	644.25	–	NAV. 87.45	10.55	478.30

AWARDED V.C. 23:5:43

GRAND TOTAL [Cols. (1) to (10)]
1924 Hrs. 20 Mins.
TOTALS CARRIED FORWARD

Unfortunately the citation then (incorrectly) stated that Gibson repeated the same tactics over the Eder but, as we have seen, that dam was completely undefended. The award of the Victoria Cross was confirmed by King George VI on May 22 and notified to Gibson on the following day when he entered it up in his log-book *(above)*. Including Gibson, 34 members of No. 617 Squadron received decorations which were approved by the King on May 26. The Distinguished Service Order was awarded to Flight Lieutenant Joseph McCarthy, DFC; Flight Lieutenant David Maltby, DFC; Acting Flight Lieutenant Harold Martin, DFC; Acting Flight Lieutenant David Shannon, DFC, and Pilot Officer Leslie Knight. Four men received a Bar to their Distinguished Flying Crosses: Acting Flight Lieutenant Robert Hay, DFC; Acting Flight Lieutenant Robert Hutchison, DFC; Acting Flight Lieutenant Jack Leggo, DFC, and Flying Officer Daniel Walker, DFC. The DFC was awarded to Acting Flight Lieutenant Richard Trevor-Roper, DFM; Pilot Officer Jack Buckley; Flying Officer Leonard Chambers; Flying Officer Harold Hobday; Flying Officer Edward Johnson; Flight Sergeant George Deering; Pilot Officer John Fort; Pilot Officer Lance Howard; Pilot Officer Frederick Spafford, DFM, and Pilot Officer Torger Taerum. The Conspicuous Gallantry Medal (Flying) was given to Flight Sergeant Kenneth Brown and Pilot Officer William Townsend, DFM. A Bar to the Distinguished Flying Medal went to Sergeant Charles Franklin, DFM, and DFMs to Flight Sergeant George Chalmers; Flight Sergeant Donald Maclean; Flight Sergeant Thomas Simpson; Flight Sergeant Leonard Sumpter; Sergeant Dudley Heal; Sergeant George Johnson; Sergeant Vivian Nicholson; Sergeant Stefan Oancia; Sergeant John Pulford; Sergeant Douglas Webb, and Sergeant Raymond Wilkinson. As soon as awards were promulgated in the *London Gazette*, the ribbon could be worn even though the decoration had not yet been given. One anomaly is that although both Flight Sergeants Deering (AJ-G) and MacLean (AJ-T) were commissioned on May 18, the former received the DFC (reserved only for officers and warrant officers) but the latter the NCO's equivalent award, the DFM. *Right:* This picture of the five Australians in the crew of AJ-P wearing theirs was taken on the roof of the Admiralty while they were on leave in London. L-R: Flight Lieutenant Leggo, the navigator; Flight Sergeant Simpson, the rear gunner; Flight Lieutenant Hay, the bomb-aimer, Pilot Officer Foxlee, the front gunner (and odd man out as he was not given either a new award or bar to his DFC), and Flight Lieutenant Martin, the pilot.

On May 21, Bomber Command HQ announced that a royal visit to various bomber stations — Wyton, Methwold, Downham Market and Binbrook — would take place on May 26-27 and that this would culminate at Scampton. All the aircrews who had taken part in the raid against the dams were to stand by at the base and King George VI particularly expressed the wish to be able to talk to Barnes Wallis. Accordingly, Air Vice-Marshal Cochrane sent a telegram (confirmed by letter on the 23rd) to Wallis suggesting that he should come to Grantham the previous evening and stay overnight. The Royal party motored the 24 miles from Binbrook, which they had visited in the morning, and arrived at Scampton at 1 p.m. Here, Gibson escorts the King from where the crews were lined up in front of AJ-G on the grass facing the squadron hangar. On the right Group Captain Charles Whitworth, the Station Commander.

'All the men who had been picked for this squadron were experienced bomber crews', recalled Dave Shannon after the war. 'All of them had completed at least one tour of operations (25 missions), some of them more. All had volunteered because everybody was given the choice. It was not an order that one joined this squadron. Gibson and Group went out to the crews and everybody was given an opportunity to say yea or nay.

'Our feelings before this raid, after the briefing, were one of elation, excitement and, to a certain extent, relief that the training that we'd been doing was coming to an end and here we could see that the actual operation was about to take place and we were to strike a blow against the Hun.

'We were on an operational station with another bomber squadron [No. 57] who were operating at night. Nobody knew what we were training for and there was a certain amount of talk about the new 617 Squadron. "They do nothing but practice fly — when are they going to do something?" So we were all very keen to get on and do it.

'Our take-off was planned for the first wave at 21.30 aiming to be over the target at about midnight. We formed up into our three vics of three and flew across the North Sea — quite uneventful — until we hit the coast of Holland and then the light flak opened up all along from there. The main hazards were light flak and searchlights although we were too low for them to hold us for any length of time. There were no attacks by fighter aircraft as we were too low for them to operate.

'Once we got into the dams, we were all told by Gibson to hold off in the hills — three or four miles back from the dam itself — and to await the result. It was then that we found out that the Möhne dam was very heavily defended with light flak guns. Gibson went through and released his mine and there was a tremendous explosion of water and debris up into the air. We waited for it all to subside only to see the dam wall was still there.

'Hopgood did his run and he got hit in his petrol tanks. One wing on the starboard side caught fire and I think his bomb-aimer was possibly hurt too because his bomb was

The crews were lined up in in the order shown in the operational table on page 46. Flight Lieutenant Hopgood (AJ-M) having failed to return, Flight Lieutenant Martin (first wave AJ-P) was introduced first *(left)* then AJ-J's Flight Lieutenant Maltby *(right)* as Squadron

Leader Young (AJ-A) had also failed to return. (David Maltby crashed in the Channel after the aborted attack on the Dortmund-Ems canal on the night of September 14/15, 1943, his body being washed ashore in Kent. Harold Martin survived the war.) Barnes Wallis is behind.

A triple bonus for Flight Lieutenant Dave Shannon: his 21st birthday; the award of the Distinguished Service Order . . . and a meeting with the King! Shannon returned home to Australia in 1945 and later entered business in London.

released late and bounced over the wall. There was a tremendous explosion. Hopwood did his best to gain height — some 400-500 feet — when the entire aircraft exploded in mid-air beyond the dam in a steep climb.

'Next to go in was Martin. He was hit several times going in but, to try to draw off some of the flak, Gibson was flying down one side of the lake, just out of range of the flak, with his navigation lights on and spotlights to try to fool the guns. Martin's bomb was released exactly on sight — again with a vast explosion of water up into the air but the wall was still there. Young was called in next; now Martin was flying down one side trying to draw the fire. Again a tremendous explosion and although Young called up to say he thought the wall would go — he thought it had been a perfect run but when it subsided the wall was still there.

'Maltby was next but still the dam wall was there.

'I was then called in by Gibson to start my run when there were tremendous excited yells over the R/T: "It's gone! It's gone! It's gone!" The wall had collapsed and water was spewing out down the valley.

'By this time, as we flew the 60 miles or so to the Eder, the mists were starting to form across the hills and down in the valleys. Gibson eventually got there — he was the only aircraft there so he called up and asked where I was. I said I was in the vicinity — in fact I was making a dummy run on what I thought was the dam but it was another arm of the dam which looked very similar. Gibson fired a Very light and all the aircraft found the dam.

'It was way down in a very steep valley and we were at about 1,000-1,500 feet. There was a castle at one end over which we had to drop immediately down the side of the hill, level out over the water, and go over a spit of sand. I tried, I think, four times [actually three] to get down but each time I was not satisfied so I told the bomb-aimer not to release. To get out we had to immediately put on full throttle and do a steep climbing turn to the right to avoid a vast rock face in front.

'Gibson said have a rest while he called in Maudslay. He did a dummy run but on the next run his bomb overshot, bounced over the wall and exploded below with a tremendous flash. [In fact Maudslay had four runs in two turns and dropped his mine after Shannon.]

'Gibson told me to have another go so I had another dummy run [actually two abortive attempts during his second turn] and then I got what I thought was an excellent run down. We released the mine and as far as we could tell there was a small breach on the left-hand side.

'There was only one aircraft left — that was Les Knight — and he had three or four runs before he could actually release. The wall gave — we were very lucky because that was the last of the nine aircraft.'

With Squadron Leader Maudslay and Flight Lieutenant Astell missing, Pilot Officer Knight of AJ-N was next. (He lost his life on a follow-up operation to the Dortmund-Ems canal on September 15/16, 1943, his body being recovered from the sea two days later.) In the background, the Queen is shaking hands with David Maltby.

The two Second Wave crews who aborted — Flight Lieutenant Munro (AJ-W) and Pilot Officer Rice (AJ-H) — are conspicuous by their absence as Flight Lieutenant McCarthy *(left)* of AJ-T (who survived the war) is next in line, Pilot Officer Byers (AJ-K) having also failed to return. The Queen is about to move on to Les Knight. With the first two crews of the Third Wave — Pilot Officer Ottley (AJ-C) and Pilot Officer Burpee (AJ-S) — all killed, save for

Sergeant Tees (see pages 101-105), Flight Sergeant Brown *(right)* of AJ-F met the King next. (He also survived the war to return to Canada.) No picture appears to have been taken of Pilot Officer Townsend (AJ-O) nor of Flight Sergeant Anderson (AJ-Y), who suffered Gibson's wrath when he returned to Scampton with his Upkeep still on board and for that reason had already been posted from the squadron.

Lunch was taken in the Officers' Mess *(above)* where selected officers were chosen to be seated within earshot of the King and Queen. In this photograph taken outside the entrance, Barnes Wallis is partially hidden behind the King. The press were not admitted that day, apart from a *Movietone News* cameraman who filmed a two-minute report.

After lunch His Majesty visited the squadron operations room where the briefing models had been put on display together with reconnaissance photographs, pairs of which have been pinned to the table to be viewed through a stereoscope. The model of the Sorpe is in the left foreground, the actual dam at the northern end being out of the picture.

Gibson had previously asked for suggestions for a design for the squadron crest and two versions had been prepared to show to the King. The first depicted a hammer parting chains attached to a figure representing Europe with the motto *Alter the Map* while the other portrayed three bolts of lightning above a broken dam with the words *Après Moi le Déluge*, a misquote from Madame de Pompadour's alleged exclamation: 'Après nous le déluge' (after us the flood). In this picture, the King appears highly amused at the adoption of words by Louis XV's maîtresse en titre as he is asked to make a choice between the two designs in front of him. (The lookalike on the right, often miscaptioned, is *not* Sir Arthur Harris.)

Paul Brickhill in *The Dam Busters* claims that 'the King called the Queen and unanimously they picked [the] drawing showing the dam and bolts of lightning' but other commentators suggest that His Majesty was non-commital and instead suggested that the opinion of the Chester Herald should be sought. The heraldic authorities subsequently pointed out the error in the motto but with the King having given his tacit approval, the design was granted without alteration and it remains the No. 617 Squadron crest to this day.

Four weeks later — on Tuesday, June 22 — Gibson travelled by train to London with more than 30 of his squadron who were to be decorated at Buckingham Palace. Gibson was also to receive a Bar to his DSO which, with his Victoria Cross, would make him the most-decorated member of the RAF at that time. Altogether there were to be awarded five Distinguished Service Orders; ten Distinguished Flying Crosses and four Bars; eleven Distinguished Flying Medals and one Bar; and two Conspicuous Gallantry Medals. *Above:* After a photo-call outside the Palace, dinner was held in the Hungarian Rooms in Lower Regent Street when Gibson signed a large photograph *(below)* of the breached Möhne dam as a souvenir for Barnes Wallis.

The Luftwaffe had ruled out a successful air strike on the Möhne dam but pointed out the danger of sabotage on the ground. Consequently, Lothar Eickhoff, the District President of Arnsberg (the county covering the Möhne dam area), acting in conjunction with the Chief of Police, arranged for vulnerable point protection to be set up at the dam. On September 1, 1939, the heads of administration in the districts of Arnsberg, Soest, Olpe, Altena, Schwelm, and Meschede had been ordered to set up emergency teams comprising 12 men including a commander and, during the course of the war, each team was overseen by a police staff officer or a police officer concerned with air defence matters. But it would all be to little avail on the night of Monday, May 16/17, 1943 when the waters unleashed their trail of destruction. This is Neheim.

Basically before the attack, while there was a simple warning plan based on the 'snowball principle', there were no instructions for those living in the valleys on what to do in the event of a flood. There was no system of special sirens to warn people in the air raid shelters to leave them or even notices indicating escape routes to higher ground. Informing the telephone exchanges and police stations was pointless as they could not evacuate people from the air raid shelters while an alert was in progress. On June 9, the SS and police compiled a provisional list of casualties which had occured within the jurisdiction of the

Oberpräsident (Lord Lieutenant) of Westphalia, of the city of Hanover, of the Rheinprovinz, and of the Reichsstatthalter (Reich Governor) at Lippe and Schaumburg-Lippe in Wehrkreis VI Münster: identified German dead 403; unidentified German dead 73; German missing 60; foreign dead 593; foreign missing 156. *Left:* Funeral cortège at Fröndenberg. *Right:* Members of the Reichsarbeitsdienst carry a victim to the cemetery in Zennern near Fritzlar. The total death toll from the destruction of the two dams has never been precisely determined but it is believed to be in excess of 1,400.

Repercussions in Germany

Back in Germany, it was not just the population at large who wondered how the dams had fallen victim to bombs so easily. Those in authority also sought an excuse or an explanation for the disaster. In Arnsberg, District President Lothar Eickhoff wrote to the Reich Minister of the Interior, Dr Wilhelm Frick, in Berlin on June 24, 1943:

'The attack by the enemy aircraft on the Möhne dam, its military success and catastrophic aftermath raise the following questions. How could it happen that this raid was carried out in the way it was? How could it achieve its success against the dam wall? It is accepted that, with the possible exception of loss of livestock, damage to property was unavoidable. However, when the disaster struck, why was it not possible at least to avoid casualties? In accordance with these questions, one wonders if anyone is responsible and, if so, where the responsibility lies — as the disregard of this responsibility leads to blame for the event as such or for its catastrophic scale. Insofar as this points to military matters, so must these be totally disregarded for they cannot form the subject of this report. Such matters can be considered here only as external, and unverifiable, pre-existing facts.

'The idea of an air strike against dams is not new and not unknown. This is shown by *L'Aviation de Bombardement* (1936), a book by the important French writer Camille Rougeron, who specialised in the field of military aviation during the pre-war years. In his book he covers just such an attack in detail. So this must have made everyone — civilian or military — at the authority responsible for the dams aware of the possibility. It was

accordingly the duty of this administration to do everything possible to prevent such an attack or to diminish its outcome.'

On August 28, 1939, the Ruhr Valley Dams Association, in consultation with President Eickhoff, had submitted a written petition to the commander of the Münster Air District and sent a copy of this letter to the Generalkommando A.K. (General HQ of the Army Corps) on September 5. In it a direct reference was made to Rougeron's book. The purpose of the petition, which clearly predicted the ensuing catastrophe, was to secure military defence for the dams but, in their reply of September 9, the commander of the Air District flatly refused to provide any defensive anti-aircraft guns for the dams.

Immediately upon the outbreak of war, with the military authorities already aware of the possibility of an air strike against a dam, the Association stressed the danger yet again. Furthermore, the attention of the military was expressly drawn to the fact that the British had carried out an attack on the largest dam in Sardinia. The Münster Air Defence District was also specifically informed about this in a letter from the Association on February 1, 1941. This stated that the decision and responsibility as to whether this raid could lead to enemy action in Germany lay solely with the military authorities; the same was also true for any counter-measures which were required to protect the dams. It was also pointed out that it was the duty of the military to inform the civil administration of the possibilities, the means, and the effects on the dams of such an attack. Such information would then enable the required defensive measures to be implemented. However, this request was not acted upon.

The above death announcements were published in the notices' section of the local newspapers *Soester Anzeiger* and *Westfälische Landeszeitung — Rote Erde* on June 11 and 12, 1943. Not all the victims from the Soest district are included.

Then followed a tough battle between the Mayor of Essen, Justus Dillgardt, who was also Chairman of the Ruhr Valley Dams Association and the military authorities in Münster. He sent strong letters and graphs showing the correlation between the content of the reservoir and the depth of the water behind his dams so as to draw attention to the increased danger of a disaster when the reservoirs were full. The Association also emphasised that the size of enemy bombs was increasing all the time; with this came the risk that the crest of the dam could be destroyed. Yet the catastrophe which had been so clearly predicted was still considered by the military to be an impossibility and on June 12, 1941, the Münster Air Defence District advised the Association that 'it is no longer necessary to send us regular reports about the height and volume of water contained in the two reservoirs'.

Upon the outbreak of war, AA guns and searchlights had been deployed but these were all withdrawn when the western offensive began in 1940. They returned in the autumn of 1940; were removed in the spring of 1941 but replaced again in the autumn of 1942. Thereafter they remained in position until the raid. Also, from the spring of 1942 until the autumn of that year, a balloon barrage was set up around the Möhne reservoir and at the beginning of 1943 torpedo nets were deployed in front of the dam. But only the Möhne was linked to the air defence system and there were no smoke generators at any of the dams until after the attack.

In his letter to Interior Minister Wilhelm Frick of June 24, 1943, Eickhoff went on:

'As the administration was convinced that an air strike against the dams was feasible and — as the attack in Sardinia shows — would take place, it was their duty to obtain clarification regarding the extent of the effect of such an attack and, in accordance with this, take the appropriate defensive measures. The documents for this needed to be provided by the military for it was only the military that knew the type of enemy weapons and the extent of their effect.

'On October 10, 1939, the Ruhr Valley Dams Association received a letter from the Reichsluftfahrtministerium (RLM — German Air Ministry), with information about the anticipated size of a breach in the wall of the Möhne dam following an air strike. The assumptions expressed by the Luftwaffe regarding the extent of possible destruction are based partly on explosive tests carried out on the Bever dam, which is out of service, at the instigation of the RLM. On October 17 the Association reported to the RLM via the Arnsberg District President with a detailed report regarding the anticipated damage from the flood waves which would follow the destruction of the Möhne dam.

Private dwellings reported as being totally destroyed numbered 95; those severely damaged 248; slightly to severely damaged 134; slightly damaged 589. Farmhouses totally destroyed 6; severely damaged 8; slightly to severely damaged 3; slightly damaged 15.

Damage to actual farmland was estimated to cover 4073 hectares (over 10,000 acres) with more than 6,000 animals drowned including 625 pigs, 571 cattle and horses . . . and 33 swarms of bees! This miraculous sight was pictured at Neheim.

'On November 14, 1939, a site inspection was carried out at all the dams within the District of Arnsberg to assess their vulnerability. The Möhne dam extends from 6.25 metres at the crest to 34.20 metres at the base of the wall. According to information from the RLM, the destruction of the wall, where this is up to 7 metres thick, could produce a gap 6.70 metres wide. The resulting water mass would, according to the calculations of the Association, be at some 625 cubic metres per second, approximately the equivalent of twice that of any anticipated maximum flooding. This was the basis provided by the responsible expert authority for the measures taken by the administration. In order to be absolutely sure, the mass of water was based at 1000 cubic metres per second. This quantity would have produced a flood of threatening proportions; but never the catastrophe that in fact ensued when 120 million cubic metres of water poured out of the Möhne reservoir, initially at a rate of over 8,800 cubic metres per second. Thus far the explosive effects of the enemy's armament had been unknown. Accordingly, the extent of the ensuing destruction to the dam wall was totally unexpected. A warning system had been set up at the dams based upon the egress of a mass of water at 1000 cubic metres per second and the speed of its progress. For years before the war the District Government of Arnsberg had devoted particular attention to the question of the defence of the reservoirs. This did not simply take into account the hydro economy but also the protection of the population from the danger that would result from damage to the dam walls.

'Instructions for the warning report system were accordingly set up with the administrative officials and took into consideration the expertise and experience of the Association. These instructions were promulgated with the circular order dated June 5, 1940 of the District President Arnsberg Nr 336/40g. As detailed therein, there is a scheme for each reservoir explaining how information is relayed by the watchmen at the dams to all places threatened by the water. This relaying of information depends essentially on the co-operation of the Reich Post. In an emergency the watchman at the Möhne dam informs the telephone exchange at Soest, number zero. The telephone exchange then calls, in the order of the danger to each, those towns and exchanges at risk along the course of the Möhne and Ruhr. The sequence is as follows: the town of Neheim, the exchanges at Werl,

Fröndenberg and Menden, the town of Schwerte, the exchange at Westhofen and the flood control centre at Hengsteysee. From this flood control centre, information is passed to the heads of administration of the districts involved, the district president, the waterworks and the other towns and exchanges further downstream. The purpose of the scheme is to ensure that the places in immediate danger receive information as rapidly as possible regardless of administrative considerations and circumstances. It was the duty of the authorities involved to be particularly vigilant so as to ensure that the warning and report system operated correctly.

'The head office of the Reich Post at Dortmund confirmed in a letter dated June 6, 1940 which telephone exchanges the watchmen had to inform, and the numbers to be dialled. This information was passed to the watchmen at the dams, in particular to the watchman at the Möhne dam. The head office of the Reich Post at Dortmund further confirms in its letter that a check on the watchmen's telephones at the dams would be regularly carried out every day when the night watch came on duty. The warning report system was set up as described above.

'The experience gained from the breach of the Möhne dam has shown that this warning system was adequate when based on water exiting at a rate of 1000 cubic metres per second. Such a quantity of water would not have surged down the valley at a speed that prevented adequate warning being given to those in danger in the valleys. However, the explosive effect of the so far unknown devices (probably mines with underwater detonators) which was used during the attack on May 17, 1943 was such that a much bigger hole was made in the wall. Instead of the calculated breach 6.70 metres in width for a wall thickness of 7 metres, the explosion tore an almost rectangular gap in the wall 77 metres wide and 22 metres deep. The amount of water that flowed down the valley was accordingly much greater and travelled at a speed of 20 - 30 kilometres per hour depending on variations in the width of the valley. The planned warning service for the areas downstream could nowhere near keep pace with this speed, let alone stay ahead of it.

'Nevertheless thanks to the well-organised warning report system and the prompt action of the district of Arnsberg (District Director Niewisch), a warning from the

Factories totally destroyed numbered 11; severely damaged 41; slightly to severely damaged 40; slightly damaged 33.

Railway bridges totally destroyed 7; railway bridges severely damaged 2; road bridges totally destroyed 18; road bridges severely damaged 7; road bridges slightly damaged 12.

24-hour special service reached the police at Neheim, the first larger community, before the arrival of the flood wave. The planned report which was to be relayed by the dam watchman to the telephone exchange at Soest and from there to the police administrations which had been precisely listed downstream was also passed in the correct manner. However, this report was delayed because the violent tremors of the dam wall knocked out the watchman's telephone and also the one at his flat; a delay therefore occurred as he was obliged to ring from elsewhere. Owing to this loss of time it was not possible for the exchange at Soest to forward the report since the speed of the flood wave in the valleys put the telephones out of action. The only official warning to reach Neheim via the district administration at Arnsberg was relayed by another route.

'Furthermore the dam watchman, Chief Forester Wilkening, who had a direct telephone connection to the control room under the dam wall, could not get through to the Soest exchange as the control room had been wrecked by bomb damage. After the loss of precious minutes he managed to get through to the Soest exchange from the railway station of the Ruhr-Lippe-Eisenbahn by going through the Körbecke exchange. He passed on the "Catastrophe Flood Warning" at some time between 01.30 and 01.35. According to the statement of the post office official, this call came through at around 01.10 or 01.15. The post office officials were hindered by the failure of the electric light and had to work by candlelight. The line to Neheim went via Menden and was poor. Perhaps the telephone exchange at Neheim was already under water thus making a connection impossible. The speed at which the flood rushed down the valley and the flooding of the roads meant that the stand-by driver was also unable to get through with the message.

'The District Government of Arnsberg immediately called for military assistance teams for the endangered localities. At 01.20 three officials of the Arnsberg district arrived at the Möhne dam, which was still under attack. A vain attempt was made to relay messages from the Hotel Möhneseeterrassen to the police administrations located down the valley. After time-consuming detours the officials of the district president reached Neheim at

03.00. At the police station, which was located in a part of the town on higher ground, they met the commander of the Order Police and the Reich Defence Commissioner, Deputy Gauleiter Hoffmann, as well as the District Vice President in order to initiate further relief measures.

'On the night of the attack I [Eickhoff] was on an official visit to Berlin. Immediately upon my return, and in conjunction with the Reich Defence Commissioner, I carried out the measures necessitated by the evolving situation. If, with hindsight, consideration is given to whether different or better means of warning could have been provided, the following point must be made: that the damage to property, deeply regretted though it is, could have been prevented only to a quite insignificant extent (for example the prompt rescue of animals in the fields) since the dwellings, industrial complexes, sheds and barns would still have been within the danger zone. The deeply-regretted loss of life within a five-kilometre danger zone below the dam could not have been prevented by any other warning system. The tremendous force of the wave made it impossible for anything at all to be saved below the dam.

'With regard to areas further down the valley, it could well have been (theoretically) possible with an earlier warning to reduce the loss of life. However, this was unfortunately not possible in the prevailing circumstances since the possible extent of the explosive effect of enemy bombs had been incorrectly given by the responsible authority: accordingly the warning system was based on water travelling at a much lower speed. It is a pity that this responsible authority did not indicate (or simply give notification) that with an explosion of considerably greater force, a correspondingly larger outflow of water could be anticipated. In that case, given the special care and conscientiousness with which such matters are always treated here, it would have been established that a warning system based on messages telephoned by the dam watchman would not keep pace with the speed of the wave. Thus, following an examination of all the technical possibilities, an even faster and more secure warning system would have been set up as far as such a thing is

Right: **Aid ranging from rescue work to assistance with clearing up was provided to all areas affected by the flooding. On May 18, Heinrich Orthwein, the Landrat (Chief Administrative Officer) of Kreis Melsungen (in the Eder valley area), ordered the following immediate measures for the affected communities of Niedermöllrich, Lohre, Altenburg, Harle, Rhünda, Felsberg, Gensungen, Böddiger, Neuenbrunslar, Altenbrunslar and Wolfershausen: 'All inhabitants between 14 and 60 years not directly affected by the Eder flood disaster at home and on their farms, and not involved in work outside the area, will be formed into working parties consisting of 10-20 men or women. An able-bodied man, or woman in the case of female working parties, is to be nominated as leader. The mayor will be responsible for urgent measures locally, and for setting up and deploying the working parties. The working parties will be considered as emergency personnel acting on a temporary basis. Anyone refusing to take part in this community work or refusing to comply with the order will be compulsorily drafted into a special working party led by a police officer or experienced SA man and forced to work. Individuals are to set aside all personal matters and any work in their own homes until economic life in the community has returned to normal. Male working parties will engage in clearing-up operations outdoors; female working parties will clean living accommodation, furniture, linen, crockery and other household items. The mayor will be held to account for any failure and severely punished.'** *Right:* **Clearing up in Niederense.**

possible. Otherwise the endangered areas would have had to be evacuated for the duration of the war.

'Immediately after the disaster I examined with the relevant telephone exchange the possibility of a warning system that would remain unaffected by a failure of the telephone network. The telephone engineer put forward the idea of burying a cable in the dam wall. Any change to the condition of the wall would also affect this cable and thereby, independently and without human intervention, set off an alarm as far away as the most distant endangered area. However, tests are not yet complete and there are difficulties concerning the composition of the material and the route for the line. In the meantime an alarm system has been set up at all the dams so that people in the valleys can proceed from the danger zone in good time.'

Left: **In the seriously affected parts of the upper Möhne and Ruhr valleys where the catastrophe could not be hushed up, this message of appreciation from the Deputy Gauleiter was published in the local press:** *'An Expression of Gratitude from the Deputy Gauleiter to the People of the Möhne and Ruhr Valleys.* **Following the raids on Dortmund and Bochum, the Möhne dam was the target of a British attack during the night of May 16/17. The floods caused by the damage to the dam resulted in the deaths of several hundred of our fellow-countrymen in Neheim-Hüsten and numerous other communities of the Möhne and Ruhr valleys. Many hundreds of dwellings were obliterated or severely damaged. These heavy losses to life and property have brought pain and suffering to many families. The depth of pain and suffering does not need to be stressed. However, out of this dreadful catastrophe has emerged not just the grief over the loss of a loved relative and the pain from the loss of a home, but also many examples of courage under trial and of unshakeable steadfastness. Your spirit of resistance, your willingness to make sacrifices and your mutual self-help have transcended the distress. Just like the people of Dortmund and Bochum you have shown that you will not be brought down. A spirit of great comradeship and true National Socialist unity pervades. And out of this, the entire population of the stricken areas has proved itself supreme through its striving to overcome the emergency. For this I express to all my gratitude and recognition. Fellow citizens! The war criminals in America and England hope to weaken and dishearten us through the gangster tactics of their terror raids, to take away our sense of duty and shake our allegiance to the Führer and to the Fatherland. They are wrong! We know what is at stake and such terror raids serve only to strengthen our resolve. Sombre but unbending we stand together shoulder to shoulder in the certainty that one day the Führer will order terror to be met with terror. And this terror will strike the cowardly murderers of defenceless German people in an even more devastating way. Heil Hitler!**

Signed: Albert Hoffmann, Deputy Gauleiter.'

Reconstruction

Quite apart from the restoration of hydro-electric supplies, the recommissioning of the waterways for barge traffic and the repair of waterworks, for reasons of propaganda the Reich accorded top priority to the speedy reconstruction of the dams themselves. The Organisation Todt had already proved itself capable of successfully undertaking large-scale construction schemes, having already carried out the building of the West and Atlantic Walls and many other projects in Russia. Accordingly the OT was given what was probably the largest — certainly one of the most important — projects of the war years.

Paramount to the reconstruction was the restoration of the rail link between Neheim and the Möhne reservoir. This line, which had been totally swept away during the raid, was essential for bringing up supplies, and it was brought back into operation by June 15.

The awesome power of the water is evident in this picture taken at Wickede where a whole section of the embankment of the vital railway line through the Ruhr valley has been washed away. Apart from the urgent necessity to restore one of the main rail links between the Ruhr and the Eastern Front, its repair was essential if work on the dams was to get speedily underway. We saw the 'young recruits' — almost all of them over 35 years of age — of the Fürstenwalder Eisenbahn-Pionier-Bataillon arriving on page 139. They completed the repair of the bridge and track in record time, even by the standards of the Reichsbahn which was used to getting lines back into service quickly, earning the battalion special praise. However, the bridge at Wickede was only one of many of the river crossings swept away in the deluge. Altogether, 25 bridges were washed away and another 21 damaged to some degree. As a result, communications across the river were severely disrupted for several weeks.

The Organisation Todt was involved in the repair of other key bridges. This is the railway bridge at Fröndenberg further down the Ruhr valley (see pages 140-142) where the OT decided to construct an emergency single-track, timber-piled bridge across the Ruhr river. Here, a loco from the Reichsbahn's Department of Works is bringing up RSJs.

By midday on June 7, the army railway engineers at Wickede completed the first stage of their task, thus enabling a single track to be laid over the bridge. A high-level commission came to inspect and approve the works. 'Load Train N', which consisted of two Type 50 locomotives coupled together, was taken across, at first slowly and then at speed.

The measuring instruments indicated a comfortable safety margin so an hour later the first passenger train crossed over.

As we have seen on page 87 the floods from the Eder destroyed the railway bridge across the river between Grifte and Wolfershausen, thus cutting the rail link between Kassel and Frankfurt. As a result, a temporary bridge had to be built straight across the valley.

Above: The tenders of the engines carrying out the load tests on the timber-piled bridge bear the words: 'Keep the wheels turning for victory; journeys lengthen the war'. *Below:* Army engineers had completed the bridge by mid-June.

The new bridge was inaugurated with a parade by the engineers of Ersatz- und Ausbildungsbataillon (Replacement and Training Battalion) 3 from Hanau-am-Main in the presence of senior officers who arrived by train. Dr-Ing. Ludwig Müller, President of the Reichsbahn directorate in Kassel, was the technical director in charge of the project.

And back at Hemfurth, in the shadow of the Eder, temporary rail, road and footbridges were built by army engineers and the Organisation Todt. The same buildings on the far bank can be recognised in the picture on page 80. Note that the house on the right has already been repaired. Hemfurth church can be seen top right.

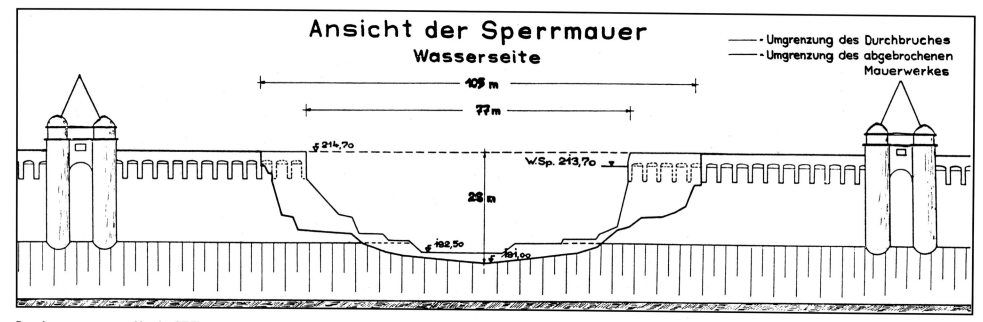

Ansicht der Sperrmauer
Wasserseite

— Umgrenzung des Durchbruches
— Umgrenzung des abgebrochenen Mauerwerkes

105 m

77 m

214,70

W.Sp. 213,70

22 m

192,50

191,00

Drawings were prepared by the OT Einsatzgruppe-Ruhr for both the Möhne (waterside) *(above)*, **showing the additional section to be demolished, and the airside of the Eder** *(below)*.

Simultaneously, clear-up work got underway at the Möhne and Eder dams themselves and detailed surveys were carried out on the two breaches — the one at the Möhne measuring 22 metres deep by 77 metres wide, that on the Eder 22 metres deep by 70 metres wide. Cracks in the walls were carefully examined and, as far as the Möhne was concerned, it soon became apparent that the structure had been subjected to such massive vibrations that a large section would have to be demolished before reconstruction could be contemplated. In the end, some 7000 cubic metres of stonework had to be removed before the engineers got down to a firm and undamaged bond.

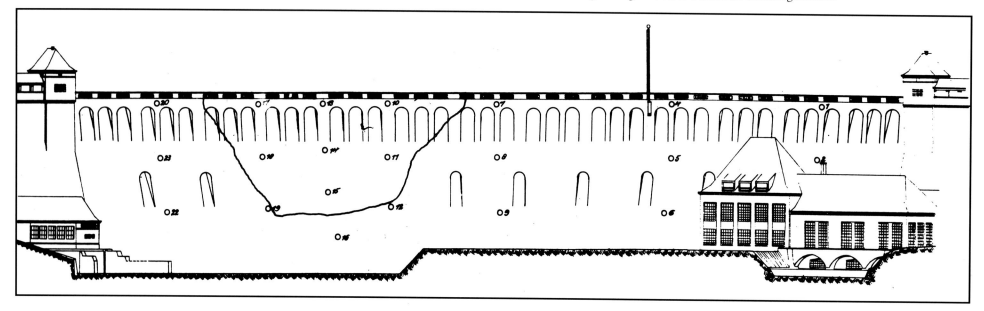

Given its vital importance to the Ruhr coalfields, the Möhne dam was the subject of a high-level decision as early as May 17 when it was resolved that repairs should be carried out with all possible speed, full responsibility for planning, construction and the appointment of staff being entrusted to the owners, the Ruhr Valley Dams Association while the Third Reich's Organisation Todt was appointed to procure building materials and the necessary specialist labour and auxiliary staff. Clearance work was already underway on May 28. First, the bottom of the breach was blasted with high-pressure hoses until the engineers got down to a firm bond at which point no further demolition was necessary. However, at the sides — especially on the northern side — it became apparent that the structure had been ruptured vertically and horizontally across a wide area and to a significant depth. There was also evidence of breaks and fine cracks in those parts of the wall which had survived. Only after 6950 cubic metres of loose stonework had been removed could the rebuilding phase proper begin on July 9.

The OT's engineers were well aware of the need to proceed quickly to seal the breach before the autumn rains so that a full reservoir would be available the following year. To speed up the rebuilding, it was initially proposed that concrete seals be inserted into the cracks caused by the explosion. However, the argument against this proposal was the uncertainty as to how the solid concrete would behave within the wall, one fear being that it might shrink once it had set. Following discussions with the Ruhr Valley Dams Association, a decision was made to cut no corners when rebuilding and all makeshift measures were accordingly ruled out. Both dams were to be repaired using the same method of construction as when the wall was originally built but such a high standard of work could only be achieved by using skilled tradesmen who would have to be drafted in from all over Germany, Carinthia and the Tyrol in Austria, and from northern Italy as only 50 German stonemasons were available by that stage of the war.

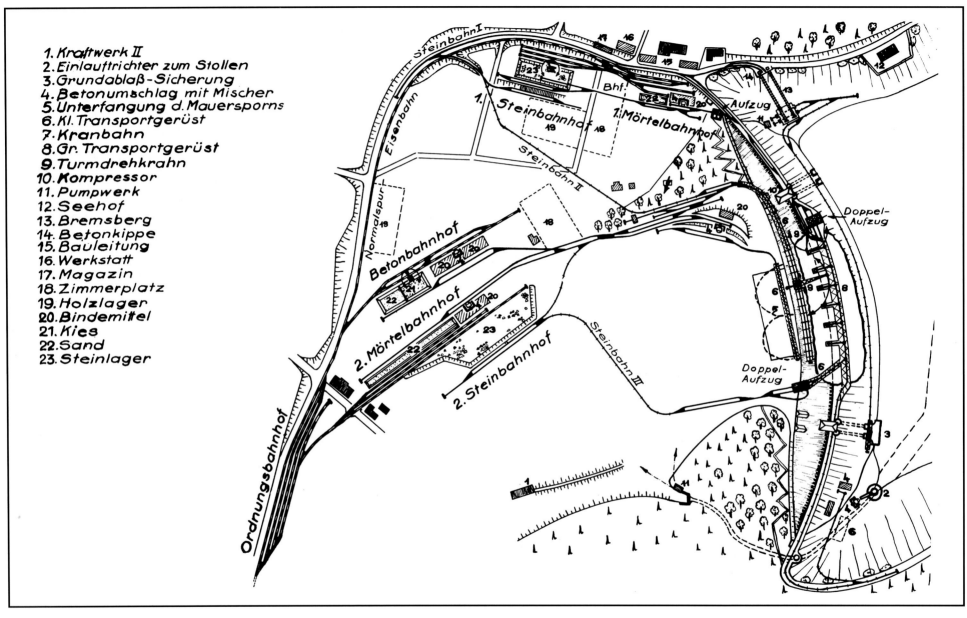

1. Kraftwerk II
2. Einlauftrichter zum Stollen
3. Grundablaß-Sicherung
4. Betonumschlag mit Mischer
5. Unterfangung d. Mauersporns
6. Kl. Transportgerüst
7. Kranbahn
8. Gr. Transportgerüst
9. Turmdrehkrahn
10. Kompressor
11. Pumpwerk
12. Seehof
13. Bremsberg
14. Betonkippe
15. Bauleitung
16. Werkstatt
17. Magazin
18. Zimmerplatz
19. Holzlager
20. Bindemittel
21. Kies
22. Sand
23. Steinlager

The construction firm, Heinrich Butzer from Dortmund, set up a narrow-gauge railway to serve the huge Möhne dam building site. A key element in the process was the Ruhr-Lippe light railway, which moved daily 100 goods wagons and 2,200 tonnes of building materials. Upon completion of work at the end of September, the final tally amounted to 5,400 wagons and 98,000 tonnes of freight. By the time the actual building work started, 300,000 cubic metres of stone had been transported along the recently completed rail link between Niederense and the building site. [1] Power station II. [2] Funnelled water inlet. [3] Bomb-proofed outlet tunnels. [4] Concrete mixing. [5] Underpinning of wall spurs. [6] Lightweight scaffolding. [7] Crane track. [8] Main scaffolding. [9] Tower crane. [10] Compressor. [11] Pumps. [12] Seehof Restaurant. [13] Jig. [14] Concrete dump. [15] Site offices. [16] Workshop. [17] Store. [18] Carpentry workshop. [19] Timber storage. [20] Cement. [21] Gravel. [22] Sand. [23] Stone storage.

The huge construction sites were a masterpiece of organisation with all red tape firmly banished. Including auxiliary workers and quarrymen, the workforce at the Möhne consisted of 2,500 men. Around 100 conscripted Dutch carpenters built a massive scaffolding, their masterpiece of carpentry — resembling a giant cobweb — gradually crept up as work progressed until it reached the height of an eight-storey building. Wood was used as an economy measure since the armament industry had first call on any precious steel. Constraints of space dictated that initially only 10 to 20 men could work side by side in the breach but, as the gap widened out towards the top, the number rose until 320 men stood shoulder to shoulder. The actual masonry work was carried out by an average of 250 stone-masons and their labourers who together laid up to 250 cubic metres of stone per day. On the Möhne, work was supervised by a foreman who had been a supervisor when the original dam was built in 1908-12.

The undressed stones used to fill the breach came mainly from the quarries which had supplied the material for the original construction. However, as the old quarries had already been extensively worked, and were unable to meet the total needs of the project, material had to be brought in from pits in the Bergisches Land region. In addition, dressed stones were used which had been originally earmarked as material for autobahn bridges. Each stone was cleaned by a high-pressure hose before being laid. Given the large number of conscripted foreign workers on the site, there was an ever-present danger of sabotage and, accordingly, technical experts carried out regular slump tests on the mortar mix. However, the foreign workers proved to be exemplary tradesmen and the only bottlenecks were the restrictions of the two hoists used for transporting materials.

Above and below: **One of the problems facing the engineers was an eight-metre deep depression which had been gouged out of the bedrock at the foot of the wall by the force of the water. The hole was filled in one operation with eight slab sections, each measuring 6 metres by 24 metres containing 1000 cubic metres of concrete.**

Wooden scaffolding had to be used in preference to tubular steel because of the constraints imposed by the war economy. (As a back-up measure, a complete section of scaffolding was kept in readiness at the timber construction yard in case the main structure suffered damage in an air raid.) As the dam wall gradually increased, the scaffolding finally reached the height of an eight-storey building, the overall height being 26.50 metres. The various platforms were 2.84 metres wide. The height of the stages was dictated by the method of working which often involved work proceeding simultaneously at two separate sections of wall. Stone and mortar were lifted up by crane and then transported to the workface in skips along a system of rails equipped with points and turntables.

The existing stonework below and at the sides of the breach was sealed by a process of injections on both sides of the wall. Liquid cement was forced into boreholes at high pressure in order to seal cracks and harden the masonry. Particular attention was paid to the joints between the old and new sections of the wall where the 105-metre-wide breach was being filled. From the end of May to October 1943, an average of 1,855 men worked on site every day in two shifts, each of 11 hours. The number of workers per day peaked at 2,192: 748 French, 460 German, 441 Dutch, 340 Italian, 183 Belgian and 20 other nationalities. Each German worker was allotted four to five foreign workers who had been mainly drawn from some 400 sites on the Atlantic Wall.

Work continued day and night when, despite the danger of air raids, the site was illuminated by a battery of low-angle floodlights, and a special alarm system with loudspeakers connected directly to the air raid warning network was installed to protect the site from surprise attacks. Precautions included the duplication of important building plant with the machines being distributed around the site to minimise disruption in the event of bombing. Thus the reconstruction of the dams continued at a pace which no one outside Germany had thought possible. The anthill of activity at the dams obviously aroused the interest of Allied aircraft but, although PR flights overflew the sites, the Germans could not believe their luck when the work was not interrupted by further raids.

Due to the fear of invisible cracks deep within the remaining parts of the wall, it was decided to reinforce the whole structure by injecting extra cement. With the aid of special equipment, holes were drilled and liquid cement injected at a pressure of six atmospheres. However, it proved difficult to even out irregularities at the point of contact between the old and the new structure and the joints were finally sealed at the crest of the dam and from the sides with cement.

Reconstruction work at the Möhne proceeded more smoothly than had been initially expected. While the breach was being filled, advantage was taken of the low water level to encase the outlet tunnels with concrete — an innovation which would render them bomb-proof even against direct hits. Reconstruction work, including repairs to the damaged outlet pipes, was completed by September 25 — six days in advance of the planned date — and just 79 days after work had started on July 9.

A similar large construction site was set up in the Eder valley with a rail terminus. Here the breach was some 230 feet wide by 70 feet deep. The labour camp lies on the hillside on the left.

Although the breach in the Eder dam was seven metres narrower than the one at the Möhne, the repairs took longer because of problems with the drainage system. Nos. 3, 4 and 5 vents — the latter a special feature of the Eder dam — were not reinstated and accordingly the position of the breach is easily recognised today. The Frankfurt firm Philipp Holzmann AG worked for the Organisation Todt on this project; the same company had been involved with the original construction. The rebuilding was carried out in co-operation with the Water and Navigation Board of Hannoversch-Münden.

After the attack both active and passive defences were deployed around the dam. First, 24 balloons were flown at low level in a tight circle around the construction site and reservoir thus affording protection up to a height of 600 metres. Another wider circle of 24 balloons at high level defended the area up to 2,000 metres. The dam and the immediate area could also be obscured by a smoke-screen laid down by a company of men equipped with 500 smoke-generators. Active defences at the dam included one company of infantry providing ground defence against an attack by airborne forces; two flak batteries each with 12 2cm guns (including some pom-poms and four 60cm searchlights); one battery with four 3.7cm guns; two batteries each with four 8.8cm guns; one mobile gun battery and three 200cm searchlights. The total number of men engaged in passive and active defences varied between 1,300 and 1,500. Here, at the far end of the roadway beside the tower, three gun positions have already been installed manned by 15-year-old Flakhelfer from the Real Gymnasium (grammar school) at Bad Wildungen.

At the Eder, unexpected difficulties arose when the drainage channels inside the wall filled up with the injected cement — something which would have prevented water venting from within the dam. Consequently, it was necessary to install a new drainage system and fresh holes were bored vertically from the crest to the shafts at the base of the wall. This, however, brought its own problems because initially the holes could not be drilled with sufficient accuracy and the matter was only resolved when a miniature transmitter in a waterproof sleeve was lowered into the holes. Then, with the help of this radio-location system, the engineers finally managed to position the holes precisely and thus drill to the correct spot but this problem held up the completion of the Eder dam considerably. Although the wall was finished at the same time as the Möhne, final reconstruction was not completed until June 1944 because of this drainage and injection work. The water level in the Eder reservoir therefore had to be increased in stages. Even after the war, more injections were required and it was not until 1947-48, following a check on the load-bearing capacity of the wall, that visitors were once again able to marvel at the spectacle of water overflowing the Eder dam.

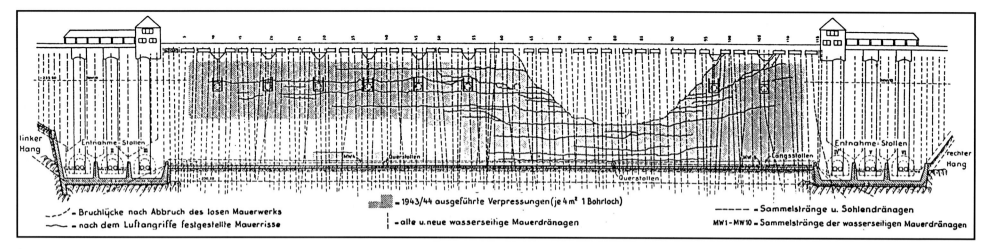

- - - - - = Bruchlücke nach Abbruch des losen Mauerwerks
───── = nach dem Luftangriffe festgestellte Mauerrisse

▨ = 1943/44 ausgeführte Verpressungen (je 4 m² 1 Bohrloch)
┊ = alte u. neue wasserseitige Mauerdränagen

───── = Sammelstränge u. Sohlendränagen
MW1-MW10 = Sammelstränge der wasserseitigen Mauerdränagen

Since the measuring devices that had been built into the wall of the Eder to check its stability had been damaged by the explosion, a new monitoring system had to be set up on the outside of the dam. Using 23 fixed measuring control points (see drawing page 180) on the open side of the construction, the OT kept watch on its stability via three triangulation points set up on brick-built platforms in front of the dam. The diagram from the waterside shows the new drainage holes which had to be bored vertically.

Escorted on his left by Einsatzgruppenleiter Adam, who was in charge of the reconstruction of the Möhne, Albert Speer arrives at the dam for the re-inauguration ceremony on October 3. On the extreme right, the managing director of the Ruhr Valley Dams Association, Dr-Ing. Max Prüss. For 20 years after war, the former Armaments Minister and Organisation Todt chief could not tell his side of the story. Speer began writing his memoirs while he was incarcerated in Spandau in Berlin and says that he finished the first draft in December 1954. On his release from prison on October 1, 1966, he spent a further two years reworking and revising his text with the help of official records and his book *Inside the Third Reich* was published in German in 1969 and in English in 1970. This is what he wrote about the events in 1943: 'As early as September 20, 1942, I had warned Hitler that the tank production of Friedrichshafen and the ball-bearing facilities in Schweinfurt were crucial to our whole effort. Hitler thereupon ordered increased anti-aircraft protection for these two cities. Actually, as I had early recognised, the war could largely have been decided in 1943 if, instead of vast but pointless area bombing, the planes had concentrated on the centres of armaments production. On April 11, 1943, I proposed to Hitler that a committee of industrial specialists be set to determining the crucial targets in Soviet power production. Four weeks later, however, the first attempt was made — not by us but by the British air force — to influence the course of the war by destroying a single nerve centre of the war economy. The principle followed was to paralyse a cross-section, as it were — just as a motor can be made useless by the removal of the ignition. On May 17, 1943, a mere 19 bombers of the RAF tried to strike at our whole armaments industry by destroying the hydro-electric plants of the Ruhr. The report that reached me in the early hours of the morning was most alarming. The largest of the dams, the Möhne dam, had been shattered and the reservoir emptied. As yet there were no reports on the three other dams. At dawn we landed at Werl airfield having first surveyed the scene of devastation from above. The power plant at the foot of the shattered dam looked as if it had been erased, along with its heavy turbines. A torrent of water had flooded the Ruhr valley. That had the seemingly insignificant but grave consequence that the electrical installations at the pumping stations were soaked and muddied so that industry was brought to a standstill and the water supply of the population imperilled.

My report on the situation, which I soon afterwards delivered to the Führer's headquarters, made a deep impression on the Führer. He kept the documents with him. (We immediately summoned experts from all over Germany who had the electrical insulation dried out and also confiscated other motors of this type from other factories, regardless of the consequences. Thus the Ruhr industries would be supplied with water within a few weeks.) The British had not succeeded, however, in destroying the three other reservoirs. Had they done so, the Ruhr valley would have been almost completely deprived of water in the coming summer months. At the largest of the reservoirs, the Sorpe valley reservoir, they did achieve a direct hit on the centre of the dam. I inspected it that same day. Fortunately the bomb hole was slightly higher than the water level. Just a few inches lower — and a small brook would have been transformed into a raging river which would have swept away the stone and earthen dam. That night, employing just a few bombers, the British came close to a success which would have been greater than anything they had achieved hitherto with a commitment of thousands of bombers. But they made a single mistake which puzzles me to this day: they divided their forces and that same night destroyed the Eder valley dam although it had nothing whatsoever to do with the supply of water to the Ruhr. A few days after this attack, 7,000 men, whom I had ordered shifted from the Atlantic Wall to the Möhne and Eder areas, were hard at work repairing the dams. On September 25, 1943, in the nick of time before the beginning of the rains, the breach in the Möhne dam was closed. We were thus able to collect the precipitation of the late autumn and winter of 1943 for the needs of the following summer. While we were engaged in rebuilding, the British air force missed its second chance. A few bombs would have produced cave-ins at the exposed building sites and a few fire-bombs could have set the wooden scaffolding blazing.'

The speedy reconstruction of the Möhne dam under the conditions prevailing at the time was a masterly performance on the part of all the engineers, construction companies and workers involved and on October 3, 1943, Armaments Minister Albert Speer, who was also head of the Organisation Todt, gave the following speech at the re-inauguration of the dam:

'Fellow workers, on May 17 this year, as the result of an air raid by English aircraft, the Möhne dam suffered extensive damage. You have in a remarkably short period of time repaired this dam, thus performing a service to the Ruhrgebiet which will be directly translated into more weapons and more munitions. On that day, May 17, my colleagues and I discussed the situation here at the Möhne dam. It was the view of all the experts that a period of at least nine months would be required to close the breach in the dam. In order to reduce this unacceptable period, we summoned the OT from its work on the Atlantic Wall. And here, as ever, the OT was not found lacking. The date of November 11 of this year, which was given to me by Task Force Leader Adam shortly after his appointment to the job of rebuilding the dams in the Ruhrgebiet, has been bettered greatly thanks to your exemplary work. Instead of the anticipated six months, you have done it in four and a half — a considerable achievement which seems hardly possible. And let us not forget your comrades at the Eder dam, some of whom are with us here today. Striving in noble competition with you, they pressed on with their reconstruction work and completed their task yesterday. Theirs is a performance of equal value to that achieved at the Möhne dam.

'I can assure you here and now that these performances, achieved in the old spirit of the OT, are quite outstanding. The Führer has kept himself fully informed of the progress and it was a particularly pleasant surprise for him when I was recently able to tell him that work was nearing completion. We believe that, with this work, we have kept part of the promise which I made to the Ruhr as the heavy raids of this spring were taking place night after night. I promised the Ruhrgebiet that it will not be abandoned by the Reich — that the Ruhrgebiet will always be rebuilt.

'And you see here before you today the first example of the fulfilment of that promise. And other examples will follow. When I look at this small band of German workers, and beside them this great achievement, I rejoice that Germans have asserted themselves as leaders. The relationship between the German and the foreign workforce, and the tireless way in which the work has been achieved with but a few German workers shows the extent of the enthusiasm with which they applied themselves.

'I thank you for your efforts and ask you to continue to do your duty for the Ruhr. There is without doubt more hard work to be done. This we will accomplish with the people of Westphalia, who have also shown that they do their duty and do not lose heart. A people that do not fail, but see matters through to their conclusion in the spirit of the OT.'

After decorating selected members of the OT for their outstanding efforts in repairing the dam in 79 days, Speer addressed the assembled workforce.

ORGANISATION TODT · NACHRICHTENDIENST

FERNSPRUCH · FERNSCHREIBEN · FUNKSPRUCH · TELEGRAMM

Nachr.-Stelle   Nr.   195   Befördert
                                  Tag   Zeit   durch

+FUEHRERHAUPTQUARTIER .=
+ OTRU NR.45/ OT ESSEN/ FUEHRERHAUPTQUARTIER 2.10.43 NR.632.

Angenommen oder aufgenommen

von   Tag   Zeit   durch

Abgang   AN DIE OT EINSATZGRUPPE RUHR.   Absendende Stelle
Tag: HEIDHAUSEN
Zeit:
Dringlichkeits-
Vermerk
                                               Fernsprech-
                                               Anschluß:

ICH HABE MIT GROSSER FREUDE VERNOMMEN, DASS ES IHRER
UNERMUEDLICHEN ARBEIT GELUNGEN IST DEN WIEDERAUFBAU DER
MOEHNETALSPERRE FERTIGZUSTELLEN. DAMIT HABEN SIE FUER DIE
DEUTSCHE KRIEGSWIRTSCHAFT EINEN ENTSCHEIDENDEN BEITRAG
GELIEFERT. ICH SPRECHE IHNEN UND ALL IHREN FUEHRERN UND
MAENNERN ZU DIESEM GROSSEN ERFOLG MEINEN BESONDEREN DANK
AUS UND ANERKENNUNG.=

· ADOLF HITLER +

In Anerkennung Ihrer
Verdienste zugeeignet :

Einsatzgruppenleiter

Adam then had the pleasure of reading out a telegram *(above)* that he had received from the Führer's headquarters the previous day: 'It is with great pleasure that I have learned that thanks to your tireless work the rebuilding of the Möhne dam is now complete. With this you have made a decisive contribution to the German war economy. I express to you and to all the supervisors and workers my particular gratitude and my appreciation for this great success. Adolf Hitler.' *Above right:* Listening attentively were Speer, Oberbauleiter Hermann Quast and OT-Leiter Voigt. *Right:* To mark the rebuilding, three large photographic albums were prepared for presentation to Hitler and Speer with one for OT archives. The pictures of the ceremony were copied from it by the author 30 years ago, since when the album has been lost. Included was this sketch of the Möhne dam by W. Henning dated September 24, 1943 — the day before the breach was finally closed.

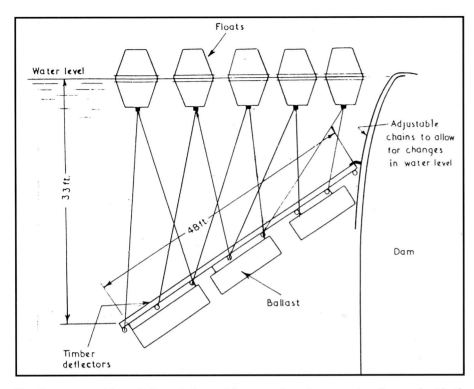

The whole deflector wall, some 400 metres long, was supported by 44 floats and 398 buoys. Including the cables, 40 tonnes of metal were used for the fixings. The individual rafts measured 10 metres long by 20 metres wide.

The Germans could not believe their good fortune when the reconstruction work at both dams progressed throughout the summer months without any interference from the Allied air forces. This gave the opportunity to install new defences against a repeat attack. *Opposite:* **The first line of defence were the formidable Flakvierling anti-aircraft guns followed in February 1944 by the specially-designed bomb deflector in front of the dam** *(above)*. **Constructed from huge timber 'rafts', this was assembled on the lakeside** *(above right)* **and then towed to the sinking position** *(below right)* **in front of the dam.**

The large-scale rebuilding work at the Möhne and Eder did not escape the attention of British photo-reconnaissance flights but the German defences were now on a new footing. The Möhne was closely defended by a large number of quadruple flak guns around the dam itself with 8.8cm FlaK set up on the Haarhöhe hill near Theiningsen. Night defences were reinforced by searchlights and even the new mobile flak guns were deployed. In addition, smoke-generating equipment and balloon barrages at high and low level were put in place.

There was also considerable expenditure on passive defences for the dam. Following the examination of the Upkeep which had been recovered at Haldern, and the statements made by the three aircrew who were now in captivity, the secret of the bouncing bomb had been revealed. Consequently, at the Delecke bathing beach, giant rafts were constructed from long, sturdy tree trunks which were then towed across to the dam by one of the lake's pleasure craft. Once in place, the 10 x 20-metre wooden rafts were weighted with concrete and sunk at an angle to form an underwater barrier to prevent bombs coming into contact with the wall. Any mine which was dropped in the future would roll away from the dam and not explode until it was at a safe distance. Divers were sent down to inspect the new underwater obstructions and ensure that they would do their job properly.

To supplement these measures, anti-torpedo nets of a robust steel construction were suspended from buoys 30 metres in front of the dam extending to a depth of 18 metres. These underwater curtains were intended to trap torpedoes or floating mines before they could hit the wall.

3.5kg contact mines. The erection of steel nets was also started on the valley side of the dam. These were 20 metres long and 15 metres wide and were intended to deflect bombs. The erectors worked almost 40 metres up and, when seen from below, they looked as if they had been caught in some giant spider's web. Finally, the two towers on the Möhne dam itself were dismantled so that they could not again be used as markers in any attack.

As a defence against low-flying aircraft, two 100-metre-high steel masts were erected on the slopes on both sides of the lakes, 600 to 800 metres up from the Möhne and Eder dams. Between these masts, a curtain of steel cables was strung consisting of a heavy cross-wire to which mine anchor-cables were attached at 15-metre intervals, each supporting seven

Guns . . . nets . . . towers . . . mines . . . smoke — the new-look Möhne dam.

The other major dams in western Germany — the Eder, Sorpe, Diemel, Ennepe, Lister and Agger — were also provided with what were, for the time, almost impregnable defences. At the Diemel lake, tests were carried out with a new type of sea mine which it was planned to bring into use at the reservoirs in the so-called 'Aktion Blumentopf' (Action Flowerpot). Four staggered rows, each with 24 mines containing 1000 kilograms of explosive, were strung across the Möhne and Eder lakes at right angles to the flight path of any attacking aircraft. The mines could be remotely detonated and the plumes of spray which would be thrown up when they exploded were intended to bring down low-flying aircraft or at the very least cause any bouncing bomb to explode prematurely or be deflected from its path. The operation of these mine traps had been expertly conceived yet the technicians had not reckoned with the forces of nature. To the alarm of people living near both dams, static electricity in the air sometimes caused odd mines to explode so the system had to be switched off if there was a thunderstorm in the offing!

Another unique form of defence was tested at the Diemel dam — No. 617's Target F — in the event never attacked. The picture *right* shows it pre-1943 and *below* the effect of detonating the anti-aircraft mines strung out in front of the dam wall. Meanwhile, in the United Kingdom, consequent upon the success of the RAF raid, the Ministry of Home Security was earnestly looking into protection measures for Britain's dams . . . and along very similar lines! As early as the day of the raid, Churchill was asking the authorities to advise what defensive measures had been implemented to protect Britain against a retaliatory attack. Altogether, 11 dams were singled out with the five around Sheffield, of which the Derwent — No. 617's practice dam — was considered particularly vulnerable, and No. 57 Anti-Aircraft Brigade, some 5,000 strong, with 28 40mm Bofors and 42 searchlights was quickly deployed in the area. And, as in Germany, other measures were introduced including barrage balloons, smoke-generating apparatus . . . and high steel towers with hanging cables. Even more coincidental, the Admiralty were considering the installation of mine-barriers, some 300-400 yards in front of the dams, to be exploded in the face of low-flying aircraft! Guns and searchlights were also deployed at the King George reservoir at Edmonton and the Queen Mary at Staines to protect London's supply of drinking water.

It was already believed that the Heinkel 177 or Dornier 217 were capable of being adapted to carry an Upkeep-type of mine and that the secrets the weapon might already be known to the Germans through the study of the wreckage of the aircraft lost. It was therefore accepted in Britain that a similar type of attack could be expected within the next three months raising the question as to whether the cost of protecting Britain's dams was too high a price to pay for the success against the German dams. Barnes Wallis was brought in to advise and he felt that the only effective defence would be to blind the pilot of an attacking aircraft. 'Permanent dazzle lights installed in concrete emplacements with bullet-proof glass screens would be quite feasible', he said, and 'practically indestructible' and could be 'brought into action at a moment's notice'. He even proposed that No. 617 Squadron be

employed to carry out a mock attack at Staines to test his searchlight idea. However, there would have been even more disquiet in Britain had it been known that in Germany the Haldern Upkeep was already being examined and its secrets unearthed, and that Pilot Officer Fraser had revealed so much in his interrogation (page 63). *Above and below:* By September, Dr-Ing. Heinz Maecker of the Ballistics Institute and Technical Academy of the Luftwaffe at Berlin-Gatow was carrying out his own primitive back garden testing à la Barnes Wallis. He also developed the deflectors which were subsequently placed in front of the dams to protect them from bouncing bombs. However, the Germans did not know the exact depth against the wall at which the Wallis bombs exploded. The captured airmen were also unable to give any accurate information regarding this point.

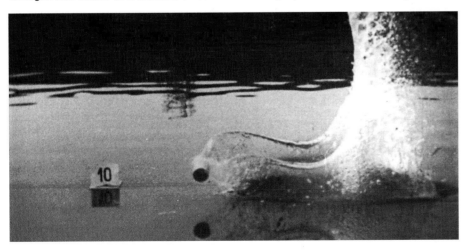

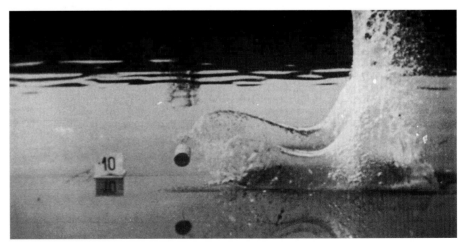

Although all these defensive measures came too late to help the Möhne and Eder dams, they did nevertheless have a deterrent effect against further raids. The Sorpe was the only one to be attacked again — in October 1944 — when No. 9 Squadron attempted a dam-busting mission using another of Barnes Wallis's inventions — the 'earthquake' bomb. This was designed to be dropped from a great height so that its velocity caused it to penetrate deep in the ground before exploding whereupon the pressure wave created would shake the target to pieces. While the 22,000lb Grand Slam was being developed (it was first tested on March 13, 1945), a scaled down version — the 12,000lb Tallboy — was put into production. From June 1944 it was also used by No. 617 Squadron against the V-weapon sites in northern France and the E-Boat and U-Boat pens along the Atlantic coast, the *Tirpitz* hiding in a Norwegian fjord being another target successfully attacked.

Sometimes confused with the May 1943 operation, this picture shows the aftermath of a further attack on the Sorpe with another of Barnes Wallis's dam-busting weapons — the 12,000lb 'earthquake' bomb. Although size and penetration were their strength, the accuracy of 'Tallboy' bombs was subject to all the vagaries of conventional bombing. Some of the Tallboys dropped on the Sorpe on October 15, 1944 were fitted with time-delay fuses which did not explode until 60 to 90 minutes after impact as Josef Kesting (whom we met earlier on page 94) explains: 'I saw the bombers come over like a flight of cranes. The first six planes were flying in a line, quite close together in a staggered formation. Escorting fighters shot up the dam at low level. The bullets rattled above us in the bushes under which we'd taken cover. It was as if someone had emptied out a sack of beans. Some of the bombs had time-fuzes and one bomb exploded later on the central roadway, blowing several people to pieces.' The craters in the picture are 15 metres deep and up to 30 metres across and numerous ring-shaped cracks appeared in the dam. On the crest the concrete wall has been smashed open leaving two craters 30 to 40 metres wide, 12 to 16 metres deep, and at the point of the third impact on the crest, the wall has been pushed aside leaving gaping holes. Bombs have hit the non-water face of the dam immediately below the crest, and caused a partial earth slip. The water level was about eight metres below the crest which meant that none spilled over into the craters. Had this happened, the body of the dam could have been undermined causing a collapse. The photo also shows the anti-torpedo netting installed after the Upkeep raid.

Werner Meschede was a 15-year-old Luftwaffe auxiliary who had been stationed at the dam since January 15, 1944. 'I was a member of No. 4 Platoon of No. 1 Battery of Flak-Regiment 892. Our platoon was on the crest of the dam with No. 5 Platoon further along. Each was equipped with three 2cm pom-poms. On that Sunday the air raid siren went off again in the morning. We trained our gun and scanned the sky. A group of bombers flew over the centre of the dam from the direction of Neheim. There was no way we could hit them at that height and so we tracked the aircraft through the gunsight. Suddenly I saw the bomb bays of the Lancasters open and the bombs drop out. We jumped off the gun in a panic and took cover on the ground. At that very moment there was a booming and thundering noise from the Sorpe dam which seemed to be shaking and vibrating. I thought I would soon be sinking into the mud and water of the reservoir. After these massive explosions, I got up again and saw that all my friends had run off. A direct hit on the crest of the dam over on the Langscheid side had wiped out No. 5 Platoon. There were several dead. There were inquiries afterwards because we had abandoned the guns but nothing came of it. The very same day, the Armaments Minister, Speer, came to the dam to get an impression of the damage and the size of the bomb craters. They covered the large crater on the crest of the dam with a camouflage net.' The bombs had been dropped by 16 Lancasters of No. 9 Squadron (No. 5 Group) but not all exploded and a Tallboy was recovered from the reservoir and defused by Flight Lieutenant J. M. Waters, RAF, and Walter Mitzke of the German civilian bomb disposal organisation in January 1959.

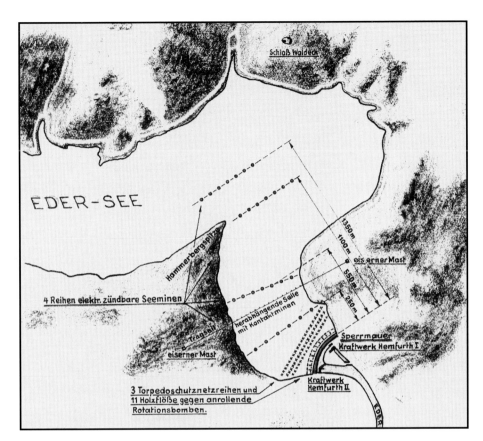

Above: **The growing defences at the dams — this is the plan for the Eder — were still under Allied observation and the Möhne** *(above right)* **was rephotographed a few days before the second Sorpe attack. Although the picture was issued as a target photo in January 1945, there is no evidence that a further Tallboy — or Grand Slam — mission was being considered. By now the greater danger to the dams came from within Germany itself where Hitler was hell-bent on laying waste all that lay in the path of the advancing Allied armies.**
Below right: **The Eder pictured on March 15, 1945, just ten days before its capture.**

The dams of the Sauerland region were not to face danger again until the final days of the war when it was suggested that they should be blown up in order to halt the American advance into the Ruhr. Such an attempt had already been tried in the Aachen area in early February 1945 when the sluice gates of the Schwammenauel dam controlling the Rur (Roer) river were destroyed. The Germans had demolished it in such a way that it created a long-lasting flood in the Roer valley which forced the Allies to postpone their crossing of that river — planned for February 10 — to February 23. Furthermore, Albert Speer had, in March 1945, already opposed Hitler's order for a scorched earth policy, Hitler's directive of March 19 having stated that 'all military, transportation, communication, industrial and supply installations, together with any material assets within the territory of the Reich which the enemy can, either immediately or in the foreseeable future, use for the continuation of hostilities are to be destroyed.' However, long after the war, the rumour persisted in the Möhne valley about plans to blow up the dam — according to the story, bombs and ammunition had been placed in a shaft in the dam wall and primed for detonation.

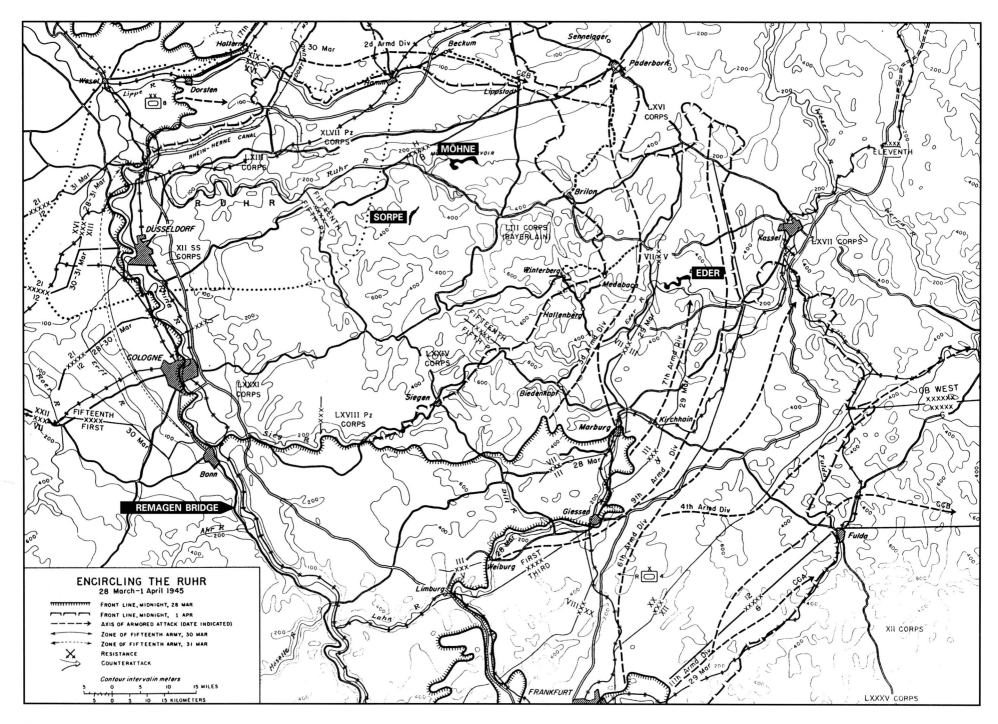

ENCIRCLING THE RUHR
28 March–1 April 1945

FRONT LINE, MIDNIGHT, 28 MAR
FRONT LINE, MIDNIGHT, 1 APR
AXIS OF ARMORED ATTACK (DATE INDICATED)
ZONE OF FIFTEENTH ARMY, 30 MAR
ZONE OF FIFTEENTH ARMY, 31 MAR
RESISTANCE
COUNTERATTACK

Contour interval in meters
5   0   5   10   15 MILES
5 0   5   10   15 KILOMETERS

The German frontier had been crossed on September 10, 1944 at Roetgen (not far from where the borders of Belgium, Holland and Germany converge) but the Rhine was not breached until the following March when the bridge at Remagen was captured intact. From that date — March 7 — the end of the war was just eight weeks away. By then the flak on the dams (the Eder *above* and the Möhne *right*) had been removed for use elsewhere in the last desperate battles . . .

The Eder dam was captured by the US 7th Armored Division (III Corps, First Army) advancing northwards on March 29 in the operation to encircle the Ruhr, but the Möhne fell within the sphere of XIX Corps of the US Ninth Army. By April 1945, the damage caused in 1943 had long since been made good; now the Möhne dam and reservoir were back in operation, albeit with the water level at just two thirds of its maximum. Below the dam thousands of foreign workers who had fled across the Ruhr were camped on the scree of stones which had been deposited by the flood. Meanwhile, the gunners of the flak battery had abandoned their posts. The Americans were in a hurry to take the Möhne dam as the previous day they had been told by German prisoners of war that preparations had been made for its demolition and that the approach road to the crest had been mined. Retreating German troops had already blown up the bridges at Delecke and Körbecke to hinder American access to the Arnsberg forest.

On April 7, the US 95th Infantry Division (Ninth Army) captured Hamm and advanced two to four miles south-west of the city. Meanwhile the 8th Armored Division had cleared Warstein and reached the northern bank of the Möhne reservoir. During the night, a 23-man patrol from Troop A of the division's 88th Armored Reconnaissance Battalion approached the dam under cover of artillery fire. The group, which was led by Sergeants Roman H. Woods from St Louis, Montana, and Emil Dragosita from Allentown, Pennsylvania, came from the flank, clambering down over the steel girders and wooden shuttering which had been placed on the valley side as a protection against bombing. The Americans covered the last few yards to the foot of the dam like acrobats, lowering themselves hand over hand down a steel cable, and then jumping over a trench before finally overpowering the guards. Only once during their climb did they come under fire.

. . . only to be replaced with dummies — the 'AD' standing for Ausser Dienst: Retired!

205

Before leaving, the Germans had left all the dam's defences intact, including the underwater deflectors, torpedo nets, contact mines, and the netting suspended from the steel masts. They had also beached the pleasure boats — known locally as the 'White Fleet' — belonging to the Möhnesee-Reederei Schmitz to prevent these potential 'troopships' from falling into enemy hands. Karl Schmitz, the owner, repaired the damage personally in the hope that he would soon be able to return his boats to civilian use. The British

forces that moved into the Möhne valley in June were most grateful for his foresight and they promptly commandeered his boats and renamed them after members of the royal family. Thus Lake Möhne acquired its own naval unit sailing under the White Ensign!

Both dams fell to US troops, the Eder to the First Army and the Möhne to the Ninth. Save for the guns, the Americans found all the defences intact. These pictures of the Möhne were taken by US Army photographers on April 19.

Still bearing its scars of the battle, the Möhne dam pictured in February 1946. Gibson's own account of the attack *(inset)* was published posthumously later that year — a narrative which the *Birmingham Post* claimed as 'the most exciting and moving in all the air literature of the two world wars'. Thus are legends born.

Pan Books

Guy Gibson V.C.

ENEMY COAST AHEAD

ONE OF THE GREAT TRUE STORIES OF WORLD WAR II   *Illustrated*

Postscript

By Winston Ramsey
Editor-in-Chief of *After the Battle*

As a schoolboy growing up in Britain in the 1950s, the publication of *The Dam Busters* by Paul Brickhill in 1951 was one of the catalysts which fuelled my interest in the exploits of the Second World War. Guy Gibson was already a legend and the deed carried out under his command, brought to the screen in 1956, made him every boy's hero. It fact, in our eyes, Richard Todd *was* Gibson but little could I have known then that some 20 years later, not only would it be my privilege to publish a facsimile of Gibson's flying log-book, but I would spend an evening with Richard Todd in preparing his own wartime biography for *After the Battle* (issue No. 5). Richard had recently remarried and I saw him at his home in Market Deeping, Lincolnshire — by coincidence not far from the No. 5 Group headquarters at Grantham which figures so prominently in the story of the raid. He was so proud to show me his new baby . . . how sad I was when I read the headline in the paper in February 1998 that baby Seumas — now 20 — had shot himself dead at the family home.

Seumas Todd as a baby with his father.

The repaired break in the Möhne has yet to have the stone coping added. The roofs to the towers had been rebuilt by 1952.

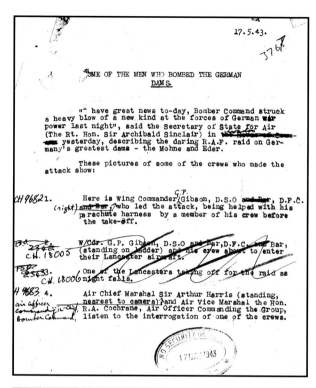

For such an important mission, the official photography was very sparse. Flying Officer Bellamy exposed just nine frames at Scampton which were forwarded to the Air Ministry in London with his dope sheet (left and centre). However, there would appear to be something amiss with his date (May 23) because four of the shots — Nos. 2, 4, 5 (or 7), and 6 (or 8) — were approved for issuing to the press on May 17 (right). (These four photos are reproduced on pages 48, 49, 30 and 111 respectively.) This date of release is confirmed on the cover of the file (right) issued to the Ministry of Information at 1900 hours on May 17.

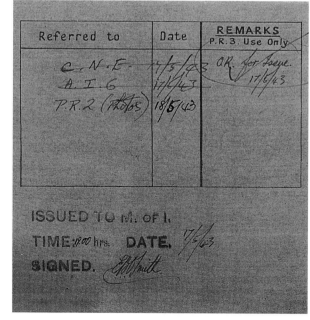

Back in 1943, moves were already afoot to make a film about Operation 'Chastise' and shortly after the raid the British Embassy in Washington received a memo from King Features in New York, one of the largest syndicates in the USA: 'No one accomplishment in the war appears to have generated public enthusiasm to the extent of the mining of the Möhne and Eder dams by the RAF. There is a demand for every scrap of information about the feat and about Wing Commander Gibson and his men.'

In forwarding the syndicate's request to London for more information, the Joint Liaison Committee Air Attaché added that 'a great deal of information has already reached us, but it occurs to me that when it is possible to collect all the data on the effect of this raid and assess the full results, it might be well worth the Air Ministry and the Ministry of Information publishing a special pamphlet about the episode, preferably written by Hilary St George Saunders (author of several publications for His Majesty's Stationery Office). . . The pamphlet should, of course, contain as much personal details about Wing Com-

mander Gibson and his team as possible. By the time this is produced, interest in this country will probably have subsided, but in view of the immense importance of the exploit, it seems to me that it would be a very good thing to record it in this way. The film division of the Ministry of Information might even be inspired to produce a reconstruction of the episode on the lines of the famous Zeebrugge film which was produced after the last war.'

By the end of July, Howard Hawks (later famous for films like Gentlemen Prefer Blondes with Marilyn Monroe) had secured a budget of $150,000 to make a movie in Hollywood of the operation. A 300-foot model dam was planned as well as nine-foot flying model Lancasters, and a machine from Canada was to be used for the shoot with in-flight sequences filmed with actors, but Hawks was desperate for more specific details which were requested through in secret cypher telegram on August 1:

'1. Approximate number of all flak batteries and search-lights and their strength and any other defences such as balloons which were at Möhne.

'2. Number of aircraft despatched to each dam and segregated losses.

'3. Is it possible to inform us approx. where in Möhne Lake the planting was done and height from which planted?

'4. Time of despatch of aircraft, time of attack, and time of return of each mission.

'5. Apart from losses, were some of those which returned badly shot up and were some crews wounded?

'6. Could we have Gibson's report upon the operation including stratagems employed in attack? Were some losses incurred before attack, how many during and how many after?

'7. For how long were crews trained before operation? When were they briefed?

'8. Could I have more pictures of subsequent floods, from Möhne dam chiefly, but also others day by day?

'9. Can Hawks use actual names of certain personnel in raid, particularly whole of Gibson's crew and perhaps other captains of aircraft? If so, grateful for these details as well.'

The Air Ministry replied a week later giving details of training, briefing and losses with the names of the airmen decorated but said that security considerations precluded supplying any information under points 3 and 6. However, when the script arrived in London in November 1943, it was severely criticised. Barnes Wallis commented that not only was he caricatured under a false name but the whole presentation was a disgraceful travesty of the work of English scientists in general, and he went so far as to call for the permission to make the film to be cancelled. Group Captain Whitworth, on the other hand, while openly critical of many inaccuracies, still felt the film should be made with the full collaboration of the Air Ministry providing the script was rewritten so that 'those acquainted with the facts and with air force custom and tradition [will not] shudder in their seats'.

It was left to Dr D. R. Pye, the Provost of University College in Gower Street, location of the Press and Censorship Bureau of the Ministry of Information, to respond, but by February 1944 it appears that Hawks had cooled to the idea in the face of all the criticism, and Pye commented that 'by now, perhaps it is rather too much past history for it to make a big hit'.

Cine footage (other than Barnes Wallis's test film) was non-existent and an American proposal to feature the raid in a Hollywood movie came to nothing. However Paul Brickhill's account detailing the wartime exploits of 'The Dam Busters' as he dubbed No. 617 Squadron, published in hardback in 1951 and paperback three years later, proved the catalyst for the Associated British Pictures cinema production, made largely at Scampton (right), which was released on the 12th anniversary of the operation. Its huge success even led to its memorable theme tune *The Dam Busters March* by Eric Coates reaching the Top 20 in October 1955.

Four Lancaster MK VII — NX679, NX673, NX782 and RT686 — were made available from the maintenance unit at RAF Hemswell, '673' being pictured on the previous page. The notion depicted in the film that the idea of the height spotlights originated from seeing two spots converging on a female singer on the stage of a London theatre is spurious; in fact, the idea came from the Director of Scientific Research at the Ministry of Aircraft Production and developed by RAE at Farnborough.

It was to be another ten years before the Dams' raid was brought to the screen after Associated British Pictures invested two years in the research and preparation. With Richard Todd in the title rôle and Michael Redgrave playing Barnes Wallis, the other characters were portrayed (with several incorrect ranks) as follows: Mrs Wallis — Ursula Jeans; Air Chief Marshal Sir Arthur Harris — Basil Sydney; Group Captain Charles Whitworth — Derek Farr; Captain Joseph (Mutt) Summers — Patrick Barr; Air Vice-Marshal the Hon. Ralph Cochrane — Ernest Clark; Flight Lieutenant Trevor-Roper — Brewster Mason; Flight Lieutenant Martin — Bill Kerr; Flight Lieutenant Hutchison — Anthony Doonan; Flying Officer (should be Pilot Officer) Spafford — Nigel Stock; Pilot Officer Taerum (promoted to Flight Lieutenant in the film) — Brian Nissen; Flight Sergeant (should be Sergeant) Pulford — Robert Shaw; Pilot Officer (in reality a Flight Sergeant) Deering — Peter Assinder, with Raymond Huntley as the official at the National Physical Laboratory.

This film became a world success and showed the breaching of the dams from the British perspective. However, it did not deal to any great extent with the destruction in the valleys and the effects of the raid on the German armament industry were ignored. Furthermore, at the time it was made, details of the bouncing bombs were still top secret.

Scampton's former CO, Group Captain Whitworth (depicted in the film by Derek Farr) served as the film's technical advisor.

The first film documentary dealing with the subject in a comprehensive way was produced by our author, Helmuth Euler, after 30 years of research. It was shown in the areas affected by the catastrophe on the 30th anniversary of the raid — May 17, 1973 — and made use of the latest information then available and no longer subject to official secrecy.

Our author Helmuth Euler films *City of Lincoln* (PA474) during the making of his own two-hour documentary, first shown in May 1973.

Over the past four decades, Helmuth has been absorbed with studying the raid on the dams near his home in Werl, and he has been interviewing participants, collecting photographs and archive material for his extensive library. Here he talks to Barnes Wallis in his Weybridge office in 1969 where the pair exchanged rare photos, films, copies of documents and other information.

But to revert to the immediate aftermath of the raid, at the same time that requests were reaching London from the USA, the Soviets were also very keen to get in on the act! On June 1, 1943, the Air Ministry received a secret coded telegram from the British Mission in Moscow to the effect that the General Staff of the Soviet Naval and Air Forces had requested full details of the successful RAF raid against the Möhne and Eder dams. 'They are showing great interest in this operation and are possibly contemplating something similar.' Full details were requested on the next aircraft leaving for Russia regarding the following:

'Full description of the weapon used;
Number carried per aircraft;
Number of aircraft attacking each dam;
Tactical approach to the target and method of dropping mine, bomb or torpedo;
Structural details of each dam;
Damage to each dam including any available photographs.'

This put the Air Ministry in somewhat of a quandary and the matter was considered at a Chiefs-of-Staff meeting the following day. The Chief of the Air Staff, Sir Charles Portal, put forward two alternatives: 'Either we should provide the information required and at the same time request the Russians not to make use of it, or we should inform them that we intended to make further use of the weapon ourselves and that we were not prepared to release information on the subject until after the operation, in which it was to be employed, had been completed'.

Sir Dudley Pound argued that there were grave dangers to security in the Russian proposal and he asked for time to look into the matter for, as far as the Admiralty were concerned, they still hoped to capitalise on the Highball anti-ship version of the bouncing bomb. The committee agreed to postpone any decision regarding the telegram

but on June 7 the Russians repeated their request, adding that they expected information by the next courier flight. After a brief discussion, the committee decided to make the information available, replying that full details and drawings could be sent to Moscow via a secret and secure route. The Air Ministry was instructed to put together the necessary papers and prepare them for despatch but, when Churchill approved the implementation of Highball, a decision was taken on July 7 to defer all discussions with the Russians as far as the bouncing bombs were concerned. With remarkable aplomb, on August 11 the Air Staff replied to a further Soviet request of August 9: 'Information will be forwarded as soon as possible, but we cannot say when air mail will leave. You should make the greatest possible capital out of our handing over this important and highly secret information.'

Filming a reunion of ex-617 Squadron personnel on a ground level return to the Möhne dam in September 1976. L-R: Fred Tees (gunner AJ-C), Geoff Rice (pilot AJ-H), Ken Brown (pilot AJ-F), Eve Gibson, Jim Clay (bomb-aimer AJ-W), Basil Feneron (flight engineer AJ-F), Harry O'Brien (gunner AJ-N) and Jan van den Driesschen, a Dutch 617 aficionado.

Above: **Guy Gibson's widow shows the author her husband's St Christopher (why was he not wearing it on his last fatal flight?) and** *below* **Basil Feneron visits his target: the Sorpe. He commented that 'we could not hear the detonation but we were caught by the blast. We flew back over the Möhne dam at 1,000 feet.'**

Len Sumpter (right), awarded the Distinguished Flying Medal for his role as bomb-aimer on Shannon's AJ-L, and Karl Schütte (centre), decorated with the Eiserne Kreuz 2. Klasse for his part in defending the dam, exchange gifts of friendship in August 1990. The illustration by Kevin Buckingham depicts the 617 Squadron Memorial at Woodhall Spa.

In May 1991, Colonel Wjenkow, Head of the Historical Branch of the Soviet General Staff in Moscow, sent the following reply to Helmuth Euler in response to the author's request for confirmation of Allied co-operation: 'Despite our sincere wish to help, we are unable to trace any drawings or information about the bouncing bomb in the war archives of the USSR. It is probable that the despatch of blueprints of the bouncing bomb was top secret and therefore no information about the discussions reached our archives'. In fact the information was never sent to Moscow because it was to be withheld until Highball was used and that weapon was never employed operationally. Indeed, the Upkeep mine itself saw no further action after the raid of May 16/17, 1943.

General Henry H. 'Hap' Arnold, the Commander of the United States Army Air Forces, also wanted specimens of the Highball and Upkeep weapons. In principle no objections were raised as the Americans had already received consent from Bomber Command together with all drawings and data. Test equipment was to be fitted to US aircraft and specimen bombs were to be despatched in crates with special markings and the most extreme security precautions observed. It was essential that Highball remain top secret lest the enemy turn the tables and use such a weapon against Allied surface vessels but, as it never reached the production stage, not even prototypes were delivered to the Americans.

It was during my research for issue 3 of *After the Battle*, in which I wanted to feature the raid, that I first visited Gibson's grave in Holland. Gibson had very little operational flying experience after the May 1943 raid as he spent the latter part of the year in North America on a promotional tour. He flew to Quebec on August 20 and arrived in New York three days later. He then shuttled back and forth between the USA and Canada; was invested with the Legion of Merit by General Arnold in Washington on October 13, before flying on to California on the 27th to see Howard Hawks to discuss the making of his film.

Gibson arrived back in the UK on December 1, 1943, and logged less than 50 hours as first pilot during the first nine months of 1944. He first flew in a Mosquito on July 10 when Squadron Leader Martin checked him out and he had only undertaken three further flights in the type before his final mission on September 19. At the time Gibson was serving as the Base Operations Officer at Coningsby when he escorted 227 Lancasters of Nos. 1 and 5 Groups as Master Bomber on an attack on the twin towns of Mönchengladbach and Rheydt. Piloting a No. 627 Squadron Mosquito with Squadron Leader James Warwick as his navigator, while returning from Germany the

aircraft crashed in flames at Steenbergen, 13 kilometres north of Bergen-op-Zoom, virtually on the same route flown when attacking the dams 16 months previously.

When interviewed by Wing Commander Jack Meadows for an article in *Aeroplane* for the May 2000 anniversary of the attack, Flight Sergeant Ken Brown — one of only two Dams Raid pilots then still alive — had little doubt as to the reasons for Gibson's crash. 'He had only had one short familiarisation trip on a Mosquito, followed by a quick briefing from a flight sergeant. His experienced navigator had never flown in one before. Gibson had not brought himself properly up to date, and his return route, once flak free, was now far from it. In the middle of it, while he was taking evasive action, his engines cut, Ken believes, because Gibson had failed to change fuel tanks. The fuel cocks on a Mosquito are behind the pilot's seat. Some pilots always reached behind to select them, largely by feel, which was not difficult. Others relied on the navigator beside them to do it. As they were also taking violent evasive action at the time, two people inexperienced on the Mosquito must have been frantically and ineffectively scrambling in the dark to find the cocks and turn them. Meanwhile, they were sitting ducks.'

Guy Gibson's final flight took place on September 19, 1944 while he was serving with No. 5 Group in a non-operational role. He asked to fly as raid controller in a Mosquito borrowed from Wing Commander Rupert Oakley of No. 627 Squadron and was given permission even though the latter felt that Gibson had not flown the type long enough to undertake such a mission. The Mosquito came down in flames near the Dutch town of Steenbergen. The Deputy Mayor, Mr A. V. Herbers, described what they found at the crash site: 'At about 23.30 a British aircraft "Merlin KB 264 Lockheed 2, Mark 33", crashed in flames. Near the crash an identity plate or disc was found with the following written on it: "J. B. Warwick Offr Pres 156612 RAFVR" and on a sock was found the name "Guy Gibson". The remains of the unidentifiable bodies were put into one coffin and buried in St Gumarus Roman Catholic Cemetery. At the scene of the crash the following items were found: a silver ring gold-plated with initials "J.B.W"; identity plate as above; an Omega wrist watch; a black tie; a booklet on fishing; an envelope with the address "S/Ldr J. B. Warwick DFC, Officer Sen. RAF Station, Coningsby, Lincoln"; a button; a forage cap; five maps, and French and Belgium bank notes. These were all sent to the Red Cross.'

Above: **The Mosquito B.XX (a Canadian-built version of the B.IV) bore the serial KB267 and the code-letters AZ-E. It came down about 1½ miles from the centre of town on the West Graaf Hendrik-Polder.** *Right:* **On December 11-12, 1985, the Royal Netherlands Air Force excavated the site which was about to be developed as an industrial park but all that was found were small pieces of wood covered with painted fabric, pieces of aircraft skin and rubber from the fuel tanks; a major part of one of the main wheels, disintegrated engine parts and a piece of tail fin bearing the letters 'KB'.**

It was not until December 1985 that the Royal Netherlands Air Force Recovery Service, assisted by the Explosives Demolition Unit, investigated Gibson's crash site. The survey had become necessary because of plans to develop the area which until then had just remained an open field. Digging went down some three metres but very little of the Mosquito was found, the largest item being a piece of the tail fin bearing the letters 'KB' of the serial number KB267. Today the site of the crash has been smothered under an industrial estate although some of the surrounding streets have been appropriately named.

On September 19, 1979, the 35th anniversary of the crash, streets on the new Reinierpolder estate were appropriately named.

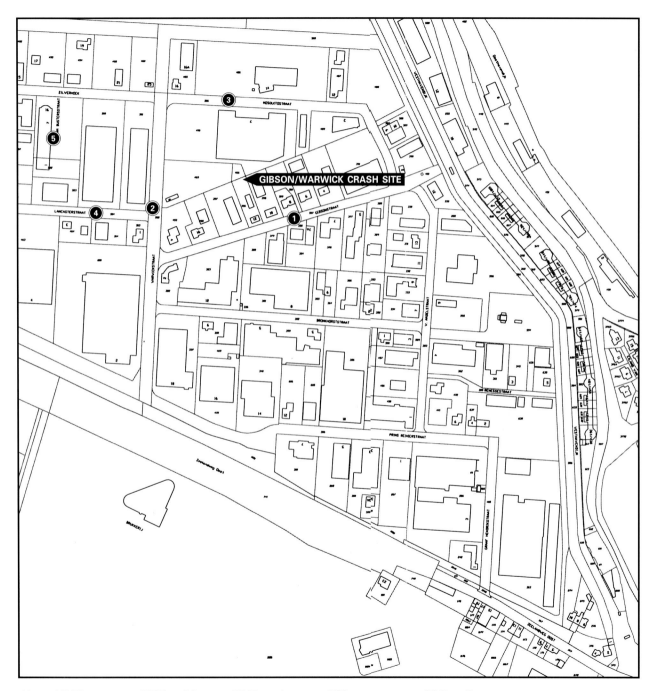

Above: [1] Gibsonstraat. [2] Warwickstraat. [3] Mosquitostraat. [4] Lancasterstraat. [5] Dam Busterstraat.

Hardly a fitting location for the death of a hero fallen in battle . . .

. . . yet in the town park this memorial was unveiled on May 7, 1990 to the memory of Gibson and Warwick. (The propeller comes from a Lancaster of No. 106 Squadron which crashed near Monnickendam in the Netherlands on December 20, 1942, when Gibson was CO of the squadron.)

Air Marshal Sir Harold Martin (pilot AJ-P) escorts Eve Gibson (left) and Ellen, the sister of James Warwick, to the grave on September 27, 1974.

During the September 1976 pilgrimage, ex-members of the squadron visited Steenbergen. L-R: Harry O'Brien, Ken Brown, Geoff Rice and Basil Feneron.

As for the fate of the aircraft used against the dams, none of the Lancasters which returned have survived. The majority were scrapped at the end of the war; Gibson's AJ-G, Martin's AJ-P, and Maltby's AJ-J all in July 1947, AJ-L, AJ-N, AJ-W and AJ-Y having already gone in 1946.

McCarthy's original aircraft (ED923) was lost on September 8, 1943 and AJ-T (ED825) three months later. Townsend's AJ-O was lost in December 1943 and Brown's AJ-F the following month. AJ-H, flown by Rice, crashed on July 21, 1944.

Pictured at the Aeroplane and Armament Experimental Establishment at Boscombe Down before delivery to the squadron (see also page 31), the carrying brackets and motor drive for the Upkeep on ED825/G are clearly visible. Unbelievably, not one of the machines which flew on the raid survives.

The first of the practice Upkeeps was recovered from the foreshore at Reculver by Malcolm Ilott of the Rayleigh Branch of the British Sub-Aqua Club in April 1975 using an HH53 helicopter from the USAF.

As far as the weaponry is concerned, in May 1972 Mike Bishop, a member of the British Sub-Aqua Club, visited Reculver and plotted the remains of over a dozen of the practice bombs — full-size and scaled down Upkeeps and Highballs — still lying on the foreshore and in March 1974 the late Peter Cornish, the BSA regional coach, passed on details to the Rayleigh Branch who were searching for an interesting diving project. The Marconi Branch also visited the beach but they considered that the rusted remains were not worth recovering, an opinion conveyed to Rayleigh by the diving officer who was also a Marconi member. However, Malcolm Ilott of the Rayleigh Branch inspected the bombs the following month and persuaded his committee that it would be a worthwhile project to try to recover an Upkeep. Initially, an attempt to raise one was made by using a 'raft' of oil drums but while the weapon was easily lifted from the seabed, the operation had to be aborted because of the difficulty of clearing the sandbank between it and the shore.

Malcolm then decided to adopt a different approach and see if he could get help to lift an Upkeep bodily using a helicopter. The RAF did not have a machine large enough but the USAF at Woodbridge agreed to provide a Sikorski HH53 'Jolly Green Giant' which had the necessary lifting capability. On April 28, 1975 — 32 years possibly to the day when some of the weapons had been dropped — the first one was successfully recovered, but not before the first strop snapped when the strain gauge in the helicopter reached 11,000lbs! The following day three more Upkeeps were lifted to safety.

Two more mines — in this case rather worse for wear — were uncovered during routine excavations along the sea-wall in October 1977. RAF bomb disposal officers (Squadron Leader Edward Toat, Junior Technician Chris Pheasey and Warrant Officer Don McGuirk are pictured) were brought in from RAF Wittering to check but, as the photo clearly shows, both weapons were inert filled with concrete.

Barnes Wallis died in November 1979 and Albert Speer — the man who was so successful in negating the long-term effect of the destruction of the dams — in September 1981. Wallis had returned to Reculver at least once — in 1976, when Raymond Hepner of Sale, Cheshire, took him back to see the test range; 20 years later Wallis's son was present on the same beach when a further operation was mounted to retrieve more of the test weapons. It was Andrew Hemsley of the Invicta Military Vehicle Society who proposed that a follow-up-operation should be mounted to recover the remaining bombs for preservation. Living close to Reculver, Andrew, together with Nigel Hay, had plotted the positions of the remaining Upkeeps and had also located a Highball as well as two of the scaled-down versions of the Upkeeps. In July 1996, Andrew approached Captain Sandy Sanderson of the Explosive Ordnance Disposal Technical Information Centre at Chattenden in Kent, to see if a recovery operation could be mounted as a training exercise. The idea found favour with Lieutenant-Colonel Robert Murfin, the commanding officer of 101 Engineer Regiment (EOD) (Territorial Army) in that it would provide a unique training opportunity enabling the regiment to exercise both its combat engineer and bomb disposal skills. It would also be a good demonstration of the ability of the reserve forces (i.e. the TA) and it was felt that as the weapons were a unique part of the United Kingdom's military history, they should be recovered for the benefit of future generations.

Detailed for the operation were 221 Field Squadron (EOD)(V) based at Rochester, Kent; 222 Squadron (EOD)(V) from nearby Dartford, and 223 Headquarters

After the war, Barnes Wallis was granted £10,000 for his work which he placed in a trust fund for the benefit of the education of the children of men who lost their lives while serving in the Royal Air Force. He continued working right up until he died aged 92, one of his dreams being a 5,000mph space-age airliner. In 1976, three years before he died, Raymond Hepner took Sir Barnes and his wife (who had never visited the test range) back to Reculver to the spot where he had witnessed the wartime trials.

Wallis's adversary in Germany, Reich Armaments Minister Albert Speer, was rewarded for his efforts (see pages 193-195) by being sentenced to 20 years imprisonment by the International Military Tribunal. Judgement day was September 30, 1946 when Speer was found guilty of violating the laws of war and of crimes against humanity. After his release *(above)* on October 1, 1966, Speer made a private trip to see the dams and whilst there, he also paid a visit to the church at Ostönnen.

Left: In June 1977, following the initiative by Andrew Hemsley and Nigel Hay of the Invicta Military Vehicle Society, another operation was mounted to recover more of the test weapons. Here, Major Nigel Francis, the OC 222 (EOD) Field Squadron and the Joint Project Controller, points out to Barnes Wallis Junior the positions of the weapons to be recovered.

First to be retrieved from the sands were two of the miniature Upkeeps — one approximately 40 inches long and 22 inches in diameter, the other 28 inches by 21 inches — and a Highball. The anti-ship version of the bouncing bomb was never used in anger but the test weapon recovered (some 30 inches in diameter) was a unique specimen.

Who could have foreseen that over 50 years after they had been dropped, so much effort would be put into recovering No. 617 Squadron's practice weapons?

Squadron (EOD)(V) co-located with Regimental Head-quarters at Catford in south London. After preliminary reconnaissance of the various bombs during November 1996, a plan was produced for the recovery of four: two miniatures and a Highball, all believed to weigh about 500kgs (half a ton) each; and one full-size Upkeep. Measuring five feet long and four feet in diameter, the latter lay over 300 metres offshore and could only be reached at a low spring tide. Even then, there would only be a 'window' to work on it of a maximum of two hours before the tide turned and covered it.

The TA units arrived on Friday, June 6, 1977 and by that evening, one of the small Upkeeps and the Highball were on display on dry land, the second scaled Upkeep being

removed from the beach early on Saturday. Andrew Hemsley had already promised that the Highball would go to the Mosquito Aircraft Museum at Salisbury Hall at London Colney as this weapon was developed primarily to be dropped by Mosquitos. One of the small Upkeeps was earmarked for display locally at Reculver, the other pos-sibly destined for RAF Scampton. At that stage, a home had not been found for the full-size Upkeep, still to be recovered, but when Wallis's son arrived to watch the pro-ceedings, he quickly laid claim to it for the Barnes Wallis Trust display at the Yorkshire Air Museum.

Further operations on Saturday had to wait for the next low tide which was due at eight o'clock that evening but as darkness fell the tide turned before it could be winched up

the beach so it was decided to halt further work until the following morning.

Sunday dawned bright and clear with minimal sea con-ditions and by 5 a.m. the sappers were already wading out with the tide, low water coming around 8 a.m. Ground anchors were secured and the Upkeep soon freed from its watery grave. However it quickly became a race against the incoming tide so a decision was taken to bring down a three-inch rope and physically manhandle the mine up the beach by parbuckling. Once it reached the shingle, a bulldozer then pulled it the last few yards to where a crane on the sea-wall hoisted it onto the back of a Bedford truck for transportation to the Defence EOD School at Chattenden.

So what other relics remain? The original plaque unveiled by the Kaiser on July 12, 1913 (see page 69) was taken as a souvenir by Flight Lieutenant K. G. Hesketh, a Royal Australian Air Force officer based at the RAAF Historical Section in Kodak House, Kingsway, London. He was an enthusiastic collector of material relating to the Australian Air Force in Europe and he spent a considerable amount of time attached to the British Army of the Rhine (BAOR). Not only did he visit the Möhne dam, where he simply unscrewed the plaque from the northernmost tower, but during subsequent travels, he secured a souvenir from the *Tirpitz* and managed to get himself shot at in the Russian Sector of Berlin while removing Reichsmarschall Göring's personal crest from his front gate! Flight Lieutenant Hesketh's collection was passed by the RAAF to the Australian War Memorial in Canberra in 1948. From time to time, German tourists who have visited Australia have contacted the author about this item of 'booty' removed from the Möhne dam. The many reports in the popular press during the post-war years — which often contained errors, myths, half-truths and lies — made the raid on the dams known far beyond the frontiers of Germany and thus served as free publicity for the region. Drawn by the events which took place during the war, many German and foreign tourists now come to see the Möhne, Eder and Sorpe dams every year.

Wilhelm Neuhaus, a farmer from Nieder-Werbe, holds up a piece of the anti-torpedo net which had been deployed in the Eder reservoir after the raid and the reconstruction of the dam. Long after the war, fields and gardens in the area around the Eder could be seen fenced off with this rust-resistant material.

There are also many reminders in the towns and villages in the Möhne and Eder valleys where plaques have been erected showing height of the floodwaters. And not only in the vicinity of the dams. In Bad Karlshafen for example, 139 kilometres from the Eder dam, the level of the River Weser rose to 8.56 metres above normal at around 11 a.m. on May 18, some 58 million cubic metres of water — a third of the contents of the Eder reservoir — ending up in the areas affected by flooding. Flowing as it did through wider valleys, the Eder flood moved more slowly than the water from the Möhne which reached Mülheim-Ruhr, 135 kilometres to the west (see page 236).

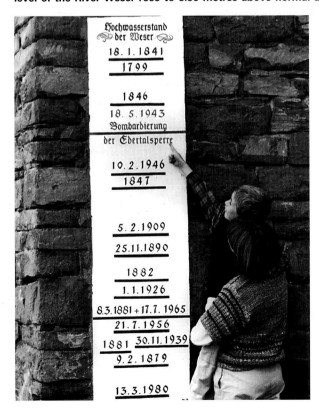

In Herstelle, Henriette Euler and young Helmuth Junior examine a board comparing the May 1943 disaster with other floods . . . before and after.

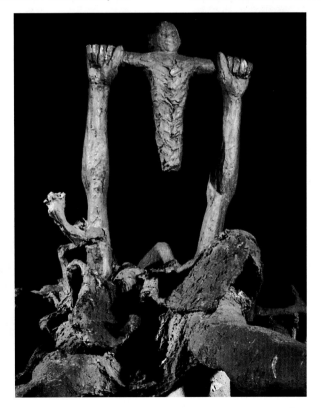

This sculpture stands near the Dorfgemeinschaftshaus in Affoldern. It is by the Swiss artist, Professor D'Altri from Zürich, and features a mother holding her child above the flood.

A bronze relief by Josef Baron in Wickede where a service of remembrance for those who died is held every year on the evening of May 16.

Left: **Scampton remained a front-line base — in Strike Command from April 1968 following the merger of Fighter and Bomber Commands — until the Vulcan squadrons were disbanded.**

Reminders of its wartime role beside the main gate: a Lancaster (R5868 from 1959 to 1970) and Tallboy and Grand Slam bombs. Lancaster NX611 *(right)* **arrived in April 1974.**

No. 617 Squadron has survived the many vicissitudes which affected the RAF in post-war years and the squadron even returned to their old base at Scampton after its brief disbandment from December 1955 to May 1958. It was re-formed at its birthplace with Avro Vulcans and a year later was awarded its standard — a rare honour which is usually only given after a unit has existed for 25 years.

When in 1961 another new weapon — the Blue Steel stand-off bomb — was brought into service with the Vulcan Mark II, the Dambusters were the first to be chosen to be armed with Britain's latest strategic nuclear deterrent until it was superseded by the Royal Navy's Polaris-armed submarines in 1969. So, 30 years after the raid, No. 617 Squadron still occupied the same hangar and crew rooms as they had in 1943. Gibson's office was maintained just as it was when he left it with his cap on his desk and Nigger's grave visible through the window.

The squadron was disbanded in January 1981 at the end of the Vulcan era and reformed in June 1983 at Marham equipped with Tornados. It moved to Lossiemouth in April 1994.

Meanwhile, at Scampton, a tribute to the squadron's wartime role remained — Lancaster NX611 standing beside the main gate. The machine had been purchased by the Panton brothers as a tribute to their third brother who had been killed on a bomber operation during the war.

In September 1983, the Lancaster was bought by Fred and Harold Panton in memory of their brother Chris who failed to return from a raid to Nuremberg on March 30, 1944. It remained as gate guardian at Scampton until it was moved to East Kirkby airfield as the nucleus of their Lincolnshire Aviation Heritage Centre in March 1988.

Scampton then . . . Scampton now. In 1953-4, when filming for *The Dam Busters* took place, its face was almost unchanged from its wartime days. We saw an enlargement of this picture on page 28.

Today the trees in front of the now-condemned Airmen's Mess on the right — used for the main briefing — are knarled and twisted, the base empty save for the odd contractor's vehicle carrying out care and maintenance.

A sad sight in December 2000. The abandoned and boarded up No. 2 Hangar — the crew rooms including Gibson's office (see page 34) stripped bare of fixtures and fittings. This shot compares with the picture of the Upkeep-armed Lancaster on page 34.

In 1996, it was intended to sell off the airfield including the hangars and non-housing buildings. To that end, chain-link fencing was erected to divide the site leaving the Officers' Mess — venue of the historic photo on page 166 — alone and inaccessible.

And look at poor Nigger's last resting place — as it was in the 1970s *(left)* and railed off in 1995 to protect it from grave robbers *(right)*. Over the years there have been rumours that this is not the actual grave dug on the night of May 16/17, 1943 . . . that instead Chiefy Powell buried the black labrador behind the guardhouse. Fortunately Jim Shortland, a No. 617 Squadron historian, raised this very point with ex-Sergeant Jim Heveron who was serving in the orderly room at the time and he confirmed that he personally helped Powell bury Nigger outside the crewrooms at midnight. Surely, today, this grave remains one of the most poignant memories of Operation 'Chastise'?

Six years on it was the actual base which was under threat when the Ministry of Defence announced that Scampton was to be axed. A vociferous 'Save our Scampton' (SOS) campaign was run by the *Lincolnshire Echo* to keep the airfield open which received one offer of support from a surprising quarter when a group of German businessmen joined and declared: 'Everyone has heard of the Dambusters. They are part of British history and their home base should not be allowed to close'. However, it did just that in November 1995 but its runways were still used every flying day during the winter months by the Red Arrows Display Team based at Cranwell, some 20 miles to the south, to avoid the crowded airspace surrounding the Central Flying School.

However, with no resident squadrons and no comprehensive maintenance budget, the technical site slowly began to take on an abandoned look as plans were set in motion to dispose of the airfield. With defence spending under constant review, it was feared that Scampton might go the way of so many other historic RAF airfields but then, in March 2000, came the welcome news that the Red Arrows would be moving in before the end of the year. The RAF Aerobatic Team was to take up residence in No. 4 hangar with combined messing facilities to be provided in the old Sergeants' Mess. Officially, Scampton was to become a detached operating base under RAF Cranwell, commanded by a wing commander from the Central Flying School.

While all this was going on, No. 617 Squadron up at RAF Lossiemouth had chalked up another first — this time for being the first RAF squadron to employ a woman as a combat pilot. At the time — February 1995 — the Dambusters were equipped with the Tornado GR1B and Flight Lieutenant Jo Salter took up her duties shortly before the squadron left for an assignment over Iraq. But that, as they say, is another story!

And in Germany, this memorial cross, erected exactly 20 years after the Porta Coeli chapel in Himmelpforten was destroyed, stands on the exact spot where the altar stood (see page 119).

The 50th Anniversary

By Squadron Leader Tony Cunnane
Red Arrows Corporate Communications Officer

I thought that there should be a special event at Scampton to mark the 50th anniversary of the Dams' Raid in May 1993, and as the 16th fell on a Sunday it seemed very appropriate that such a well-known and controversial operation should therefore be remembered by means of a religious service with a theme of reconciliation. The Station Commander and Padre both agreed so I sent a fax to the Reverend Chris Hutchings, the Editor of the BBC Television 'Songs of Praise' programme, and asked if he would be interested in producing a programme from one of Scampton's hangars. Chris was so enthusiastic about the idea that he very quickly telephoned me to say that not only would the BBC be very keen to do such a programme but they would like the programme to go out live at the exact time that the crews of No. 617 Squadron had been preparing to take off, 50 years earlier.

When I first started planning the event, I was put very firmly in my place whilst discussing the arrangements with one of the Dambusters' aircrew. I commented that the event would *celebrate* the 50th anniversary of the raid. 'Squadron Leader', he said gravely. 'We do not celebrate an event which cost the lives of 53 of our colleagues and countless lives on the ground'. I felt quite humble.

Left: **May 16, 1991 — the two *City of Lincolns* pictured over the city whose name they bear. After the christening of the British Airways Boeing 747 at Coningsby, she flew in formation with Lancaster PA474 to Scampton, five miles north of the city, where the BBC were broadcasting a band concert from one of its hangars.**

There was room in the hangar for 2,500 people including the Central Band of the Royal Air Force. The last flying Lancaster, with the Battle of Britain Memorial Flight at nearby RAF Coningsby, which proudly bears the name *City of Lincoln*, and a Tornado from the present-day 617 Squadron together with a British Aerospace Hawk and other Scampton-based training aircraft, would together form a colourful backdrop for the TV cameras. Many of the surviving aircrew from the Dams Raid would be in the congregation including some from New Zealand, Australia, Canada and USA.

Then, by happy chance, came an opportunity to include in the programme another *City of Lincoln* aircraft — but this one certainly would not fit inside the hangar!

This part of the story began in 1991 when one of British Airways' newly-delivered Boeing 747 Dash 400s was officially named *City of Lincoln* at a formal ceremony at RAF Coningsby. The naming ceremony for G-BNLT (Lima Tango) was carried out by Her Majesty's Lord Lieutenant for the County of Lincolnshire, Sir Henry Nevile. The two *City of Lincolns* were parked nose to nose for the ceremony.

After the naming, Lima Tango flew over to RAF Scampton where, somewhat improbably, the aircraft was parked outside a hangar while BBC Radio broadcast a band concert from within. An audience of over 2,000 listened to the concert and then had conducted tours of the county's most recent acquisition.

Above: **Two years later, in preparation for the special 50th anniversary service which had been arranged for Sunday, May 16, 1993, the 'Mark II' version of the *City of Lincoln* was escorted to Scampton by the RAF Aerobatic Team, the Red Arrows. Before it landed, the Jumbo had overflown the RAF bases at Wittering, Cranwell and Waddington.**

231

G-BNLT, flying the British Airways and RAF ensigns, carefully taxies past the Central Flying School buildings at Scampton in readiness for the special charity flight laid on for disabled and under-priveleged children on Sunday afternoon.

Two years after that first visit to Scampton by the Jumbo, the Lincolnshire-based crews of British Airways were, quite independently, organising a charity flight for 250 disabled and under-privileged Lincolnshire children. Lima Tango, The *City of Lincoln*, would return to Scampton and take the children on a two-hour flight including low-level flypasts over all the major towns and villages in the county. It soon became apparent that the charity flight could be run on the same day as the 50th anniversary 'Songs of Praise'.

On the morning of May 15, 1993, Lima Tango rendezvoused with the Red Arrows at the southernmost point in Lincolnshire and then flew northwards in close formation passing over the RAF stations at Wittering, Cranwell and Waddington, and finally the 900-year-old Lincoln Cathedral before landing at Scampton.

For this special positioning flight, the Civil Aviation Authority insisted that Lima Tango should have on board just three qualified pilots: the Captain in Command, one of BA's most experienced Dash 400 pilots; the First Officer, a former RAF fighter pilot who would fly the actual formation on the Red Arrows; and an RAF Wing Commander, the Red Arrows' senior flying supervisor. Wing Commander David Hamilton said afterwards: 'Shortly after taking off from Heathrow I had to go back for a call of nature and I took the opportunity to walk through the cabins. It was the weirdest sensation I have ever had — walking alone through that enormous aircraft and finding nothing but empty seats. It was a great relief to get back to the flight deck and find that there really were two pilots on board as well!'

Red Arrows' Team Leader, then Squadron Leader Adrian Thurley said: 'It was quite an economical way to fly because the huge bow wave which precedes a 747 was literally pushing us along through the air and I found that we had to reduce power quite considerably to maintain the assigned true air speed of 330 knots.'

Bearing an uncanny resemblance to his counterpart, Richard Todd, one of the 2,000 guests at the 50th anniversary service, is pictured alongside the painting of Guy Gibson just inside the main entrance to the Officers' Mess.

The service for the 'Songs of Praise' broadcast was conducted by the Reverend (Squadron Leader) Andy McMullen, and was transmitted live from No. 1 Hangar.

In the early afternoon of May 16, Lima Tango took off from Scampton with 413 persons on board, the largest number of people ever to be loaded onto a single aircraft at an RAF base. The local radio station, BBC Radio Lincolnshire, broadcast live from on board the aircraft during the flight and listeners to the programme were able to ring in to the radio station as the aircraft passed overhead and talk live on air with the crew and passengers.

Later, at 6.16 p.m., 50 years later almost to the hour that the 19 Lancasters had rumbled across Scampton to take off for Germany, 'Songs of Praise' went live on air with a flypast over the hangar by the Red Arrows. Almost 2,000 of the audience had some connection either with the airfield or RAF Bomber Command during the Second World War. The programme was seen live by eight million people in UK and the recording was received in many countries throughout the world via satellite TV.

Many people attended the ceremony at Wickede marking the 50th anniversary of the Möhne disaster. Following an ecumenical service on the market square, the townspeople made their way to the bank of the River Ruhr. Here wreaths were placed at the memorial *(above)*, which had been erected in 1958 for the 'Wassertoten', as the flood victims are known locally.

This bronze memorial was dedicated on May 16, 1993 in Neheim's pedestrianised high street. It commemorates 'the victims of the floods and war, aggression and terror' and is also an 'exhortation for peace and understanding'.

In Germany, memorial services in the name of peace were held at many of the places affected by the floods along the valleys. In memory of that terrible night, church bells were rung in the Eder valley to coincide with the precise time the dam was breached.

At Wickede in the Ruhr valley, the villagers attended a memorial service held in the market square to commemorate the 50th anniversary of the disaster. An ecumenical service of reconciliation between former enemies was celebrated by the Roman Catholic Dean Karl Mause, the Protestant pastor, Peter Fischer, and the Reverend Simon, Chaplain of the nearby British Army base at Werl. After the service, the villagers, accompanied by representatives of the local associations with their banners, the churches and the local authority, made their way to the memorial where wreaths were laid in memory of those who perished in the floods.

That same day in the pedestrian precinct at Neheim, a memorial was inaugurated in front of the Sauerländer Dom by the parishioners of St Johannes Baptist. The 5.5-metre-high bronze memorial, which tapers towards the top, was erected at the instigation of Pastor Franz Schnüttgen specially to mark the 50th anniversary, and is the work of the artist Bernhard Kleinhans. The central relief shows the breached dam and portrays a moving scene of drowning people. The inscription above recalls the night of May 16/17, 1943 with the words: 'We mourn the 1285 women, men and children who lost their lives in the floods'. At the top of the memorial is a lantern showing a light which is intended to symbolise the lines of the prayer from the burial service: 'Herr laß unseren Toten das Ewige Licht leuchten' — O'Lord, let light perpetual shine upon them.'

The relief depicts the broken dam wall with victims being swept away by the flood. Although the inscription states '1285' deaths this cannot be relied upon as a precise total for any of the valleys has never been determined. Also the number of victims in the Eder and Fulda valleys has not been included in this figure.

Sir Barnes Wallis; 'The most regrettable thing about the whole episode was the fact that numbers of women and children were sheltering in their bomb-proof shelters in the valleys and were trapped and drowned and for that we are deeply sorry. But it was not part of our intention; we thought that by destroying the dams we could stop the manufacturing of steel.' This is the dam at the Kahlenberg power-station in Mülheim-Ruhr, some 135 kilometres (over 80 miles) west of the Möhne dam and not far from the River Rhine.

Acknowledgements

The author is indebted to many people who contributed information, photographs, their valuable time and assistance, over many years to make this book possible. In particular, the expertise of Michael Ockenden in translating the text into English is gratefully appreciated.

Detlef R. Albrecht, Manfred Bäcker, Evelyn Bäppler, Gerard Bellebaum, Karl Bergmann, Helmut Bladt, Udo Bleidick, Grete Blumenroth, Ignaz Böckenhoff, Karl Bömer, Dick Breedijk, Dr Volker Brendow, Lotte Buerstätte, Gertrud Caspari, Dr A. R. Collins, David Collins, Newark Air Museum, Alan Cooper, Squadron Leader Tony Cunnane, Günter Danzglock, Werner Dettmar, Jan van den Driesschen, Bernard Droste, René Elshout, Karl Ludwig Ensuleit, Henriette Euler, Walter Fischer, Eckhard Fisseler, Heinz Gerlach, Dipl.-Ing Gluch, Jürgen Grewe, Otto Grünewald, André Guillon, Albert Günther, Nigel Haines, Commonwealth War Graves Commission, Gerhard Hallen, Ulrich Hake, Wilhelm Hellwig, Didier Hindryckx, Major Tonie Holt, Vicki Irwin, Australian High Commission, Friedel Junker, Hermann Kaiser, Dr Jörg Kaltwasser, Dr Erwin Kegel, Paul Keiser, Karl Kleinenbroich, Manfred Kemper, Werner Kittler, Frank-Roland Klaube, Dr J. Kloosterhuis, Leo Klerks, Dr Gerhard Köhn, Hartmut Kraatz, Heinz-Wilhelm Kramer, Günter Krause, Friedrich-Wilhelm Kretzer, Norbert Krüger, Randolf Kugler, Hans Lauer, Anne Marie Laurenz, Klaus Leber, Heinz Leiwig, Leon Lejeuné-Steils, Heinrich Lehn, Dr Richard Litterscheid, Luise Lorenz, Prof. Dr Ing. E. H. Heinz Maecker, Otto Mantel, Rolf Matzen, Mike McCormac, Jan-Olov Molin, L. C. Morrison, Air Historical Branch, London, Alfred Müller, Ingeborg Münzing-Ruef, Wilhelm Neuhaus, Wilm Nölke, Franz Josef Obermeier, Harry O'Brien, Fred and Harold Panton, Hans A. Peters, Joachim Prölss, Friedhelm Quast, Hermann Quast, Roswitha Reiming, Anton Riediger, Walter Rocholl, Theo Röttlingsberger, Wilfried von Rüden, Andy Saunders, Manfred Schaake, Kurt Schiefelbein, Wolfgang Schilling, Hermann Schmidt, Heinz Schnelle, Herbert Scholl, Dr Johann-Henrich Schotten, Harry Schürmann, Karl Schütte, Engelbert Schwingenheuer, Jim Shortland, Karl Heinz Stammschulte, Albert Stieglitz, Bernd Stobrawa, Hubert Stolle, Len Sumpter, Christoph Tauchert, Gerhard Teriet, Christan Tilenius, Raymond F. Toliver, Bill Townsend, Alan Thompson, Josef Vogel, Sir Barnes Wallis, Alan D. Walton, Fred Wauters, Siegfried Welt, Brigitte Weller, Dr H. Wilhelm, Les Wilson, Heinrich Windgassen, Klaus Winter, Dr Ursula Wolkers, Paul Wunderlich.

The following organisations gave invaluable help:

Associated British Pathe Limited; Australian War Memorial, Canberra; British Aerospace; British Aircraft Corporation Limited, Weybridge; British Museum, London; Bundesarchiv Aachen; Bundesarchiv Berlin; Bundesarchiv Freiburg in Breisgau; Bundesfilmarchiv Berlin; Canadian National Archives; Commonwealth War Graves Commission; Elstree Studios, Borehamwood; Ennepe Wasserverband Gevelsberg; Foto Hahn; Friedhofsamt Soest; Foto Fritz; Hessisches Staatsarchiv Marburg; Hygiene Institut des Ruhrgebietes Gelsenkirchen; Imperial War Museum, London; Institut für Geophysik Universität Göttingen; Institüt für Weltwirtschaft Universität Kiel; Institüt für Zeitgeschichte Munich; Internationaler Suchdienst Arolsen; Kurmuseum Bad Wildungen; Landesarchiv Berlin; Luftwaffenmuseum Berlin-Gatow; Ministry of Defence, London; Militärgeschichtliches Forschungsamt Freiburg im Breisgau; National Archives, Washington; Public Record Office, London and Kew; Radio Canadian Army Europe; Regionalmuseum Fritzlar; Royal Air Force Museum, Hendon; Ruhrtalmuseum Schwerte; Ruhrverband und Ruhrtalsperrenverein Essen; RWW Mülheim; Schicht 1 Schwerte; Stadtmuseum Saporoshje; Stadtwerke Remscheid GmbH; Science Museum, London; Sternwarte-Planetarium Bochum; Verkehrsmuseum Nuremberg; Volksbund Deutscher Kriegsgräberfürsorge Kassel; *Waldeckische Allgemeine*; *Waldeckische Landeszeitung*; Wasser- und Schiffahrtsamt Hannoversch-Münden; *Westfälischer Anzeiger und Kurier*; *Westfälische Landeszeitung – Rote Erde*, Wetteramt Essen; Wupperverband Wuppertal.

Also the town archives in Affoldern, Arnsberg, Baunatal, Bergisch-Gladbach, Berlin, Düsseldorf, Edertal, Ennepetal, Essen, Felsberg, Fröndenberg, Hagen, Hamm, Herdecke, Kassel, Korbach, Marburg, Melsungen, Münster, Solingen, Witten.

Index
Compiled by Peter Gunn

Note 1, Page numbers in *italics* refer to illustrations.
Note 2, References to Möhne and Eder dams, and No. 617 Sqn are not indexed. Please refer to relevant chapter headings.

239